UNDERSTANDING
THE GREAT PHILOSOPHERS

Books by HENRY THOMAS

UNDERSTANDING THE GREAT PHILOSOPHERS
THE LIVING WORLD OF PHILOSOPHY
MATHEMATICS MADE EASY
SCIENCE SUBJECTS MADE EASY
STORIES OF THE GREAT DRAMAS AND THEIR AUTHORS
THE STORY OF THE UNITED STATES
THE COMPLETE BOOK OF ENGLISH
THE STORY OF KNOWLEDGE
THE STORY OF THE HUMAN RACE
THE WONDER BOOK
THE POETS OF THE FUTURE

Books by HENRY THOMAS and DANA LEE THOMAS

LIVING ADVENTURES IN PHILOSOPHY
LIVING ADVENTURES IN SCIENCE
FIFTY GREAT AMERICANS
FORTY FAMOUS COMPOSERS
LIFE STORIES OF THE GREAT INVENTORS
LIVING BIOGRAPHIES OF GREAT PHILOSOPHERS
LIVING BIOGRAPHIES OF RELIGIOUS LEADERS
LIVING BIOGRAPHIES OF GREAT SCIENTISTS
LIVING BIOGRAPHIES OF FAMOUS RULERS
LIVING BIOGRAPHIES OF AMERICAN STATESMEN
LIVING BIOGRAPHIES OF FAMOUS MEN
LIVING BIOGRAPHIES OF GREAT COMPOSERS
LIVING BIOGRAPHIES OF GREAT POETS
LIVING BIOGRAPHIES OF GREAT PAINTERS
LIVING BIOGRAPHIES OF FAMOUS AMERICANS
LIVING BIOGRAPHIES OF FAMOUS NOVELISTS
LIVING BIOGRAPHIES OF FAMOUS WOMEN

UNDERSTANDING THE GREAT PHILOSOPHERS

by Henry Thomas, Ph.D.

Doubleday & Company, Inc.
Garden City, New York

184

Contents

PART 5   *The "Enlightened" Philosophers*

PART 6   *Modern European Philosophers*

PART 7   *Modern American Philosophers*

PART 8   *The Completed Circle*

Introduction

PHILOSOPHY MEANS the "love of wisdom"—that is, the passionate desire to solve the four outstanding enigmas of life: who we are, where we come from, where we are going, and what is the best way to get there. The chief purpose of philosophy is to establish mental serenity through the contemplation of wisdom. A knowledge of philosophy will enable us to become better acquainted with ourselves and our proper place in the world.

And the object of the present book is to make the journey to the understanding of the world's wisdom both interesting and easy. Our aim will be to turn the complex questions of the head into the simple answers of the heart.

Most of the current books dealing with the history of philosophy have erred on two important points:

1. They are too fragmentary. They give only a part of the picture instead of the entire picture. In their survey of the world's wisdom, they omit the wisdom of the Orient. They begin their story with the discussion of Greek philosophy, ignoring the fact that it was the Eastern thinkers—of Egypt, Persia, India, China, and Judea—who served as the sources for the inspiration of the Greek and the later philosophers. It is impossible to understand the wisdom of Plato, Spinoza, Schopenhauer, Kant, Nietzsche, Bergson, Emerson, and James without an understanding of their indebtedness to the wisdom of the Orient.

2. Most of the histories of philosophy are too controversial. They emphasize the discord rather than the concord between the various schools of thought. Many a student of philosophy comes out more perplexed at the end of his study than he was at the beginning. He feels as if he has been carried through a journey, not over a definite road that leads to a distinct goal, but over a bumpy road of sudden detours and impenetrable

jungles. At every new turn he finds himself completely lost. No part of the new road seems to have any connection with any part of the older road. As one of the students in a course on the history of philosophy has remarked, "All I have learned in this course is that every philosopher disagrees with every other philosopher. As a result, I don't know what it's all about."

The aim of the present book is to avoid the two defects of incompleteness and of emphasis upon discord instead of concord. This book will tell the *whole story* of philosophy from its beginning in the Orient down to the present day, and it will point out the *essential unity* rather than the superficial diversity in all the leading philosophical systems. The book proposes, in short, to give the reader a complete and definite view rather than a fragmentary and blurred picture of the world's wisest thought. *Understanding the Great Philosophers* is intended as a clear and consistent guide for everyday living.

We shall therefore begin with oriental philosophy, tracing the stream of thought through Greece and Rome and western Europe, on to America, and back again to its origin in the East. And as we complete the circle, we shall try to point out how all the great philosophers have emphasized one truth, just as all the great religious leaders have emphasized one God.

And as we try to clarify our conception of the world through philosophy, we shall discover the close relationship between philosophy and science on the one hand, and philosophy and religion on the other. Indeed, we shall see that philosophy is a bridge between science and religion. Philosophy is assertive toward the skepticisms of science, and skeptical toward the assertions of religion. And thus it leaps ahead while science follows, and follows cautiously while religion leads the way. It tries to spur science into adventure, and to translate religion into reason. But above all it tries to point the way, both through the limited certainty of science and through the infinite mystery of religion, to a wiser, saner and happier life.

This, in brief, will be the substance of our book. The treatment will be largely biographical and anecdotal. We shall present here not merely wisdom in the abstract, but the wise thoughts and the sparkling humor of men who lived. And as we examine the lives and the thoughts of the wisest men of the ages, we shall find that philosophy is not, as a wag has remarked, the process of looking in a dark room for a black cat that isn't there, but rather the effort of the human mind to discover the divine pattern and the ultimate meaning of life.

Our book, therefore, will take us on a mental flight over the entire world of thought. I can promise you an exciting journey of discovery and adventure and delight.

So let us take off to the first stage of our journey—the brilliance of the eastern landscape that emerges from the mists of the dawn.

PART
1

The Wisdom of the East

CHAPTER I

The Philosophy of Egypt

As soon as Man began to think, he must have asked himself these perplexing questions: Who am I? What sort of place is this world? What am I doing here? And ever since that earliest period of human thought, the great philosophers have been asking the selfsame questions.

The first great wise men of history lived in Egypt. This ancient country may be regarded as the pioneer teacher of mankind. When the primitive races drifted from place to place in search of food and shelter, many of them passed through a corridor now known as the Valley of the Nile. This valley, the land of Egypt, served as a gathering place for thousands of people who came from mountain, forest, desert, ice field, and seashore. Here in their new home they sharpened their wits through an exchange of their various experiences. And thus their minds were fertilized with new ideas, cults, and customs. Egypt therefore became the cradle of civilized thought.

It was to Egypt that many of the philosophers of the ancient world traveled for their inspiration and training. The wisdom of the Egyptians was proverbial among the ancient Greeks. Plato—the greatest philosopher of Greece and perhaps of the entire world—acknowledged the Egyptians as his leaders to the sublime.

And through Plato and the other Greek philosophers, all modern thinking may trace its origin to the wisdom of the Egyptians. The Greeks borrowed their philosophy from the Orient, and we in turn have borrowed our philosophy from the Greeks. The stream of wisdom, beginning with the Nile, has flowed steadily down through the ages. There are no new thoughts under the sun. Whatever we regard as a new thought is merely an old thought dressed in a different style and seen under a different light. As Byron reminds us, every so-called modern system of philosophy "is but the same rehearsal of the past."

A brief survey of early Egyptian thought will demonstrate the truth of this observation. We shall find the legacy of Plato and Aristotle in the philosophy of Ptah-hotep; the heritage of Schopenhauer and Tolstoy in the wisdom of Ipuwer; and the inspiration of Spinoza and Kant in the vision of Ikhnaton.

Let us glance at some of these Egyptian sources of ancient and modern philosophical thought:

II   *PTAH-HOTEP*

Our knowledge of this philosopher, who lived about twenty-three hundred years before Plato, or 2700 B.C., is rather scanty. Yet we have enough excerpts from his Manual of Wisdom to give us a fairly adequate idea of his philosophy.

Ptah-hotep was Governor of Memphis and Prime Minister to the King. Toward the end of his life he retired from office and devoted himself to the instruction of the young—especially his son. His purpose as a father on earth, he said, was "to imitate a wise and loving Father in Heaven."

Ptah-hotep believed in chastisement as a spur to virtue. The rule of heaven and earth, he said, is to learn through suffering. Men began as brutes—here Ptah-hotep anticipated Darwin—and it was only through a slow and painful process that they learned to become human.

And every child, at the beginning of his development, is more or less brutal. If you spare the rod, therefore, you spoil the child. The youngster must be taught to obey the whip like a refractory horse. Indeed, the teachers of ancient Egypt were called the "Royal Stable of Instructors." Very often, said Ptah-hotep, the best lecture is a good spanking. "For the children seem to have their ears on their backside."

But in addition to punishment, the child is in need of advice. He must acquire a philosophical outlook on life. This philosophical outlook, said Ptah-hotep, "is the best inheritance I can leave to my son."

He begins his Manual of Wisdom with a request to be relieved of his political duties. "My King and Lord, the end of life is at hand. Old age is descending upon me. The feebleness of my childhood has returned. He that is old lies down in misery every day. The eyes have become dimmed, the ears bereft of their hearing. My energy is diminished, my heart finds no rest . . . Allow thy servant, therefore, to give over his princely authority to his son."

And then Ptah-hotep explains that the purpose of his Man ual is to enable his son to be a good man. Even in that early period of history, Ptah-hotep made no claim to originality. He was merely restating old truths in a new way, he said. "Let me speak to my son the words of those who hearken to the wisdom of the men of old time—those that once heard the words of God."

Following this introduction, Ptah-hotep goes on with his Manual of the Good Life:

"Be not proud because thou art learned, but discourse with the ignorant as with the sage. You have much to learn from one another. For no limit can be set to knowledge, neither is there any philosopher who possesses full wisdom. Tolerant speech as between equals is more rare than emeralds."

But more important even than tolerant words are gentle deeds. "Live in the house of kindliness, and men shall come and give gifts of themselves."

Ptah-hotep advocated "kind words, gentle deeds, and a tongue that knows when to be silent . . . Never speak in harshness or in haste. Beware of making enemies with thy words. Never overstep the truth, and never repeat words that have been spoken to thee in confidence—whether the speaker be a peasant or a prince. Telling tales out of order is abhorrent to the soul."

This picture of a wise son, as we shall see, is very close to Aristotle's picture of the gentle man—that is, the perfect gentleman. "Learn to bear thyself with equanimity in the tempests of life," advised Ptah-hotep. "Let nothing overturn the even balance of thy character. A good character is the most precious gift in life."

Sail through life on an even keel. "Be not too timid to speak the truth, nor too rash to utter a falsehood. And teach thy son to do likewise." Do not coddle him if he is perverse. "If he be heedless and trespass thy rules of conduct, and is violent, if every speech that cometh from his mouth is a vile word, *then beat him* that he may become more careful of his words and his works."

Above all, Ptah-hotep urged the learning and teaching of the virtue of self-control—a doctrine that was to become one of the cornerstones of Plato's and Aristotle's philosophies. "Fit thy deeds to the occasion and thy words to the point. The wise man never speaks of things about which he knows nothing. And once again let me caution thee—curb thy temper and thy tongue."

Like most of the other wise men of Egypt, Ptah-hotep believed in one God. It is not historically true that the Hebrews invented the idea of monotheism. They borrowed this idea from the Egyptians and—as we shall see—from some of the other oriental nations. The belief in one God, one Father of all mankind, seems to have taken root in many places as a result of the father-and-son relationship in the early development of the family. The philosophers were the first to recognize the unity of the human family under a single godhead. While the common people talked of the gods—just as we talk of the angels —the wiser men spoke of God.

This god of Ptah-hotep and the other early philosophers of

Egypt was known as Osiris. The story of Osiris is somewhat similar to that of Jesus. He came down to earth in order to serve mankind, he was killed by the unbelievers, and he was resurrected to guide mankind for all time. At the feast of his resurrection, the populace thronged to his tomb, scattered flowers over the ground, and sang a Song of Love to their savior on high.

To Ptah-hotep the myth of Osiris represented the struggle between good and evil. "For a time evil may conquer, but good shall prevail in the end." This Egyptian philosopher declared that God is Eternal. He holds His people responsible for their acts, but He guides their upward climb toward heaven.

For the soul of man, like a flame, tends ever upward. "Man dies, to live again." It may well have been the Egyptian thinkers who first implanted in St. Paul—a profound student of oriental learning—the thought "O death, where is thy sting? O grave, where is thy victory?"

For it was Ptah-hotep and the other early Egyptian philosophers who first recorded man's belief in resurrection. It was this belief that prompted the Egyptians to preserve the bodies of their dead. They placed all sorts of utensils in the tombs for the use of the dead during their long wait for their return to life. The philosophers refined this popular idea with the explanation that the objects deposited in the tombs were symbols to comfort the living rather than tools to help the dead.

In ancient Egypt, philosophy was closely allied to religion. One of the most interesting symbols painted on the walls of the tombs was a picture of the deceased rising to his feet with his arms outstretched in the form of a cross. This idea of the cross—which had its origin in Egypt about three thousand years before the Christian Era—had an uplifting rather than a saddening connotation. It represented mankind as reaching up toward life rather than sinking down toward death.

This, in brief, is the optimistic phase of early Egyptian philosophy, including the work of its founder, Ptah-hotep. But

Egypt also had its share of pessimistic philosophers. One of the earliest exponents of this negative aspect of wisdom was a skeptic who may be regarded as the philosophical godfather of Schopenhauer.

III   *IPUWER*

This ancient unbeliever bemoans the fact that he is unable to make offerings to God because he doesn't know where God may be found. He deplores the waves of adult crime and juvenile delinquency that have swept over the land. Anticipating Schopenhauer and Tolstoy, he advocates race suicide as an end to human misery. "Would that there might be an end of men, no conception, no birth. If the earth would but cease from noise, and strife would be no more, how good a thing it would be for all!"

And then he goes on to enumerate the corruption of his age in words that arouse an echo in *every* age, including our own:

"To whom can I speak today? Brothers are evil and cheat one another. To whom can I speak today? Hearts are thievish, every man seizes his neighbor's goods. To whom can I speak today? The gentle man perishes, the arrogant aggressor lives in triumph. To whom can I speak today? When a man's conduct should arouse indignation, it arouses mirth; when his thievishness deserves the whip, it is rewarded with riches and fame."

Following this outburst against the evils of his day, Ipuwer composes a eulogy to death—the gentle release from the sickness called life:

"Death is before me today like the recovery of a sick man, like going forth into a garden after sickness. Death is before me today like the fragrance of lotus-flowers, like sitting under the sail on a windy day. Death is before me today like the course of a mountain-stream, like the return of a man from the warship to his house. Death is before me today like the longing of a man to see his home after many years of captivity."

Unlike the sun dial, this philosopher recorded the dark rather than the bright hours of life. Yet he, too, was always in search of the God whose existence he denied. This ancient Shelley was such a fierce denouncer of injustice because he was such an ardent believer in the ultimate triumph of justice. His hatred was but the reverse side of his love. At heart he was inflamed with the passion of a Messiah. He envisioned a spiritual leader who was to become the philosopher-king of Plato, the Redeemer of the Hebrew prophets, and the Saviour of the Gospel. "This leader," wrote Ipuwer, "brings cooling to the flame of injustice. He is the shepherd of all men. When the herds in his pasture have gone astray and their hearts are afraid, he passes the hours in bringing them together again. He smites the evil ones and rescues the good. Where is he today? Is he asleep perchance? But take comfort; when the time is ripe, he shall awake!"

Ipuwer was the first social philosopher in the history of the world.

But Ipuwer and Ptah-hotep merely paved the way for the greater philosopher who was to come after them.

IV IKHNATON

This Egyptian king may be regarded as the founder of the supreme concept in human thought: One God, One World, One Universal Law—the harmony of mankind.

The real name of this philosopher-king—he lived about fourteen hundred years before Christ—was Amenhotep IV. He assumed the name Ikhnaton, which means "dedicated to God." Though he was only thirty when he died, he left behind him a testament of wisdom for all time.

He was inspired by the earlier Egyptian philosophers and by the Theban Book of the Dead. This book was a sort of "negative confession" that the souls of the dead were supposed to recite on their Day of Judgment. It was a declaration that they had refrained from breaking the Commandments of God:

"Hail to thee, Great God, Lord of Truth and Justice! I have been brought before thee, my Master, that I may behold thy Glory and give my testimony . . . I have not injured any man, I have not oppressed the poor . . . I have not imposed labor upon any man beyond his strength . . . I have not neglected my duties, I have not committed anything that is an abomination to God . . . I have not refused food to the hungry, I have not brought pain to anyone or caused anyone to weep . . . I have not given short weight, and I have not deprived the little ones of their milk. I have not taken anything that belongs to man or God . . . I am pure. I am pure. I am pure."

But this declaration of goodness—or rather, negation of evil—was made a mockery by a corrupt priesthood. The priests as a rule adhered to the doctrine of many gods instead of one God. They were interested in selling charms (the more gods, the more charms) rather than in teaching virtue. They told their followers that if anyone forgot to recite his declaration but displayed the magic trinkets bought from the priests, the gods would forgive him for his sins.

And thus the moral principles of Egypt had degenerated into magic formulas. But it was the goal of Ikhnaton to put an end to this corruption. Though it brought about his early death, he inaugurated a religious and ethical revolution. Like Isaiah, Socrates, and Jesus, he was a martyr for the truth.

This truth, as Ikhnaton saw it, envisioned one supreme God whose Heaven lay tenderly over the body of the Earth. "From this divine embrace all things are created with a body composed of earthly clay and a soul compounded of heavenly fire." This undying fire, declared Ikhnaton, resides not only in every human creature but in every created thing—in the palm tree that gives restful shade, the river that waters the plain, the spring that slakes the thirst, the flower that brings fragrance and beauty to the human heart, and even the lowly onion that brings the zest of spice to the banquet of life.

This belief of Ikhnaton in one supreme power is the first *formal* expression of monotheism in history. Yet with its idea of God-in-everything, the philosophy of Ikhnaton is somewhat closer to pantheism than it is to monotheism. Ikhnaton may therefore be regarded as the original source of Spinoza's pantheistic philosophy.

The Egyptian king expressed his religious philosophy in a poem dedicated to the glory of God. It is one of the world's sublime songs:

"Thy dawning is beautiful in the horizon of the sky,
O living God, Beginning of life.
Thou hast created all things, thou guidest all things,
Thou bindest all lands and all nations by thy love

. . .

Bright is the earth when thou bringest the dawn.
The earth awakes in festivity,
And all its creatures lift up their voices
In a song of adoration to thee, the bringer of light.
All the living things of the earth and the air and the sea
Are filled with the flame of thy glory.
Thou art the creator of the plant in the earth,
And the seed in the womb.
Thou hast planted them and brought them to life.
When the fledgling bird stirs in the egg,
Thou givest him breath that he may burst his shell
And come into light.
All things are alive and thou art the life of the world.

. . .

How manifold are thy wonders, O Lord,
The One Living God of the Universe!
Thou art the Father and lover of all men,
In Egypt, in Syria, and in every other land."

Here we get the first glimmer of an international brotherhood that includes the members of one human family throughout the world. "There is a Nile for the Egyptians here below," declares Ikhnaton, "and a Nile of living water in the sky for all the strangers of all the other nations, and for the cattle that go upon their feet in every land."

In the sky, said Ikhnaton, there are many mansions along the banks of the River of Life. And God dwells in all of them, for His dwelling is in the human heart.

Thus, almost at the dawn of history, the philosopher-king of Egypt envisioned one human family, and one God—the compassionate Father of all, the Lord of Love.

Ikhnaton ordered the destruction of the monuments raised to the gods of the more primitive religious creeds, and he closed their temples. He abandoned the royal city of Thebes as unclean, and built himself a new capital which he called the City of God.

For a while he flourished in this new city and made it a center of literature and art. But the priests of the older cults, enraged at the loss of their revenue from the selling of magic charms, brought about his destruction. Jesus was not the first victim of the money-changers in the temples of the world.

This brief survey of Egyptian thought—the earliest recorded philosophy in the world—reveals an important truth: the old is the same as the new, the new is the same as the old, and all our modern wisdom is but a restatement of the wisdom of the ancient seers.

We shall see this truth repeated in many different guises and under many different lights as we follow the stream of philosophy from the earliest sources down to the present day.

CHAPTER II

The Philosophy of Persia

IN NEARLY EVERY modern system of philosophy we find the echo of an ancient sage who quietly observes: "I too have said it." One of our most baffling problems today is the meaning of the struggle between good and evil. This philosophical problem was puzzled over during the time of Zoroaster—or to use his Persian name, Zarathustra—who lived about one thousand years before Christ.

Zoroaster not only formulated the problem but tried to find an answer to it. This answer, as we shall see, has been accepted by many great thinkers including our own American philosopher, William James.

Yet even in Zoroaster's day, the question of good and evil was regarded as an ancient problem in philosophy. "Long before my own time," he wrote, "a shepherd by the name of Yima arose to teach the people how to make the light prevail through the conquest of the dark." Zoroaster called himself merely an interpreter of Yima, who in turn was "an interpreter of God."

This early Persian interpretation of God marks an interesting chapter in human thought. Zoroaster was the founder of a new religion of righteousness, and a new philosophy of harmony. His idea of righteousness became corrupted into ritual—his adherents worshiped the name and perverted the teaching of their leader. But his theory of harmony arising out of discord has remained an inspiration to the philosophers down to the present day.

Let us look at this half-legendary Persian with his strange life and even stranger thought.

II

At the time of Zoroaster's birth—the exact date is unknown —Persia was a country of despotism, cruelty, and war. The ruler called himself King of Kings. His word was the law of the land. It meant death for a subject even to "think" unkindly of his monarch. For his ministers—"the King's Eyes and Ears"—were trained to ferret out the very thoughts of the people. One day the king shot an innocent young man to death before the eyes of his father. When the monarch turned to the father for his comment, the poor man threw himself on the ground and exclaimed: "Hail, O King, for thy perfect archery!"

Another man, the father of five sons, lost four of them in battle. When he begged His Royal Highness to spare the fifth son from the Army, the king ordered the young man to be cut in two and placed on each side of the road, so that the marching soldiers could see the practical results of a subject's disobedience to the king.

As for the "gentler" half of the royal court, one of the queens ordered her lady in waiting to be flayed alive and the skin to be made into upholstery for her footstool.

This was the state of affairs in Persia at the time of Zoroaster's birth.

There are many legends about Zoroaster, several of them dealing with his "miraculous" birth. "The Lord of Light hearkened to His people and sent them a Strong One who would bring them salvation."

According to one legend, he entered the body of his mother—a woman of the nobility—in the form of a flash of lightning. This was a symbol of his life's mission "to bring light to the children of darkness." The moment he came into the world he burst into laughter, "and the spirits of evil that surrounded his cradle fled in tumult and terror."

Thereupon all nature rejoiced. The very leaves of the trees rustled in a song of glory, and the winds and the rivers joined in the universal song.

After a while the evil spirits returned and tried to kill the infant. But he was under the special protection of God, and all their efforts failed.

As the infant grew into childhood, they continued their evil designs. At one time, they threw him into the path of a herd of stampeding cattle. "But guided by the hand of God, one of the oxen stood guard over him while the rest of the herd rushed by on either side."

At another time the spirits of darkness imprisoned him in a den of wolves. But once again, "the hand of the Lord rescued him and brought him back into the light."

Through the mists of these legendary stories we can gather perhaps a single ray of truth. Zoroaster seems to have been a lively child full of mischief out of which he managed "miraculously" to escape.

At the age of seven he was put into the care of a number of wise men who taught him the ways of God. Among these teachers, according to some of the ancient scholars, were the Egyptian sages and the Hebrew prophets. Again there may be a grain of truth in the chaff of these fables. Whether directly or indirectly, the wisdom of Zoroaster was inspired by the thoughts of Ikhnaton and the other oriental philosophers.

His teachers, we are told, had a double duty to perform. They saved his body from the poisoned barbs and his mind from the poisoned lies of the evil spirits. And at the age of fifteen he completed his education. He was now ready to assume "the parchment of wisdom and the girdle of religion."

For the next fifteen years he refined his character in the "sacred waters of compassion." To translate this into more prosaic terms, he devoted himself to social service. "He ministered to the sick; he fed the hungry; he comforted the aged; he lightened the loads of the beasts of burden; and he cleared the obstacles from the roadways of life for his fellow travelers on earth." In other words, he took a postgraduate course in the science of interdependent living.

And then, at thirty, he was ready to become the prophet of a new religion and the professor of a new philosophy. "For he had seen a new light upon the peak of the Mountain of Sabalan—the light that glowed upon the face of Ahura Mazda, the Lord of the Universe." Here, in a cave where Zoroaster had spent many an hour of meditation, Ahura Mazda had "revealed himself" to him as the one God, though known by many names and interpreted in many ways through his various attributes. These attributes were not, as most people believed, different gods, but one God seen under different aspects. Thus, Ahura Mazda explained to Zoroaster, he might be regarded as a sevenfold personality—representing Righteousness, Eternal Light, Omniscient Wisdom, Supreme Power, Divine Piety, Infinite Mercy, and Everlasting Life.

Yet these seven aspects of God, as Zoroaster learned, were but as seven drops in the ocean of his glory. And he, Zoroaster, had been chosen to teach this glory to the world.

But as soon as he came down from the mountain, Zoroaster found himself confronted by the spirits of evil. "Let us kill him!" they cried. "For if this all-too-righteous prophet lives, evil dies. And without evil we, too, die."

Once more Ahura Mazda saved His prophet. But now Zoroaster was assailed by a new doubt. "Why this evil in a world governed by the goodness of God? What, indeed, is the meaning of evil in this life of ours? How can I explain the meaning of good and evil for the better understanding of my fellow men?"

As he pondered upon this problem—we are told—"Ahura Mazda came to his help and gave him the answer to the mystery of the world."

III

Zoroaster compiled his ideas on religion and philosophy in a book called Avesta. It is better known to the modern world as the Zend-Avesta—the "Interpretation of Wisdom." This book, of which we have only a handful of fragments, deals with the nature of God, the duty of man, and the purpose of life. Like the poet Browning, whom he anticipated by about three thousand years, Zoroaster declared: "Life has a meaning, and to find it is the quest of my soul."

First he defined the nature of God. Ahura Mazda is the Lord of Creation and Life, Matter, and Spirit. He is the form-less, boundless, and deathless agent of eternal Law the pat-tern of the universe which holds true for all mankind at all times. He has assigned different peoples to different times and different places, so that all of us may behold him *and work along with him* from our various stations and viewpoints. And he has implanted in each of us a special love for our own coun-try and our own God. Actually there is only one country and one God. But our diverse habitations and interpretations enable us to piece together our fragmentary ideas into the one Eternal Truth. This Eternal Truth is the lesson we have to learn in the School of Life. Whoever has succeeded in learning it is a true believer—whatever the form of his religion or the name of his God.

There is a beautiful Persian legend about an angel whom the Lord sent down to earth in order to discover whether it contained a single devout soul—"a soul whose prayer is a prayer for the entire world." The angel traveled all over the earth and visited thousands of temples and shrines. Yet he failed to find anywhere the object of his search—a man of perfect under-standing and complete faith. "There is great nobility in most of the religions," observed the angel, "and much fervor in many of the prayers. But nowhere have I seen a man who has enshrined all his fellow creatures in his heart."

And then, as the angel was returning to heaven, he came across a savage praying to a wooden idol "on an island in the distant seas." He looked into the heart of the savage "and saw therein a compassionate image of the human race."

And the angel came to the Lord and said: "I have discovered one devout man on earth. But this man is an idol-worshiping savage."

"Then the earth shall be redeemed," said the Lord. "For there lives upon it one civilized believer in God."

To understand God, observed Zoroaster, we must learn to understand our fellow men. And on the road to understanding there are a number of signposts pointing toward our goal. Most important among these signposts are Justice, Service, Faith, and the Pursuit of Perfection.

The first signpost to the goal is Justice. This was one of the doctrines that was to guide Plato to his own system of philosophy. The Greeks were great admirers of Zoroaster and regarded him as "among the wisest men of the ancient world." Zoroaster's idea of Justice is the elimination of wrong through the true knowledge of what is right. The light that reveals this knowledge is the Eternal Harmony of God. "If you know the truth, you know God." The whole world is a moving pattern weaving its way toward the divine.

"Through the Supreme Truth, the Law of Justice," declared Zoroaster, "man is able to come into union with God."

The principle of Justice through the knowledge of Truth is symbolized among the devout followers of Zoroaster by the "Sacred Flame." This is to be regarded not as a physical fire but as the "countenance of God enshrined in the human heart."

The first signpost to the divine, therefore, is the shining light of Justice fed by the Fire of Truth.

The next signpost to the divine is Service. Our entire life, declared Zoroaster, is meant to be an adventure in serving one another. In the philosophy of Zoroaster we find a story similar to that of Adam and Eve in the Old Testament. Before he could make the perfect man, Ahura Mazda created a man and a woman of ordinary clay and placed them in an earthly Paradise. The word Paradise, it is interesting to note, is Persian; it means a "nobleman's garden." When the first human couple came into this Garden of Nobility, Zoroaster tells us, they obeyed the Laws of Service. They thought good thoughts, they spoke good words, they performed good deeds, and they served one another, their children, and their children's children.

But when the first couple died, their offspring began to quarrel among themselves. They forgot the Law of Service and fell into evil ways of aggression. And in punishment for their sins, Ahura Mazda sent upon them a flood of melting snows and destroyed them all with the exception of a few who were still devoted to justice, compassion and service. "Out of these faithful few," declared Ahura Mazda, "I will try again to build the righteous man."

And thus Ahura Mazda keeps experimenting through all eternity with this human clay. For the development of the righteous man who is to teach the lesson of mutual service is not the matter of a few generations or centuries. It is an eternal job of man's progressive journey on the road to God.

Hence the second signpost along the road to the divine is Service to God through Service to our fellow men.

The third signpost along this Godward road is Faith. "The faithful man is he whose ears have heard the whisper of the Lord." And within the heart of such a man the Lord implants an instinct for loyalty toward his home, his community, his province, his country, the entire world.

For a man's faith in God is translated into his love for mankind. "Ahura Mazda embraces all humanity in his universal love." The best way to show your belief in God is to imitate His love. "The warmth of love will melt all the doubts within your heart."

But this love, this faith, must be active rather than passive. It must be manifested not merely in thoughts and in words, but in deeds. Paving the way for Plato, Zoroaster said that love leads to justice and service. And inspiring the still later thought of St. Paul, he said that neither justice nor service nor faith can prevail without the all-pervasive spirit of love.

Thus Zoroaster's third signpost to the divine is Active Faith through Deeds of Love.

His fourth signpost to the divine is the Pursuit of Perfection. This, said Zoroaster, is the purpose of creation and the meaning of life. Indeed, it is the very core of the Persian philosopher's teaching. He brooded long upon the problem of imperfection in a world which we so ardently desire to be perfect. And the answer he found to the problem is this: It is up to us to help *make* the world perfect. This is the only reason for our life on earth.

And thus we come to Zoroaster's famous doctrine of the struggle between good and evil. We are soldiers enlisted for life in this struggle. We are meant to be co-fighters with God in making the world better, in abolishing the bad and establishing the good.

This idea has exercised the best philosophical minds of the centuries, from Zoroaster to William James. As Zoroaster first explained it, the world is a battleground between Ahura Mazda, the Spirit of Light, and Ahriman, the Power of Darkness.

Light and darkness, good and evil, according to Zoroaster, are both equally necessary to make the pattern of the universe complete. A world without evil is just as impossible as a life without pain. It is the contrast between the two, and our participation in bringing harmony out of chaos, that makes life so interesting. The value of goodness consists in the overcoming of evil, just as the value of health consists in the overcoming of pain. How could we enjoy rest if we never experienced labor, or appreciate the glory of the day if we never knew the terror of the night? A life of light without shadows would be no more interesting than a living death. It is our striving out of the shadow into the light that makes our life so zestful. "A perpetual holiday," as George Bernard Shaw expressed it, "is a good working definition of hell."

In other words, it is the spirit of darkness, negation, disharmony, that helps to make our life so meaningful. And this meaning consists in our effort to conquer the darkness, negation, and disharmony of the world. Goethe borrowed this idea from Zoroaster when he depicted Mephistopheles—or Ahriman —as the power that evermore denies. Yet Mephistopheles admits that he is "the power that produces good while scheming evil."

This, according to Zoroaster and Goethe, is true because God *wills* us to transform evil into good. He places obstacles in our path to make our adventure through life less monotonous and more worth while. In the popular expression of our own day, we are put here to make the world a better place to live in—a precise echo of Zoroaster's thought. As St. Augustine put it, "God permits evil for the sake of a greater good."

Each of us, therefore, is "a laborer in God's vineyard." It is a thought that gives a sobering purpose to our life. "God and you and I work hand in hand to bring order out of chaos, beauty out of ugliness, peace out of war." All of us, Zoroaster declared, are the builders of our own fate.

And when the job of our own life is finished, said Zoroaster, each of us is called to account for his work. Those who have failed in their duty—"of good thoughts, good words and good deeds as weapons against evil thoughts, evil words and evil deeds"—are punished for their sins in their life after death. This ultimate punishment for every sin is a part of Zoroaster's conception of a world moving toward harmony—a place where all wrongs are righted at last.

But no punishment, declared Zoroaster, goes on forever. In the end, after we have paid our necessary dues, all our united destinies are woven into the pattern of a complete, harmonious, and righteous world. To quote Tennyson—this poet's mind was saturated with the philosophy of Zoroaster and the other oriental thinkers—"we trust that somehow *good* will be the final goal of ill."

And thus—according to Zoroaster—when men pray to God, "Deliver us from evil," God replies, "Deliver *yourselves* from evil. Working together, you with my help and I with yours will gradually transform the world into a Paradise for noble souls."

"Thus spake Zarathustra" of the divine and human collaboration in the crusade for a better world. Many of the ancient and modern philosophers have accepted this doctrine. A few have questioned it, though they have found no answer to their own question. One philosopher, Nietzsche, perverted the doctrine from a crusade of God and Man against the Devil into a conspiracy of the Devil and Man against God. But all agree that Zoroaster was one of the first supreme teachers of the human race.

There is a revealing legend about the death of this Christian who lived before Christ. He leaped up to heaven, we are told, in a flash of lightning. Translated into prosaic words, this legend probably means that he was burned to death when a group of fanatics set fire to his house. He seems to have suffered the fate frequently shared by the saviors of mankind. "But death," Zoroaster had declared, "is not the end of life."

CHAPTER III

The Philosophy of India

THE FRENCH SAVANT, Victor Cousin, regarded India as "the native land of the highest wisdom." And Schopenhauer observed that in the entire world "there is no study so beneficial and so elevating as that of the Upanishads"—the earliest book of Hindu philosophy.

The word "Upanishad" consists of two parts—*upa*, "near," and *shad*, "to sit." It describes the philosophy that the pupils received from their teacher as they sat at his feet. Suppose we join these pupils and learn something about the wisdom of their master.

Or rather, masters. For the Upanishads represent the ideas of several philosophers who taught over a period of three hundred years—from 800 to 500 B.C. Those thoughts were collected into a series of discourses that tried to penetrate through the mists of the intellect to the reality that lay beyond.

We know nothing about the lives of these philosophers; but we do know that at least one of them was a woman. The early Hindus believed that the best ornament for a beautiful body is a beautiful mind.

The Upanishads deal with the philosopher's eternal quest to piece together the fragmentary puzzle of our existence into a complete and understandable picture. A certain king, we read in one of the Upanishads, asked a "knower of the soul" to explain to him the riddle of the universe. Said the king to the philosopher, "In this foul-smelling, perishable body, this jumble of skin, bone, muscle, marrow, semen, blood, tears, mucus, bile, and phlegm, what is the good of the gratification of desire? In this body that dies like the gnats, the mosquitoes, the worms, the grass and the trees, what is the good of the gratification of desire? In this world of the drying up of seas and the crumbling away of mountains, in this cycle of existence which compels us to be born only to die, and to die only to be born again, what is the good of birth and death and desire and its fulfillment, only to lead to other desires without meaning or end?"

Here the king was expressing the universal Hindu belief in, and revulsion against, the idea of reincarnation—the rebirth of the individual into a repeated succession of sufferings under different forms of life. And the philosopher's answer to the king was threefold:

1. Let us not try to understand the complex mystery of the whole with the fragmentary instrument of the mind. You and I, exalted king and humble sage alike, are like prisoners looking at a vast landscape through a narrow slit in the wall of our cell. The cell is our body, and the slit through which we see the world is the window of our senses. At best we can see but a small segment of the entire circle of the horizon. Thus, the first step to the understanding of the world is to realize how little you can understand.

2. But the best way to see the meaning of life is to look not outward, but inward. In order to know the world, learn to know yourself. Examine your own soul, and you will get a small reflection of the universal soul of life. In order that the reflection may be unruffled and clear, cleanse your soul with silent meditation and gentle deeds. And so the second step to the understanding of the world is to put your mind at peace.

3. And, when your mind is at peace, you will find that the impersonal part of your own soul, freed from its temporal desires, is at one with the impersonal soul of the world. Thus, at our noblest and selfless best, all of us are blended into a single unit of life. "Just as the flowing rivers disappear into the sea, losing their name and form, just so the wise man, released from

name and form, goes to the divine ocean of life" known variously as the universal soul, Brahman, or God. This, according to the Upanishads, is the final step to the understanding of the world, and the ultimate purpose of life.

And so the philosophers of the Upanishads would say, together with one of their disciples, Ralph Waldo Emerson, "What's your hurry, little man?" Where are you rushing? To the fulfillment of your desires? But every fulfillment is merely a transition to other unfulfilled desires. It is an interminable and insatiable quest. When you have amassed ten thousand pieces of gold, you hunger for a hundred thousand. When you have amassed a hundred thousand you crave for a million. And so on and on.

Or are you trying to fly away from yourself? This, too, is an impossible aim. For "he who flies across the sea will find a new sky, but not a new mind." When you try to escape from yourself, "you are the wings on which you fly." Your true self, your larger self, will carry you and confront and upbraid you wherever you may go.

The wise thing, therefore, is to recognize your limited capability as an isolated self, and your infinite capacity as a part of the Universal Self. You are a seed in the forest of growing trees, a drop in the waters of the boundless ocean, a spark in the fire of eternal life.

> All is one, and one is all;
> Things are different but in name;
> Both the torch-light and the sunlight
> Are one liquid living flame.

The philosophical writers of the Upanishads believed in only one kind of sacrifice—the slaying of your selfish desires upon the altar of your universal self. This doctrine is closely allied to that of Bertrand Russell's idea of enlightened selfishness. You can best serve yourself by serving others. It is even more closely allied to the Christian teaching that you can find yourself only by losing yourself. Our business in life, declares the Upanishads, is to aspire to the vision of this all-inclusive self. You become immortal by eliminating all your mortal—that is, all your selfish—desires.

And if you try and fail, don't despair. You will be reborn to try again and again. And in the end you are bound to succeed.

In other words, the writers of the Upanishads advanced the idea of progressive transmigration—the passage of the individual soul from life to life until it is cleansed through the fire of experience and becomes absorbed into the universal soul.

In this absorption you do not lose your individual personality; you merely lose your individual or self-centered separateness from God. Thus, in losing yourself, you find God.

II

This philosophy of the Upanishads persisted as an interesting theory for many years. It remained for Buddha (563–483 b.c.) to submit the theory to a practical test. The life of Buddha, as well as his teaching, served as an example of the submergence of individual selfishness into universal selflessness. He exchanged a crown for a beggar's bowl, and found his greatest happiness in rising from riches to rags.

His life, in brief, is the story of a man who refused to be a prince in order to become a vagabond teacher of love. The word "love" has been twisted into many meanings, ranging all the way from the salacious to the sublime. In the story of Buddha we shall find it revealed in its most exalted form. The universal love of Buddha made him the pioneer democrat of history. He regarded all men as kings, and himself as their one willing slave.

His father, Shuddothana, was the Rajah of Kapilavastu—

a kingdom in the foothills of the Himalayas. The name given him at birth was Siddartha Sakya-muni Gautama Tathagata, which means "Gautama, the prince of Sakya who will reach the goal of perfection through the knowledge of truth." He later came to be known as Buddha, "the Enlightened One," just as Jesus of Nazareth came to be known as Christ, "the Anointed One."

As a child, however, Buddha was called Prince Gautama. And, according to the Hindu legends, he was a most extraordinary prince. Just before his birth, we are told, his mother had dreamed that she would bring forth a child the like of whom the world had never seen. And Gautama came into the world "unstained like other infants with the impure waters of childbirth, but shining like a jewel upon a golden cloth."

As soon as he was born, "a light flashed in the sky, the lame walked, the deaf heard, the gods bent down from heaven to smile upon him, and the kings came from many lands to honor him."

He was brought up to look upon himself as the perfect prince of a perfect country in a perfect world. His parents protected him from every contact with the pains and miseries of mankind. When he was a child, "forty thousand dancing girls entertained him"; and when he came of age, "five hundred of the loveliest ladies in the world were paraded before him." He selected the winner of this "Miss Universe Contest" as his bride.

This marriage was as happy as his bachelorhood. The gods he had been taught to worship seemed to be propitious to this "favorite Child of Fortune." It was planned that he would inherit his father's kingdom and enjoy a life of extraordinary health, happiness, and good repute.

But he had come under the influence of the philosophers in the Upanishads. The race, he learned, is not always to the swift, nor the battle to the strong, nor the gift of happiness to the well-born. He took to walking into the streets of the city, and he discovered "the festering sores upon the body of mankind." His disciples have touchingly described these adventures he made into "the more sorrowful byways of the world." One day, we are told, he asked Channa, his charioteer, to drive him through the city. In the market place he saw an old man who stumbled painfully along the street. "Such," explained his charioteer, "is the way of life. We must all come to this as we draw near the end."

On another drive he saw a beggar whose festering body showed through his rags. "This, too," said Channa, "is the way of life."

On still another occasion, he saw an unburied corpse rotting on the ground. "This," said Channa, "is the *end* of life. It is the penalty we pay for our birth."

"Then," wrote Gautama, "I began to ask myself: 'What if I, being myself subject to birth, and having seen the wretchedness of life, were to seek out the happiness of the unborn—the cessation of all life, the supreme peace of Nirvana?'"

This was the beginning of Buddha's philosophical quest.

III

Thus far Gautama had been childless. His married life, with all its happiness, had been "like a counterfeit jewel without the beauty of a precious stone." He decided to leave all this tinsel and to set out in search of Truth.

But just before his departure, "the gods granted him their final gift"—a son. Another tie to bind him to the "glory of a prince favored by the gods." He had reached the fulfillment of his greatest desire, a life born out of his own loins.

Yet even this tie was not strong enough to stay him from his course. He was no longer satisfied with the fulfillment of his desires. His aim now was to find the meaning of all desire, to put an end to the turbulence of the mind that chased after illusory goals which, in turn, led only to other illusory goals. An endless struggle over the hurdles of pain.

His decision to leave his glory for the life of a hermit was like a sudden conversion, a rebirth into a new life. In the middle of the night he stole into his wife's room and looked for the last time upon her and their child. The Buddhist writers give us a striking picture of this scene:

"In the bedroom a lamp of scented oil was burning. On the bed strewn with heaps of jasmines the mother of the child was sleeping, with her hand on the baby's head. The Master, standing with his foot on the threshold, looked and thought, 'If I move aside the Queen's hand and take my son, the Queen will awake, and this will be an obstacle to my going. When I have become a Buddha, I will return and see him.' And he descended from the palace."

It was still dark when he ordered his charioteer to saddle two of his swiftest horses. On their way out of the city, legend tells us, the Spirit of Evil tempted him—as it was later to tempt Jesus—with the promise of powerful empires and uncounted wealth. But Gautama rejected the offer, galloped into the forest, and "crossed a wide stream with a single leap." For a while he was assailed with a desire to look back. But he stifled his longing and at dawn arrived at a place called Uruvela. "This," he said to himself, "is a beautiful spot. Clear flows the river, cool are its bathing places, and peaceful are the surrounding villages." He chose this place as the first school for his lonely meditation. Removing his precious jewels, he gave them, together with his sword and his horse, to his charioteer. And then, meeting a peasant at daybreak, he exchanged clothes with him and went off in search of a cave where he might settle down to a hermit's life of ascetic meditation.

Here he lived for six years, clothing himself in a tunic of matted hair and sustaining himself upon seeds and grass and a handful of rice. At night he laid himself upon a bed of thorns. Battered by the wind and the rain, he began to resemble a withered old tree. Like many of the other yogis of India, he was determined to learn wisdom through suffering.

But it didn't work. "My body," he said, "became extremely thin . . . When I thought I would touch the skin of my stomach, I actually felt my back . . . The bones of my spine were like a row of spindles to the touch. And, as in a deep well the sparkle of the waters is seen, so in the depth of my eye-sockets the sparkle of my sorrow was seen."

No, the way to the spirit did not lie through the mortification of the flesh. Asceticism was not the teacher of enlightenment. "By this sort of austerity I did not attain to noble insight." On the contrary, his self-imposed suffering had only weakened his intellect and increased his ignorance. He had started his hermitage in order to rise above the knowledge of the Upanishads. He had succeeded only in stooping to the ignorance of a starving dog.

So he abandoned his ascetic life. He refreshed himself with food and drink, and sat down under a fig tree to take stock of himself. And of the world. "What," he asked himself, "is the reason for my discontent—for all human discontent? What is the source of suffering, sickness, the infirmity of old age and the ugliness of death?"

All night he sat meditating under the tree. And then, with the rising of the sun, "his mind became flooded with the Truth." The cause of human sorrow, he suddenly realized, is the endless succession of births and deaths in the turbulent stream of existence. Life, desire, frustration, death—leading to another life, desire, frustration, death—repeated over and over again without cessation or rest. "Thus, with mind concentrated, purified, cleansed . . . I saw creatures passing away and being reborn, high and low, good and bad, rich and poor—yet all unhappy, none at peace."

The trouble with human life, as Gautama now envisioned it, was its endlessness. Every creature is reincarnated—an unshakable Hindu belief—into another creature. There is no rest for anyone, even in sleep, which is but a transition from day to day, or in death, which is a transition from life to life.

If only birth could be stopped! (This idea, as we shall see, lies at the core of Schopenhauer's philosophy.) But why is it not stopped? Because, as Buddha's vision revealed to him, of the law of *karma*—the retribution for the sins of our present life through our rebirth into another life.

And how can birth, or rather rebirth, be stopped? By living a life of perfect justice, compassion, and patience toward your fellow creatures. By stilling your personal desires in a single aim to serve not only all mankind but all kinds of living things.

For we cannot escape our karma. Every unkindness in this world is punished, not in a future hell but in a future life on earth. The only way to escape this punishment is to live a blameless life. Then, and only then, can we free ourselves from the chain of continual rebirth and arrive at the peace of *nirvana*.

With this vision that descended upon him under the sacred bodhi, or fig tree, Gautama became Buddha, "the Enlightened One." He went to a public park in Benaros and began to teach nirvana to the world.

IV

The idea of nirvana—the central point in the Buddhist philosophy—has frequently baffled the Western mind. Let us, however, try to understand it as Buddha understood it. And then, perhaps, we shall see its application to our own problems at the present time.

In the first place, nirvana is not a negative state of extinction but a positive state of existence. A facetious Western critic has described it as "a sort of incomprehensible infinity comprised within an inconceivable eternity." And this critic has pictured the individual soul when it is absorbed into nirvana as "a liberated prisoner who beats the drum of Nothingness in the orchestra of everlasting Silence." This cynical picture is far removed from the concept of nirvana as envisioned in Buddha's philosophy. Nirvana is not the final annihilation, but the great liberation—the shedding of the excess baggage of our personal desires so that we can come unhampered into the freedom of identity between ourselves and the universe. It is the great emancipation from a living death into eternal life. So long as we keep on yearning after earthly things, we stay bound to the earth. We are transferred from life to life, from prison cell to prison cell, "and there is no release until our cravings end." Buddha has beautifully expressed this idea in the following passage:

> When the fire of lust is extinct, that is Nirvana. When the fires of hatred are extinct, that is Nirvana. When pride is extinct, that is Nirvana. There is only one thing I teach— the extinction of suffering.

In other words, Buddha teaches not the end of our personality, but the end of our personal griefs—the ultimate joy of our oneness with God.

As for the nature of God, Buddha confessed that he knew nothing about it. This problem, he believed, is beyond our human knowledge. How can the atom know the nature of the substance of which it is but an infinitesimal part? "Suppose," he said, "you have been wounded by a poisoned arrow, and your relatives have secured a physician in whom they trust. Do you ask them what sort of person he is, what he looks like, what he thinks about the world, or whether the color of his skin is light or dark? You are interested only in his power to heal."

In the same way we are all stricken with the poisoned arrow of life. Let us not be too inquisitive about our Healer; let us merely be concerned with His plan for our healing.

And the divine plan for our healing, as Buddha explained,

is based upon the fact that our existence means unhappiness due to our selfish craving, and that we can destroy this craving by following the eightfold path of good conduct. In other words, we can avoid the pain of our karma—or repeated punishment through our repeated "sinking" into the ocean of life —if we practice the eight Buddhist Commandments:

1. Learn to understand yourself.
2. Be patient.
3. Speak kindly.
4. Act nobly.
5. Work honestly.
6. Do your best at all times.
7. Be alert to your neighbor's needs.
8. Look compassionately upon the world.

Buddha condensed these eight Commandments into three words: Pity, Piety, Love.

Buddha pitied all living things because he identified himself with them. In the process of our reincarnation, he believed, every one of us passes through many forms of existence—animal as well as human. "All of us, therefore, are related in a common bond of suffering." It is a sin to kill; and this applies not only to your fellow men but to all your fellow creatures. When a Brahman proposed to purify himself in the sacred waters of the Ganges, Buddha said: "Purify yourself, rather, in the sacred waters of your kindness."

He believed in a classless, casteless society of equals. "Go into all lands and teach this lesson. Tell them that the poor and the lowly, the rich and the high, are one, and that all creatures are united in this world as all drops of water are united in the sea." When we have learned to pity not only ourselves but all living things, then at last we shall reach the peace of nirvana.

Buddha's piety, like his pity, was a result of his belief in universal fellowship. He did not believe in formal religion. The trouble with most religions, he said, is their separateness. The adherents of every different sect believe that they alone possess the one sure way to salvation. This results in continual arguments which in turn incite us to intolerance, persecution, and war. "Let us stop quarreling about our differences and begin to concentrate upon our common relationship in the family of life." The value of a man's faith must be judged not by his exclusive feeling of superiority but by his inclusive sense of equality. Buddha himself has been pictured by his followers as "a binder-together of those who are divided, an encourager of those who are friendly toward one another, a peacemaker, a lover of peace, impassioned for peace, a speaker of words that make for peace."

Buddha taught the piety of a single and simple faith—universal fellowship. And this faith enabled him to be patient with his more quarrelsome fellow creatures. He returned good for evil and answered abuse with a smile. One day a foolish young man gave him a severe tongue-lashing. He listened to it in silence; and when the young man was finished, he asked quietly: "Son, if a man refuses a gift offered to him, to whom does the gift belong?"

"To the man who offered it," replied his assailant.

"In that case, my son," said Buddha, "I refuse to accept your abuse. Keep it for yourself."

His faith consisted of divine favoritism to none, and equal gentleness to all. He looked upon himself as a teacher and not as a savior. He never pretended to be a spokesman of the Lord. He merely said that he had found a natural law which brought supreme happiness to himself and which, therefore, might bring supreme happiness to all.

And this natural law may be ultimately defined by a single word—love. (St. Paul was to make the same discovery later on.) Buddha distinguished between two kinds of love—the kind that leans and the kind that lifts.

The love that leans is the love of the little self. It is interested in what it can get rather than in what it can give. It is the love of animals toward their masters, of children toward their parents—and frequently, of married people toward one another. It is the kind of affection that is marred by jealousy and can easily be turned into hate.

But the other kind, the love that lifts, is the love of the greater self. In a passage which has been called "the inspiration of the thirteenth chapter of (St. Paul's) First Corinthians," Buddha wrote:

"Just as with her own life a mother shields from hurt her only child, let all embracing thoughts for every form of life be thine—an all-embracing love for the entire universe, unstinted love unmarred by hate."

An all-embracing love. One of the best modern expressions of this Buddhist idea may be found in Edwin Markham's poem, *Outwitted:*

> He drew a circle that shut me out—
> Heretic, rebel, a thing to flout.
> But Love and I had the wit to win:
> We drew a circle that took him in!

As for the rest of us, we are still trying to catch up with Buddha after twenty-five centuries of jealousy, hatred, and strife. Except for a few rare souls—like St. Francis, Spinoza, Walt Whitman, or Albert Schweitzer—we have not yet mastered the nirvana of bliss through the miracle of love.

V

Buddha's manner of teaching was as simple as his thought. Followed by his disciples, he walked from town to town, dressed in a yellow cloak and equipped with a beggar's bowl for such food as he might get on the way. He generally gave his instructions in a garden or a clearing in the woods. His first words were the Buddhist greeting of universal fellowship:

"Peace to all living things." His talks were not exhortations, but rather conversations. "Don't accept what I say, but think it out for yourself."

On one occasion, his son came to see him. The young man had been brought up with the belief that a great inheritance awaited him. "I have come for my inheritance," he said to his father. "Pray give it to me."

"You do well, my son, to ask for your inheritance. Here it is." And turning to one of his disciples, Buddha said: "Give my son his cloak and bowl, and admit him into our order of the universal fellowship of life."

His own life came to an end when he was past eighty. He had given up a throne to live among the dispossessed; and his very last act was to bless an outcast who had come to him for words of comfort. While the two men were eating at the house of a blacksmith, Buddha felt suddenly ill. Dragging his tired body into the fields, he asked his disciples to place him upon a bed of leaves. He implored them not to blame the blacksmith for his illness.

Then, as his life was ebbing away, he called to his side the outcast who had come to him for the alms of a few gentle words. The hand of the dying prince sought the hand of the beggar. "All of us," he whispered, "are drops of water flowing toward the ocean of eternal peace. Let us try earnestly to deserve it."

CHAPTER IV

The Philosophy of China

As WE HAVE observed in the earlier chapters of this book, the thoughts of the great philosophers—Ikhnaton, Zoroaster, Buddha—are never outdated. They are just as ultramodern today as they were several thousand years ago. While our scientists are charting the ways of travel between the earth and outer space, our philosophers are still trying to point out the ways of communication between human hearts.

And philosophers are the most patient of men. Spiritual progress, they realize, is not measured by a single life span, or a century, or even a thousand years. The journey to understanding is extremely long; and its milestones must be counted against the background of eternity,

This idea has been expressed by Spinoza within comparatively recent times. Yet it is as old as the teaching of the earliest Chinese philosophers. The wise men of China checked all human activity upon a time clock in which a thousand years are but as a single day.

The ancient Chinese, according to Diderot, were among the most civilized nations in history. They regarded their scholars rather than their soldiers as their greatest heroes. At the time of Confucius—who lived in the sixth century B.C.—they boasted a culture that was twenty thousand years old. At first, their legends inform us, the Chinese lived like prowling animals in the forest. But gradually there arose among them a dynasty of "thinking men" who taught their people to live together in peace. It seems that the makers of the Chinese sagas had a vague idea of evolution thousands of years before Darwin.

The "thinking men" of China possessed not only a stock of wisdom but a sense of humor. One of the earliest Chinese philosophers dreamt that he had been changed into a butterfly. When he told about this experience to his disciples, he added: "And now, my friends, I can't tell whether I am a man dreaming that I am a butterfly, or a butterfly dreaming that I am a man."

Another of the Chinese philosophers, whose humor was social rather than individual, described a pure democracy as a country where "the poets are free to write without being hungry, the historians to tell the truth, the poor to grumble at their taxes, the teachers to teach without censorship, the young people to speak of anything, and the old people to find fault with everything."

This combination of wit and wisdom came to full flower in the philosophy of Lao-tse and Confucius—two of the "Supreme Lights of China."

II

The exact dates of Lao-tse are unknown. Some scholars believe that he was an older contemporary of Confucius. Others maintain that he lived two or three centuries after Confucius, at a time when the ideas of Buddha had begun to trickle into China. These scholars point out that the philosophy of Lao-tse is in some respects very close to that of Buddha. But the wisdom of life seems at times to have been handed down from mouth to mouth, and at other times to have come independently to individual souls in a revealing flash. And so the similarity in the ideas of any two philosophers does not necessarily mean that one of them has been influenced by the other. Just as the same sort of flower may grow in widely scattered places, the same sort of inspiration may arise in sages who live in different climes at different times.

We shall, therefore, accept the theory of the scholars who place Lao-tse in the century of Confucius. According to those scholars, he was born about 600 B.C. and, "thanks to his tranquil philosophy," lived to the age of eighty-seven. Toward the end of his life, we are told, he received a visit from Confucius, who asked his advice about the surest way to successful leadership. Lao-tse's answer was cryptic and brief:

"When the hour of the great man has struck, he rises to leadership. But I have heard that the successful merchant carefully conceals his wealth; that the great man, though abounding in achievements, is simple in his manners and appearance. Get rid of your pride and your many ambitions. Your character gains nothing from all these. Such is the advice I can give you —not how to become a great leader, but how to remain a good man."

Confucius is said to have returned from the visit a better and wiser man. Speaking to his friends about this visit, he said:

"I know how birds fly, fishes swim, and animals run. I also know how the runner may be snared, the swimmer hooked, and the flier shot by an arrow. But there is one thing I do not know—how the dragon mounts on the wind through the clouds, and rises to heaven. I can compare Lao-tse only to the dragon."

Yet Lao-tse was cryptic only in his shoptalk with other philosophers. In the explanation of his ideas to the general public, he could be crystal clear.

Let us briefly examine these ideas:

The philosophy of Lao-tse was based on his concept of Tao, or the "way of wisdom." There is perhaps no finer piece of literature, observes Dr. Will Durant in his *Story of Civilization*, than Lao-tse's "Secret of Wisdom." This secret lies in a contented obedience to nature. "All things in nature," declared Lao-tse, "work silently. They come into being and possess nothing. They fulfill their function and make no claim. All things alike do their work, and then we see them subside. When they have reached their bloom, each returns to its origin. Returning to their origin means rest, or fulfillment of their destiny. This reversion is an eternal law. To know this law, and to accept it with a mind at peace, is wisdom."

The age-old quest of philosophy as well as of religion is peace of mind. Like Rousseau, who rediscovered this secret about twenty-four hundred years later, Lao-tse found no value in rivalries for riches or power. "I have nothing that may arouse my own pride or other people's envy." A man who has reached this pinnacle of wisdom "is beyond all considerations of profit or injury, of exalted or lowly rank; he is the noblest man under heaven."

According to Lao-tse, the noblest man is he who regards himself superior to none; the richest man is he who is free from hunger for riches; and the most blessed man is he who desires the same blessings for all. "To succeed" was for Lao-tse a plural instead of a singular verb. He believed in universal rather than in individual success. The greatest happiness of any one is to rejoice in the happiness of all.

And the ultimate goal of life *is* the happiness of all. The way of wisdom, therefore, is to regard each day as sufficient unto itself—and each night, too, as sufficient unto itself. The days and the nights are all leading us, in ways that we may not even realize, toward the final goal of universal joy. Our senses are too imperfect to tell us the entire story. Yet here and there we get a revealing glimpse of Tao—the one True Way. Just as the night brings to our vision the miracle of the stars that are concealed in the glare of the day, may not death bring to our vision an equally great miracle concealed in the glare of life?

Lao-tse leaves the question without an answer. Sufficient unto the day of life is our little knowledge thereof. To try to know more is too great a burden for our puny minds.

The Tao of Lao-tse has much in common with the nirvana of Buddha. To attain peace of mind, the wise man—he need not necessarily be the most educated man—will avoid trying to keep up with and get ahead of his neighbors. The struggle for wealth is bound to weaken your moral fiber. In your too great desire to love yourself, you will only succeed in hating yourself. In your search for power, you will only weaken your soul. The higher you try to rise, the more precipitous your ultimate fall.

As a matter of fact, explains Lao-tse, the mightiest things are the humblest. Take, for example, the simple substance, water. "It is strong enough to sweep away mountains, yet it seeks the lowest levels. Do thou likewise. For this is *Tao*." Ambition, cupidity, aggression, power—those are the ways that lead to war. Tao is the way that leads to peace.

The wise man, therefore, accepts his life and his fellow men with "a gentleness that conquers strength." True greatness can be achieved only when you do not strive to be great.

III

The philosophy of Lao-tse, as some one has observed, is a philosophy for old men. Young blood requires action; it is too restless for contemplation. Confucius realized this and tried to apply the wisdom of Lao-tse to practical life. How far can we follow the "sweet reasonableness" of contentment and still play an active part in our competitive world? This was the question Confucius endeavored to answer. And the quest led him into an unusual career—from philosophy to politics, and from politics to poverty.

He was born in the kingdom of Lu—the present province of Shantung—in the year 551 B.C. His father, a professional soldier, was seventy when Confucius was born. The child, legend informs us, had "the back of a dragon, the ears of an elephant and a mouth like the sea." Moreover, his coming into the world "was proclaimed by the spirits of heaven who perfumed the air around his crib." Owing to these "early symptoms of a great life," his father named him Kung Fu-tse—the Chinese for Confucius—which means "the Sage Master Kung."

At the age of three, Confucius lost his father. While at school, he worked in his spare time to help support his mother; and thus, from early childhood, he learned the practical hardships of life.

Yet he found the opportunity to become an expert flute player. "Philosophy and music," declared the wise men of China, "go hand in hand."

At seventeen he got a civil service job as a clerk in the office of the national grain supply. At nineteen he married; at twenty he begot his only son; and at twenty-three he divorced his wife. Apparently he felt that philosophy and marriage did *not* go hand in hand. Even in those days it was hard to support a wife on the wages of wisdom.

Leaving his home, he became a traveling schoolteacher. "I live now," he said, "in the north, the south, the east and the west." The subjects he taught were "history, poetry and propriety." Like Buddha, he tried to avoid disputes with other teachers. "Let us emphasize our agreements instead of debating our differences. What all men see alike is likely to be right."

Yet his tolerance did not extend to the stupidity and the insubordination of some of his pupils. He believed in using the rod in order to spur the child. Moreover, he was in favor of punishing the parents of delinquent children as well as the children themselves. On one occasion, when an adolescent was arrested for stealing, Confucius advised the judge to send the father along with the son to prison. "If the father had *taught* him well, the son would have *acted* well." Confucius believed in the integrity of the family as the basis for an upright state. Honesty, as well as charity, should begin at home.

Like all great philosophers, Confucius was far ahead of his time. And like most people ahead of their time, he was reviled and hooted out of many towns and villages. The people repaid him with stones for his nuggets of gold. "We want none of his subversive thought!" cried the people and the rulers alike. When he reached the province of Wei, the king made him the butt of an atrocious jest. He took out his courtesan for a drive in his royal carriage and forced Confucius to ride in a cart directly behind. And the cart bore a conspicuous sign: "Behold virtue trailing after lust!"

Yet here and there Confucius found a few who recognized in him the wisdom of a sage and the gentleness of a saint. "He moves along the path of humility and courtesy," wrote the father of one of his pupils. "He has heard of every subject, and retains with a strong memory. His knowledge of things seems inexhaustible. Have we not in him the rising of a great man?"

Another of the minority who understood Confucius was an old man whose grandchildren had been enrolled among his pupils. This old man had often listened to the lessons of the wandering teacher. He advised his fellow townsmen to sit, like himself, at the master's feet. "My friends, why are you distressed at his misfortune? The world has always failed to recognize the true values of life. Heaven is using this man as a bell to ring out God's message."

But the majority of the people, like their rulers, persisted in their internal bickerings and external wars. They had no ears to listen to Confucius. He was like a human creature in a jungle of beasts. Once, as he passed through a mountain wilderness, he saw a woman kneeling in tears at the side of a fresh grave. "What," he asked, "is the cause of your grief?"

"My son has been killed on this spot by a tiger. Before him, my husband met the same fate. And before my husband, his father died the same way."

"Why, then," asked the teacher, "have you not moved to a civilized community?"

"Where, sir," asked the stricken woman, "can you find one?"

This question stumped Confucius. He decided, then and

there, to go in search of a civilized community—or at least to find a ruler who might be willing to direct his people toward a more civilized life.

For about twenty years Confucius had been a wandering teacher of the young. From now on, he made it his business to teach the grownup children of the world.

IV

Confucius had entered upon one of the most difficult jobs in the world—to teach philosophy to kings. The first ruler who considered his application as a mentor in the art of government was the Prince of Chi. When the prince asked Confucius how a king could best govern his country, the philosopher replied: "By allowing everybody, from prince to pauper, to live in harmony, and especially by eliminating the causes that produce paupers." The prince was eager to retain him as his adviser; but the prime minister dissuaded him. "These scholars are impractical dreamers. Their heads are so far up in the clouds that their feet have lost touch with the ground."

Confucius did not get the post.

He tried again in another place—his native province of Lu. This time he had better luck. The Prince of Lu appointed him chief magistrate of Chung-tu, his capital city. "Whereupon," write the Chinese historians, "dishonesty and licentiousness were ashamed and hid their heads. Loyalty became the glory of men, and chastity the splendor of women."

We may take this statement with a grain of salt; yet there is little doubt that Confucius did instill in the public a reverence for honesty. He tried to base his administration upon a code of mutual generosity. Before his arrival at Chung-tu, the city had been infested with petty thieves and robbers. When he came into office, the leading citizens asked him what to do about the situation, and he replied: "The only way to put an end to stealing is to put an end to your own greed. If you are not greedy to have *too much,* others will not suffer from having *too little.* And thus there will be no temptation to steal."

Individual integrity, he said, stems out of social justice. "If we live in a country which is just, we can wear our honors with humility and bear our sorrows with equanimity."

But the world was not yet ready for the millennium. The prince of the neighboring province of Chi, envious of the greatness of Lu under the influence of Confucius, hit upon a simple plan to undermine the philosopher's standing with the prince. He sent the prince a present of eighty "song and dance" girls. The plan worked. The Prince of Lu "preferred beauty to duty." He found a shapely ankle more appealing than a virtuous heart. "Master," he said to Confucius, "it is time for you to go."

The aging philosopher took his staff and set out once more upon the road. He gathered his disciples as he went along, taught them in the morning, and spent his afternoons and evenings collecting "the wisdom of the past for the instruction of the future." He laid no claim to originality. He called himself "a transmitter and not a maker of thoughts." He devoted the last years of his life to the editing of the great Chinese classics —not as a historian, but rather as a teacher. He selected those works that were most likely to "inspire the young, equip their minds with greater knowledge, and mold their hearts to gentler thoughts."

In other words, he advocated not self-renunciation, as taught by Lao-tse, but self-control. "If men will learn to govern themselves justly for but a single century, all violence will disappear from the earth."

Accordingly, he laid down a set of rules for the self-discipline of the people. He subjected every act of life to the strict observance of an elaborate code of etiquette. Confucius preferred to call it a code of ethics. It was a strange and complicated and, to the Western mind, somewhat amusing set of daily rites. For example, he prescribed the different kinds of food that people must eat on different occasions and at different stages of life; the sort of costumes they must wear on sacred and on secular days; the number of bows they must make when they saluted one another; and how they must walk through the streets—"the men on the right side, and the women on the left." He was especially strict about the conduct of children toward their parents, not only during the lifetime of the parents, but even after their death.

Yet Confucius had a good reason for his ceremonials. Their observance enabled the peasant in his hut to become a personage of dignity no less than the king in his palace. The Confucian system of prescribed etiquette made the Chinese one of the most punctilious nations in history. But it also gave them a sense of self-respect and a feeling of respect for others. "Be loyal to yourself," said Confucius, "and considerate toward your neighbors." This was the sum and substance of Confucian morality. Instead of an anemic sort of selflessness, he implanted in his people the ideal of an intelligent selfishness. By multiplying your generosity to others, observed Confucius, you lay up a capital of generosity for yourself. For in the long run, every act of kindness is repaid in kind.

Confucius tried to turn his people into a race of aristocrats—not a conceited minority of intolerant snobs, but a civilized majority of courteous gentlemen. He himself treated the prince and the pauper with equal courtesy—the prince for the majesty of his rank, and the pauper for the misery of his suffering.

As for the elaborate ritual in honor of the dead, Confucius imposed it as a substitute for—or, rather, as a realistic form of —our human hope for immortality. When a disciple asked Confucius, "What about death?" he replied: "I cannot even understand life; how, then, can I understand death?" But, he said, we can keep the memory of our departed parents alive by including them in our family councils and enfolding them in the deathless embrace of continuity. In this way we can hope that we, in turn, are going to live in the memory and affection of our children. "Is not this in a sense the meaning of immortality?"

The philosophy of Confucius aimed at the continuity of affection in the family of mankind. Like Walt Whitman, he loved to hobnob with his "less fortunate brothers" and to share their burdens. One of his disciples upbraided him for this "too democratic" habit; but Confucius replied: "With whom then should I associate if not with suffering men?"

This fellow-feeling for others was, to Confucius, the stamp of the Superior Man. Confucius spoke of the Superior Man about twenty-five centuries before Nietzsche told of the Superman. But the ideal man of Confucius regarded all others as capable of becoming his equals, while the ideal man of Nietzsche looked down upon all others as his underlings.

The Superior Man, according to Confucius, cherishes four principles: good learning, good conduct, good nature, good will. And these four principles may be reduced to a single word —justice. Love your friends, said Confucius, but discipline your enemies. Do not hate your enemies, for hatred only begets hatred. On the other hand, do not repay hatred with love, because your love will be misinterpreted as weakness; and this will encourage your enemies to further hatred. It is brutal to avenge an injury, but it is foolish to forgive it. Judge it fairly and act accordingly, with due regard to your own dignity and your enemy's rights.

Confucius did not believe in turning the other cheek. He was too realistic for that supreme sort of love. "It is true that love can overcome hatred as water can overcome fire. But too strong a fire can dry up a pool of water." The tiny reservoir of love within the human heart is not strong enough to overwhelm the flaming hatred of aggressive power. So let us recognize this fact, said Confucius, and look upon others not as we want them to be but as they really are. "This is the true meaning of justice."

When urged to give a more specific definition of justice, Confucius replied: "Is not justice the same as reciprocity?"

And then he defined reciprocity as the Golden Rule of the earlier oriental philosophers: "Do not unto others what you do not want others to do unto you." This is the negative form of the Golden Rule of Christianity. But it is more in keeping with the realistic philosophy of Confucius. "Don't spoil others with too much love, or condemn them with too much hatred. Just follow the path of the Golden Mean between the two extremes."

For, declared Confucius, we are dealing not with angels, but with men who are half-good and half-bad. Let us try to encourage the good, and discourage the bad, through the principle of reciprocal justice. "With the establishment of this principle," he said, "the whole world will become a Republic . . . Men will converse sincerely with one another and cultivate universal peace . . . Selfish schemings will be repressed . . . Robbers, thieves and traitors will no longer infest the earth. This is the purpose of my teaching—the vision of what I call the Great Harmony of Mankind."

V

Confucius was a strange figure as he taught this philosophy on the roadside, a statesman without a state, tall, gaunt, his head almost hairless and his body gnarled and knotted with privation. Once he lost his way to a meeting with his disciples. They were able to find him from the description of a traveler who had seen "a monstrous man with the appearance of a stray dog." When Confucius heard about this description, he exclaimed, "Capital! No painter could have done a better job!"

He lived to the age of seventy-two. As the end was approaching, he spoke to Tse-Kung, his favorite disciple: "No intelligent ruler arises; there is not one who loves wisdom as he loves lust; my time is come to die."

He died in obscurity. It was centuries before the world began to recognize his wisdom. And then his people accepted his greatness, and exaggerated it, and finally deified it. The story of Confucius is one of the ironies of history. This man, who in his lifetime was an agnostic, was raised after his death to the status of a god.

For several centuries he was worshiped, until the leaders of the Communist Revolution consigned him once more to obscurity. And thus his country moved back from the Age of Confucius to the Age of Confusion.

CHAPTER V

The Philosophy of Israel

THE PROPHETS of Israel, like the sages of Egypt, Persia, India, and China, were philosophers as well as religious teachers. And in the story of the Hebrew philosophers we can trace a progressive ethical journey from vengeance to justice, from justice to mercy, and from mercy to love.

We can follow this progress as we watch the growth of the Hebrew idea about God and his relationship to man. The Old Testament, we must remember, is not one book but a collection of thirty-nine books written over a period of about twelve hundred years. It therefore varies considerably in its ethical as well as in its theological contents. The human concept of the divine is far less civilized at the beginning than it is toward the end of the Bible. In the earlier books, God is pictured as the avenging Lord of Battles. In the later books, he is depicted as the compassionate Prince of Peace.

So let us join the prophet-philosophers of Israel as they embark upon their journey to better understanding.

II

In the books of Moses, the Lord appears not as the sole guardian of the universe, but as the most powerful among a number of tribal divinities. All of these divinities are warlike, jealous of one another's prerogatives, protective of their own tribes, and aggressive toward all other tribes. Thus the God of Israel is a celestial King reigning over a small group of people whom he has taken under his special protection.

And just as this King was regarded as supreme among all the other kings of heaven, his nation strove to be regarded as supreme among all the other nations of the earth. This, in brief, is the philosophical picture of God and the Hebrews at the time of Moses.

Moses lived about twelve hundred years before Christ. He was the leader of a nation that endeavored to gain a foothold in a warlike world. The Hebrew arrival in Canaan represented a transition from a nomadic, or wandering stage of history, to an agricultural, or settled stage. The settling of the Hebrews in Canaan meant that the earlier inhabitants of Canaan had to be dislodged. It was therefore a matter of dog eat dog. Cruelty, vengeance, and victory were among the principal virtues taught to a race of warriors anxious to find a home for themselves.

This, in part, explains the savagery of the early Israelites and their conception of a rather savage Lord of Hosts. The God of Israel at the time of Moses was a Spirit who guided his people out of the desert into a permanent home. A terrible God of the wilderness; an Arabian bedouin type of God; a God who leaps over the mountains, rides across the sand dunes, and reclines in tents of gorgeous colors. A God who watches over his people while they sleep, leads them into battle, smites their enemies without mercy, changes his mind like the wind, is quick to avenge an insult, and is not above telling a falsehood when it serves either his own or his people's purpose to do so. A warrior-God who demands absolute obedience from his soldiers. "The only way to victory is to fear and obey the Lord."

Yet Moses, like the other sages of the Orient, was far ahead of his day. And he began to ascribe to the conventional picture of the Lord some of his own gentler characteristics. And so we see in the books of Moses the glimmerings of a new concept of God—a God who softens his vengeance with the spirit of justice. It is a primitive sort of justice—an eye for an eye, a tooth for a tooth, a life for a life. But it is a universal rather than tribal sort of justice, often embracing the alien as well as the Jew. The God of Moses—and the ethics he prescribed for his people—insisted upon charity to the poor, gentleness to the orphan, and generosity to the slave. "On the seventh day of the week—the Sabbath—thou shalt not work nor compel thy servants to work. And in the seventh year of their labor thou shalt set thy servants free."

The picture of God as developed in the books of Moses marks a definite step from the savage toward the sublime. Indeed, it is the picture of Moses himself magnified to superhuman proportions. Thus the philosophy of Moses carried his followers a good way along the road from vengeance to justice.

III

The later prophet-philosophers went far beyond Moses in their quest for justice. They were a strange and uncouth lot, those Hebrew radicals who, over a period of several hundred years, tried to teach virtue to a vicious world. A few of them were of noble birth; but for the most part they were peasants, workers or herdsmen who had "answered the summons of the Lord." Abandoning their fields and their workbenches, they went to live like wild animals in the mountains. For sustenance they ate roots and honey and at times even grass and flowers. Now and then they emerged from the wilderness to bring "the word of God" to their countrymen. It was a mission imposed upon them from heaven, they declared, and they had to accept it against their will, their comfort, and the very safety of their lives.

These men not only expressed strange ideas, but they had a most amazing way of expressing them. Isaiah, for example, walked naked through the streets of Jerusalem in order to show that the city would be stripped naked for her sins. Another prophet defiled his food before he ate it, as a sign that God would defile his nation. All in all, they were an object of ridicule to most men, particularly to those who belonged to the so-called better classes.

But a few of the more thoughtful people began to see the prophet-philosophers from a new angle. These dedicated men always took the part of the oppressed against their oppressors. They displayed a courage that was superb. They were not afraid to stalk into the palace of the king and to denounce him for his tyranny. In short, they had a consuming passion for justice.

God's equal justice, they declared, extended not only toward the children of Israel but toward all mankind. The God of the later prophets was no longer the King of a single nation but the Father of the human race.

IV

Yet to Amos—the first among these later prophets—God is a strict and demanding Father. Though impartial to all, he exacts the selfsame obedience from all.

Amos, a shepherd who lived about four hundred years after Moses, embraced the whole world in his vision. All nations, he said, are equally accountable to the one God of the universe. He will punish them all alike for their transgressions. But he will save them all alike—the Gentile as well as the Jew— if they turn to the ways of righteousness. "Seek the Lord and ye shall live . . . Ye who have abandoned justice, seek Him who hath made the stars and who turneth the shadow of death into morning . . ." For he is the Lord of universal life.

This universal God, in the philosophy of Amos, is not a jealous God. He is not interested in flattery or in sacrificial feasts. "I hate, I despise your feast days," saith the Lord. "Though ye offer me your meat offerings, I will not accept them; neither will I regard the peace offerings of your fat beasts."

What, then, does God require? A friendly relationship

among all the members of the human family. An honest deal throughout the world. "Let justice roll on as a flood of waters, and righteousness as a mighty stream."

V

"Not vengeance, but justice," declares the Lord in the Book of Amos. Justice receives even greater emphasis in the teaching of Isaiah.

Isaiah, who lived about fifty years after Amos, was one of the profoundest philosophers in history. Unlike Amos, he was no shepherd suddenly appearing out of the wilderness to deliver his message and then disappearing again. He was an aristocrat by birth and a statesman by profession. But the rulers of Israel rejected his statesmanship just as the rulers of China rejected the statesmanship of Confucius. "Those who govern," declared Isaiah, "rarely understand the wisdom of government."

The idea of government, as taught by Isaiah, was based upon justice tempered with mercy and devoted to peace. He denounced the hypocrisy of the priests, the aggressiveness of the warriors, and the cruelty of the kings. He lashed out against the craving for wealth that incited the rich to add "field to field and house to house" at the expense of the poor. He declared that the weakness of his nation, of all nations, lay in their rejection of the spirit and their reliance upon the sword.

In short, he gave to the world a new philosophical concept of religion. He revealed the beauty of holiness. And he showed the way to a new patriotism. Although passionately devoted to his own country, he embraced all other countries in the universality of his thought. He still regarded the Hebrews as the chosen people—chosen, however, not to conquer but to teach. To suffer, if necessary, in their teaching; but to become God's messengers of good will among the nations. "And the wolf shall dwell with the lamb, and the leopard shall lie down with the kid, and the calf and the lion's whelp and the fatling together . . . For the earth shall be full of the knowledge of the Lord, as the waters cover the sea."

Isaiah was history's first internationalist. He foresaw, far in advance of his own and even of our present day, the time when the nations would lose their lust for power, through the curbing of their dictators and money-lords and landlords, and through the dispensation of equal justice to all the peoples of the earth. "All the nations," declares the Lord, "shall be unto Me for a blessing. For all of them are My children, the work of My hands."

And then Isaiah rises to the peak of his prophetic philosophy. "And it shall come to pass in the end of days . . . that all the nations shall reach unto the mountain of the Lord and say, Come ye, and He will teach us of His ways, and we will walk in His paths . . . And He shall judge between the nations, and decide for all peoples; and they shall beat their swords unto plowshares, and their spears into pruning hooks. Nation shall not lift up sword against nation, neither shall they learn any more war . . . For then all men shall know that the Lord is good and that His mercy endureth forever."

There is a bitter footnote to the story of Isaiah. His generation repaid him for his vision with the usual wages of ingratitude. "They cut him asunder," the historians tell us, "with a sword."

VI

It is in the philosophy of a later prophet, Micah, that we get the clearest picture of ethics as an education in mercy. We learn from the Book of Micah that Micah believed, as had Amos and Isaiah, that God is no lover of sacrifices or rituals or the bending of the knees in prayer. "Wherewith shall I come before the Lord, and bow myself before the High God? . . .

With burnt offerings, with thousands of rams, or with ten thousand rivers of oil?"

No, not these are the gifts that will please the Lord. "He hath showed thee, O man, what is good. And what doth the Lord require of thee, but to do justice, to love mercy, and to walk humbly with thy God?"

This idea has been prevalent in our best ethical and political thought from the time of Micah to the present day. We find it re-echoed in the Talmud, in the Koran, in the poetry of Shakespeare, Milton, Pope, Browning, and Walt Whitman, in the novels of Hawthorne, Dickens, and Tolstoy, and—as we shall see—in the philosophy of our latest and most modern thinkers.

And only a few years ago, when Franklin D. Roosevelt ran for re-election to the Presidency, he climaxed his final campaign speech with the foregoing quotation from Micah. This, he said, is our best guide to successful political leadership in the twentieth century—justice, guided by mercy, and administered in humility.

VII

But there is one further step in the ethical thinking of the Hebrew prophet-philosophers—their summons to the all-embracing power of love. We find the seeds of this idea in the philosophies of Isaiah and of Micah. Their God is a Lord not only of justice and mercy, but loving-kindness as well. This philosophy comes to full flower at the time of Jesus. It was no accident that Jesus proclaimed the gospel of love as the guide for all mankind. He had heard this gospel from the Hebrew philosophers who taught in the synagogues while he was growing up. The words he spoke at the Last Supper—"Love ye one another"—were familiar to his disciples. They had heard them from Hillel, an older contemporary of Jesus. And Hillel, in turn, had inherited the idea from Isaiah and Micah. When asked to summarize the Old Testament in a few words, Hillel said: "The Bible teaches us one thing above all—'Love thy neighbor as thyself.'"

"And who is my neighbor?" inquired one of his pupils.

"Every human being on the face of the earth," replied Hillel.

VIII

To summarize the philosophy of the Hebrew prophets, their ethical concept advanced with the advance of their civilization, from vengeance, to justice, to mercy, to love. These prophets were not so much messengers of divine wisdom as men of superior insight. They could foretell the future because they understood the past. They had learned from history the important lesson that hatred begets hatred, war engenders war, and injustice brews the poisons of rebellion and revenge. They recognized, and are still teaching the world to recognize, the inflexible law of cause and effect. He who judges without mercy will himself be unmercifully judged. "As surely as the rivers flow downward to the sea, so surely will injustice flow downward to destruction."

This was the ethical truth as envisioned by the prophet-philosophers of Israel. Their God, in the end, was a just but merciful and loving redeemer of all mankind. Even the skeptics and the pessimists among the Hebrew philosophers believed in the compassion of God and the triumph of the good. "All is vanity," wrote the author of Ecclesiastes. Wealth, power, pride, aggression, cunning, renown, the ambitions of youth, and the disillusions of old age—these shall all alike become shadows and dust. But one thing shall endure—the knowledge that the world has been created by wisdom and is guided by love.

And the author of Job, who depicts goodness as conquered by evil, declares that this conquest is but temporary. "I know that my Redeemer liveth!" cries Job in the depth of his suffering. "And though worms destroy this body, I shall see him face to face." Our life on earth, with all its bitterness, is but the beginning of an immortal adventure. And the climax of this adventure will be good, the imaginable best.

For we are in the hands of the best possible guide, observes the writer of Job, along with the other Hebrew philosophers. So let us follow in His footsteps toward the summit of love.

"And love shall make us free!"

PART
2

Greek and Roman Philosophy

CHAPTER VI

The Greek Philosophers
Before Socrates

MANY STUDENTS of philosophy credit the Greeks with the beginning of wisdom. This, as we have seen, is a serious error. The love of wisdom, like the sun, rose in the East and then spread to the West. We cannot fully understand the philosophy of the Greeks unless we recognize its indebtedness—or at least its relationship—to the philosophies of Egypt, Persia, India, China, and Israel. Ptah-hotep had taught the idea of a divine Father in Heaven as a guide to His children on earth. Ikhnaton had advanced from this idea to the concept of one God and one World. Zoroaster had tried to explain the problem of good and evil with the theory that we are co-workers with God in the building of a better world. Buddha had conceived the vision of the democratic fellowship of mankind. Lao-tse had demonstrated the wisdom of equanimity, the calm acceptance of our destiny without fury or fret. Confucius had proclaimed the Golden Rule of reciprocal justice. And the Hebrew prophets had extended this idea of individual justice to include social justice refined into compassion and love.

These and many other threads of philosophy came to Greece from the Orient. It was the genius of the Greeks to weave these threads into an intelligible pattern of wisdom. Sometimes they used different terms for the Eastern ideas. Thus, they translated justice into harmony, reciprocity into civility, equanimity into self-control, and humility into modesty— "The highest kind of knowledge is to realize how little we know."

Above all, the Greek philosophers saw life from a somewhat unique angle. Living on a peninsula that seemed to have sprung like a jewel out of a blue sea under a blue sky, they emphasized the brighter instead of the darker aspects of life. They were poets rather than prophets. And so they revised the oriental view of philosophy without, however, changing its meaning. The oriental sages had taught the beauty of holiness. The Greek philosophers emphasized the holiness of beauty.

II

The preoccupation with beauty, however, came late into Greek life. The earliest Greek philosophers, several of whom lived in overseas Greek colonies rather than in Greece itself, were concerned not so much with the nature of God as with the structure of the universe. Their quest for the truth led them in a different direction from that taken by the oriental philosophers. They moved on from theological speculation to scientific inquiry. They began to look for structural unity in a world of eternal beauty.

III   *THALES*, (*THA-lees*) *about* 600 B.C.

The first of the Greek philosophers, Thales, was born in Miletus, a Greek colony in Asia Minor. He traveled widely and came under the influence of several of the oriental philosophers. But instead of searching for God, he was more curious about the substance of God's world.

To be more exact, Thales believed in the gods rather than in God. He accepted without question the polytheistic religion of the Greeks, whose divinities were regarded as a superior race of mortals. But like the oriental philosophers, he tried to find one supreme element out of which both heaven and earth had been created.

This element, he concluded, was water. Moisture, he said,

is life, and the absence of moisture death. Living things grow
out of the wet seed; dead things shrivel up into dry dust. When
water evaporates, it becomes air and fire; when it congeals,
it becomes ice and rock. Hence, he declared, water is the underlying central principle out of which all things are made—
from the subtle ether in the heavens to the solid mountains
on the earth.

Moreover, Thales was a "hylozoist"—a Greek word which
means a person who believes that all things are alive. Very
likely he borrowed this idea of life-in-all-things from the Egyptian philosophers.

For a philosopher, Thales was as worldly as he was wise.
Though regarded as one of the Seven Sages of Greece, he had
a practical as well as a speculative mind. One day, as Aristotle
tells us, "he was reproached for his poverty, which was supposed to prove that philosophy is of no use. According to the
story," continues Aristotle, "Thales knew by his skill in the stars
while it was still winter that there would be a great harvest
of olives in the coming year. Accordingly, having saved up a
little money, he gave deposits for the use of all the olive presses
in Chios and Miletus, which he secured at a low price because
no one had the foresight to bid against him. When the harvest
time came and many presses were wanted all at once, he
leased them out at whatever price he pleased; and thus he
suddenly became a rich man. He did this, not because he loved
money, but because he wanted to show how philosophers can
become rich if they want to. Their ambition, however, is to
acquire wisdom rather than wealth."

IV ANAXIMANDER, (A-NAK-si-MAN-der) about 575 B.C.

Most of the early philosophers who followed Thales were
still interested in the scientific principle of unity—a simple
"stuff" or formula that would explain all existence. Thus the
pupil of Thales, Anaximander, believed that the "stuff" out of

which all things were created was not water but a subtle substance which he called the "infinite." Out of this infinite, forever alive and forever in motion, came the heavens overhead and the oceans underneath. Out of the oceans, as they evaporated under the sun, emerged the first living creatures of the sea, and from them evolved their descendants, the birds and the animals, until the final earthly creation was reached—man.

Here we have the first European hint of the Darwinian theory of evolution. But we have already noticed an earlier hint of this theory among the Chinese philosophers. Again we see that a good many of the so-called modern ideas are merely revivals of the ancient wisdom of the East.

V   ANAXIMENES (*An-ax-IM-en-eez*), *about 475* B.C.

The other early Greek philosophers continued the search for the one elemental substance of the universe. To Anaximenes, who lived about a century after Anaximander, this elemental substance appeared to be air. He saw the air as boundless, timeless, and alive. In its eternal motions, he said, it condenses into material objects such as fire, wind, cloud, water, earth, metal, and stone. All these "solid" condensations of the air constitute the body of the world. But the more "subtle" aspect of the air is the *soul* of the world. Like the oriental philosophers, Anaximenes believed in a world composed of matter and spirit. "And the spirit of the world is forever alive."

VI   HERACLITUS (*Her-ak-LIE-tus*), *about 475* B.C.

Heraclitus, a contemporary of Anaximenes, believed that the original element of the universe was neither water nor the infinite nor air, but fire. "The world ever was, now is, and ever will be, an eternal living Fire." And this primeval fire keeps forever changing into all sorts of creatures and things. "Fire is the underlying principle, and change is the everlasting law."

We see nothing but eternal change—declared Heraclitus—a continual disintegration of smoke pouring out of a continual fire. This everlasting flame is the seed out of which all things grow and into which all things return. "Nothing is permanent." Even the most solid objects are as fleeting as the wind-blown images in a cloud of vapor.

And what causes all these fleeting images? Strife—the division of unlike things in order that they may be reunited into like things. In other words, life is a single harmony made up of many conflicting notes. For harmony—the blending of all discords into a single concord—is the ultimate aim of nature. "Listening not to me but to the truth," said Heraclitus, "it is wise to acknowledge that all things are one."

Here we find the selfsame quest for unity that dominated the thought of the earlier Greek and oriental philosophers. And here, too, we see the first Greek translation of "justice," or adjustment, into "harmony"—an idea that we shall find predominant in the philosophy of Plato.

Unity, justice, harmony—a single law that governs the pattern of the world we live in—this was the aim of all the best philosophic and scientific thought of the early centuries. And this aim remains unchanged in the twentieth-century world of Albert Einstein and Bertrand Russell. Einstein, like the earliest philosophers, devoted his life to the search for a single permanent formula that would explain all existence. And Russell observed that "the search for something permanent is one of the deepest of the instincts leading men to philosophy."

VII *EMPEDOCLES* (*Em-PED-ok-lees*), *about 445* B.C.

All things, agreed Empedocles, are one. They are separated into opposites by strife and brought again into unity by love. Love is the "cement of harmony" that holds the world together. And in this "harmonious togetherness" there is no such thing as original creation or ultimate destruction. For something cannot be created out of nothing, and something cannot be decomposed into nothing. That which we call creation or destruction, life or death, is merely a rearrangement of ever-living material into a new order.

This living material, said Empedocles, consists of four elements—fire, air, water, and earth. These elements are the "roots" of things. Out of their various combinations arise all the objects of the world.

And these objects arise—here we have another step toward the Darwinian theory—through the medium of selection. Nature experiments in its evolution of all living creatures. Some of the creatures in this experimental process "grew with neckless heads; some, with double faces and double chests; ox-things with men's faces; and contrariwise there sprang up ox-headed men." And those organisms that adapted themselves to their environment were able to survive; but those that failed to adapt themselves were weeded out. Thus the survival of the fittest became the determining factor in the struggle for existence, until finally nature produced the animals and the men most closely attuned to the world in which they lived.

Yet all this selection of nature is not haphazard. On the contrary, it is patterned after the unifying principle of adjustment, or justice, or love—"the bringer-together of all separate things."

VIII *DEMOCRITUS (De-MOK-rit-us), about 430* B.C.

Democritus continued the search for unity. He was a pupil of Leucippus, the scientist who founded the atomic theory. This scientific theory was based upon the "original substance" idea of the earlier Greek philosophers. At that period the scientists and the philosophers worked hand in hand. But the scientists were more interested in the procedure of *analyzing,* or taking things apart, while the philosophers were more concerned with the process of *synthesizing*, or putting things together.

And thus Leucippus had declared that the substance which goes into the structure of the world consists not of one element or even of four elements, but of an infinite number of "atoms." This word comes from the Greek *atomos*, which means "incapable of being cut." An atom, according to Leucippus, is a particle of matter so small that it cannot be cut, or divided, into lesser particles.

Democritus developed the atomic idea of Leucippus to something that closely resembles our own modern idea of a material world of atoms. These two Greek thinkers, the scientist Leucippus and the philosopher Democritus, may be called the grandfathers of our atomic age.

Yet the atomic world, as Democritus saw it, was not altogether materialistic. Though this philosopher maintained that atoms cannot disintegrate, he insisted that each atom is alive—it "has a soul that guides its motion." In other words, Democritus was not far from the discovery that the permanent nucleus of the atom is not matter but energy.

This idea was inherent in the materialism of all the scientific philosophers we have discussed in the present chapter. Their belief in a "living soul" that permeated all matter was but a prelude to the theories of the later Greek philosophers. It is not a far step from the materialism of Democritus to the idealism of Plato.

But side by side with the materialists from Thales to Democritus, there was a group of Greek philosophers who were closer to the thinking of the Orient. These, too, made their distinct contribution to the philosophy of Plato. Let us briefly examine two of them—Xenophanes and Pythagoras.

IX   XENOPHANES (*Zen-OFF-an-eez*), *about* 500 B.C.

The materialistic philosophers of ancient Greece believed

that all matter is alive. Yet they talked about a living creation without a living Creator. Xenophanes tried to supply this want. He picked up the thread of oriental philosophy and returned to the conception of one world under the guidance of one God. "The original source of the universe," he said, "is God." Here we have the first Greek acceptance of the oriental idea of monotheism. "God is One, without beginning or end." He is the Mind which *governs* the world, and the Body which *constitutes* the world.

This idea of monotheism is based upon the pantheism of the oriental philosophers, and in turn becomes the basis for the pantheism of Spinoza. God is *in* everything because he *is* everything. Xenophanes ridiculed the popular representation of God as the enlarged figure of a man. "Why, if cattle or horses or lions had hands and could paint with their hands, the horses would paint the forms of gods like horses and the cattle like cattle, and each would give them bodies like his own." Sixteen centuries later, Spinoza paraphrased this idea about our mistaken picture of God in human form. "I believe that a triangle, if it could speak," said Spinoza, "would declare that God is eminently triangular; and a circle, that the divine nature is eminently circular; and thus would every one ascribe his own attributes to God."

This utterance of Xenophanes, as echoed by Spinoza, was to inspire Voltaire to one of his famous witticisms: "God created man in his own image, and man responded by returning the compliment."

No, the God of Xenophanes—the First Principle of creation—does not resemble mortals "either in shape or in raiment or in voice or in mind." On the contrary, he is all shapes, all raiments, all voices and all minds. Men are no closer than animals to the true picture of God. He is All-in-all, All-in-one. His thought embraces all thoughts of all creatures at all times. And the universe is but the concrete reproduction of his thought—

written in syllables of aspiring lives and flaming stars so that all who have eyes may see.

X   *PYTHAGORAS* (*Pith-AG-o-ras*), *about* 500 B.C.

Pythagoras, like Xenophanes, believed in the "invisible unity" of God. The visible world, he said, is a distorted image of his light as seen through the nebulous haze of our senses.

Pythagoras was a disciple of the Hindu belief in the transmigration of souls. The soul, he declared, is immortal; it travels from creature to creature and from life to life in its upward journey to the divine. "All living creatures are our kindred, and ought to be treated as our own flesh and blood." Like St. Francis, Pythagoras is said to have preached to animals as well as to men.

The philosophy of Pythagoras is based upon mysticism and mathematics. Bertrand Russell, his disciple in mathematics if not in mysticism, has called him a combination of Mary Baker Eddy and Albert Einstein. It would be a little more accurate, I believe, to call him a combination of Buddha and Bertrand Russell. Pythagoras, however, was more scientific than Buddha and more religious than Russell. The world, as he conceived it, is a mystical structure of numbers, or harmonies, a unit of heavenly bodies moving rhythmically together and producing sounds (the music of the spheres) in their motion. The philosophy of mathematics—of the interrelationship that exists between all numbers—was to Pythagoras the answer to the mysterious order and beauty of the universe.

And the order and beauty means the harmony of the universe. The principles of mathematics are, according to Pythagoras, the principles of music. The harmonious relationship of numbers, he said, is the same as the harmonious relationship of tones. Indeed, "mathematics is the highest philosophy, and philosophy is the highest music." For all three of these subjects aim at a better understanding of a perfectly organized and concordant world.

In his effort to reach this better understanding and to help build a world based upon philosophy, mathematics and music, Pythagoras organized a Society of True Friends. The society was open to men and women on equal terms. They held their property in common—Pythagoras looked down upon private property as the root of all evil—and they tried to live a life of frugality, courage, loyalty, obedience, and faith. They regarded these virtues as the steppingstones from a lower to a higher incarnation in our soul's journey from life to life, and from a "liking for one another" to a "likeness of God." All good deeds, Pythagoras said, are blended into an equation of fitting numbers and a composition of harmonious tones. "And this harmonious intermingling of all human activity is the highest good."

Pythagoras was the greatest of the Greek philosophers before Socrates and Plato. He exerted a profound influence not only upon these two Greek thinkers, but upon several of the later religious philosophers such as St. Augustine, Descartes, Spinoza, Kant, Emerson, and William James. And, as we have already noted, the skeptical mathematician, Bertrand Russell, acknowledged his indebtedness to the devout mathematician, Pythagoras.

This brief sketch of some of the early Greek sages will help us to understand the stream of philosophy that began in the Orient with theology, or the speculation about God, and moved over to Europe with the added contribution of science, or the examination of nature. We shall now see still another contribution to the ever widening current of wisdom—psychology, or the study of the human soul.

CHAPTER VII

Socrates (469–399 B.C.)

SOCRATES brought philosophy down from heaven to earth. "I am chiefly concerned," he said, "not with the mystery of God but with the mind of Man." Whenever he conversed with anyone, he asked him, "*To ti?* What is it? Just what do you mean by what you are saying? Define your terms. You talk a great deal about such matters as justice, honor, truth, courage, goodness, patriotism, friendship and love. Just what do you have in mind when you utter these words? Explain yourself; and in order to do so, try to *understand* yourself."

He called himself the human "gadfly." He stung people into thinking. The young loved him because he stimulated them. And the old hated him because he irritated them; they had become settled in their thoughts, and they didn't want to be disturbed.

Yet nobody could dismiss from his mind this most picturesque character in the history of Athens. He was half-satyr and half-saint. From his bald head to his bare feet, he looked like a squat bronze image. His cloak was simple, his beard was unkempt, and his bulbous nose seemed ready to pry into everybody's business. But his keen eyes had a compassionate look, and his thick lips were parted in a cynical yet friendly smile.

They were always busy, those eloquent lips, questioning people, destroying their complacency, and exposing their ignorance. He was just as ready, however, to acknowledge his own ignorance. He had been reputed "the wisest man of Athens." But, he declared, his so-called wisdom consisted merely in this: "I know that I know nothing."

His physical endurance was equal to his mental prowess. While serving in the army as a young man, he walked barefoot over the snow and ice. The other soldiers grumbled as they shivered in their fleece-lined boots, but Socrates rebuked them for their complaints and sang as he marched.

His comrades marveled at his strength and adored him for his gentleness. He was always ready to help them when they were sick, to dress their wounds, and to save their lives at the risk of his own.

Yet even in his youth, there was something "queer" about him. He told his friends that he often heard a voice from heaven—the Hebrew prophets had made a similar claim—and that this voice told him what to do, or rather what *not* to do. He was subject to periodic trances, standing at times for hours absorbed in his thoughts. Plato, in his *Symposium*, describes one of these trances:

"One morning, while in the army, he was thinking about something which he could not resolve; he would not give up, but continued thinking from early dawn until noon—there he stood fixed in thought; and at noon attention was drawn to him, and the rumor ran through the wondering crowd that Socrates had been standing and thinking about something ever since the break of day. At last, in the evening after supper, some of the soldiers out of curiosity brought out their mats and slept in the open air that they might watch him and see whether he would stand all night. There he stood until the following morning; and with the return of light he offered up a prayer to the sun, and went his way."

II

The thoughts that occupied him most of the time were concerned with man and the state. Who is the best man? And what is the best state? He devoted his entire life to the examination of these two questions. He tried politics for a while, but discovered that "in [Athenian] politics no honest man can live long." The radicals had found him too conservative; and the conservatives, too radical. He then became a public teacher —or rather, a public questioner—roaming over the streets in search of a single wise man.

He found no such man anywhere. All those to whom he spoke knew nothing but believed they knew everything. "In this particular," he declared, "I have a slight advantage over them. For I neither know nor think that I know."

Yet in his mission to spur people into better knowledge, he gathered around him a fascinating group of young intellectuals—optimists, pessimists, skeptics, cynics, socialists, anarchists, aristocrats, reactionaries, and liberals. They debated the immediate questions of the day as well as the general problems of all time—such as personal morality and national responsibility. His purpose, declared Socrates, was not to give answers but to pose questions that would lead his pupils, as well as himself, to further thought. "For it is only through knowledge that we can arrive at individual virtue and collective justice."

He received no pay for his self-appointed mission. To support his wife and his children, he carved statues; but he was no genius as a sculptor and found few buyers for his work. As for his own needs, they were very simple. He could live on a crust of bread, a handful of olives, and a sip of wine.

He enjoyed his cups and could outdrink all the other guests when invited to a banquet. But he never got drunk. Plato gives us a vivid picture of a philosophical festival at which everybody became intoxicated with wisdom and wine. That is, everybody but Socrates. The festival lasted all night. And at dawn, all the guests save Socrates were under the table. But Socrates, throwing his tunic over his shoulders, left the banquet hall and went into the streets for his daily debate with his disciples.

In his outspoken discussions he spared no one. Are you a teacher? Have you conquered your own ignorance before you attack the ignorance of your pupils? Are you a doctor? Have you healed yourself to prove that you can heal your patients? Are you a statesman? Can you control your own passions while you try to govern the passions of other men? A little less arrogance, please, and a little more humility. Learn to know how little you know.

He was especially caustic about the Athenian form of democracy—the election of aggressive vulgarians by a mob of ignorant voters.

And it was this open criticism of his government that led to his imprisonment and death. The leading politicians accused him of subversion of the state and disbelief in the gods. Actually he tried to improve the state through better education, to abolish the superstition about many gods, and to establish the religion of one God.

Yet we must try to understand his accusers before we condemn them. Socrates himself tried to reason about them without blaming them unduly for his death. Like another martyr to the truth who died four centuries later, he forgave his judges because they knew not what they did. He realized that they had gone through one of the terrible periods in history—a bitter defeat after a war of twenty-seven years against Sparta, a revolution of the oligarchic (today we would call it the fascist) party, and a still shaky counterrevolution of the democratic party. Tempers were hot, offices precarious, and life itself extremely unsafe. The judges looked upon Socrates, a man who tried to think and to make others think, as a danger to the state. It was sheer blasphemy to declare that Athens ought to be governed not by the loudest mouths but by the wisest minds.

Socrates was quite prepared, therefore, when he came into the public square one day and found the following indictment posted upon the walls of the principal buildings:

Socrates is guilty of a double crime: first, for not wor-
shiping the gods whom the city worships; next, for corrupt-
ing the youth. The penalty for this crime is death.

The chief instigators of the indictment were Meletus, a
fanatical poet, and Anytus, a leading politician whose son had
come under the influence of Socrates.

III

Socrates was tried by a jury of five hundred farmers and
tradesmen chosen by lot. Most of them were uneducated; they
knew Socrates merely as a "funny clown" who taught youngsters "to prove they were right when they were wrong, and to
whip their parents because their parents had whipped them."
They were quite obtuse to the eloquent arguments of their
prisoner.

The philosopher knew he was doomed from the start. Yet
he was determined to have his say.

The words he spoke at the trial, and in the prison between
his trial and his death, have come down to us in three of Plato's
immortal dialogues—*Apology, Crito* and *Phaedo*. Plato was one
of the wealthy young pupils of Socrates. He was present at
the trial, and described the events several years later. The style
in these dialogues is the style of Plato, yet the thought is the
thought of Socrates. It has the tang of the barefoot commoner,
instead of the polish of the well-dressed aristocrat. Socrates
drew his figures of speech from the activities of everyday life,
the lowlier occupations rather than the politer pursuits. The
blunt familiarity of these dialogues is Socratic rather than
Platonic.

But let us return to the trial, condemnation, and death
of Socrates, one of the most tragic and sublime stories in the
world.

"You accuse me," said Socrates to his judges, "of corrupting the youth for my personal gain. But I am in utter poverty by reason of my teaching. I search for the truth, and invite others to join me in the search, because of my obedience to God. I obey my God as a philosopher, just as I obeyed my commander as a soldier.

"As for corrupting my pupils, I am old enough to know that in hurting others I should only be hurting myself. And no man in his right senses would want to bring injury to himself. I therefore deny that I have ever willingly harmed anybody in the world.

"The fact of the matter, O judges, is that you are against me because I have unmasked your pretense of knowledge along with my own pretense—and I have disclosed the face of ignorance underneath. I have done this not to degrade you but to uplift you, to lead you to greater wisdom and to better action because of your superior wisdom.

"Some of you will ask: 'Are you not ashamed, Socrates, of a course of action which is likely to bring you to an untimely end?' My answer is that you are mistaken. A man who is good for anything ought not to consider whether he is going to live or die; he ought only to consider whether he is right or wrong. I fear disgrace, but I do not fear death.

"For the fear of death is sham wisdom and not real wisdom; it is a pretense that we know the unknown. No one knows whether death, which we dread as the greatest evil, may not be the greatest good.

"But this I do know—that to disobey a superior, whether God or man, is evil; and I will never avoid a possible good, which is death, or accept a positive evil, which is disobedience.

"Men of Athens, I honor and love you, but I shall obey God rather than you. And God commands me to teach philosophy. If you let me go free, I shall continue to instruct men and to obey God. I shall tell all those I meet that it is shameful to accumulate wealth instead of acquiring wisdom. For this is the divine command I have received.

"But if, instead of letting me go free, you prefer to put me to death, you will inflict a great injury—not upon me but upon yourselves. For it is more evil to kill than to die. My plea to you, therefore, is to spare yourselves the sin of offending God by killing me. I am seventy years old, and in any case I have but a short time left. It is of little consequence whether I go now or next year. But it is of the greatest consequence whether you decide to kill or refrain from killing me.

"I therefore commit my cause to you and to God. And before you make your decision, I caution you to consult your own interests as well as mine."

When Socrates had finished his plea, the jury voted to condemn him to death. In accordance with the law, however, the prisoner had an opportunity to propose his own penalty as an alternative. It was up to the jury to decide between his proposed penalty and theirs.

When he stood up to submit his alternative suggestion, Socrates still refused to flinch. "I have devoted my life to your service," he said. "Too honest a man to be a politician, I have gone about privately to persuade you that you must try to be right rather than to be rich. What do I deserve for this? Maintenance at the public expense, so that I may continue to persuade you for your own good.

"I know, however, that you will not grant me this reward. I therefore propose to pay a fine of thirty minae [about $1500]. I have no funds of my own, but Plato and three of my other pupils have generously offered to raise this amount."

This fine, as Socrates expected, was promptly refused. It was too paltry an alternative for the death penalty. He was sentenced to drink the hemlock.

"I accept the verdict," he said. "I would rather die having spoken what I think, than live and speak what you want me to think. The divine voice which I often hear, and which always warns me of approaching evil, has given me no warning at this trial. How can I explain this silence? I will tell you. It is an intimation that what has happened to me is good, and that those who think that death is an evil are in error.

"For death is one of two things: it is either a state of utter unconsciousness, or it is a migration of the soul from this world to another. Now, if you suppose that it is an unconscious sleep without dreams, death will be a supreme blessing. For nothing even in the life of a king is sweeter than a night of sleep undisturbed by a dream. And an eternity of death is but a single night. But if death is a journey to another place where all the dead abide, what good can be greater than this? What would not a man give if he might converse with the noble spirits of the past? If this is true, let me die again and again. I shall then be able to continue my search into true and false knowledge. And in that world, they will not put me to death for asking questions."

The words of Socrates passed over the heads of his accusers. But before they led him back to his cell, he had a final statement to make to the court. "I am not angry with you, my judges; you have done me no harm, although you did not mean to do me any good. The hour of departure has arrived, and we go our ways—I to die, and you to live. Which of these is better, only God knows."

IV

While he was awaiting his execution, several of his friends visited him in his cell. One of them, Crito, came with a complete plan for his escape. The jailers and even the judges, Crito assured Socrates, would be glad to shut their eyes. They had done their duty to condemn the philosopher, but they would like to have him die in exile rather than in Athens.

But Socrates refused to be persuaded. He insisted upon obeying the laws of the state. These laws had protected him when he was free; and therefore he must now protect them when he was in chains.

For no state can exist when the law is set aside. "Even when unjustly condemned, a man must submit out of love for his country. He should do no violence to his country, just as he should do no violence to his father. Even when struck or reviled." Do not return evil for evil, declared Socrates, anticipating the Sermon on the Mount. Persuade your country to be better, if you can, but obey it if you cannot persuade it. Hence Socrates refused to disregard the law—to become an outlaw through his escape. "This, dear Crito, is the voice which I seem to hear murmuring in my ears, like the sound of the flute in the ears of the mystic." The philosopher is resigned to his death.

V

We now come to the last day of his life. It is one of the black days in history. Yet the radiant composure of Socrates glows like a beacon through the night.

Several of his friends have arrived at the prison to spend the last few hours with him. Of all those present, he is the least perturbed. He has sent his wife away—he doesn't want any wailing women around. He prefers the presence of men with whom he can discuss philosophy. And in the course of the discussion, he professes his belief in the immortality of the soul. "Be of good cheer," he tells his friends, "and remember that you are burning or burying only my body. I, myself, shall leave you to converse with other friends in another world." The true philosopher, he declares, will rejoice in death, since it liberates his soul from the sordid demands of his body.

The scene that follows is one of the supreme dramas of history:

"When he had finished speaking"—this passage is from Professor Jowett's translation of Plato's *Phaedo*—"he arose and went into a chamber to bathe . . . We remained behind, talking and thinking of the greatness of our sorrow; he was like a father of whom we were being bereaved, and we were about to pass the rest of our lives as orphans . . .

"Now the hour of sunset was near. When he came out, he sat down with us again . . . Soon the jailer entered and said: 'To you, Socrates, whom I know to be the noblest and gentlest and best of all who ever came to this place, I will not impute the angry feeling of other men, who rage and swear at me when, in obedience to the authorities, I bid them drink the poison—indeed, I am sure that you will not be angry with me; for others, as you are aware, are to blame.' Then bursting into tears, he turned away.

"Socrates looked at him and said: 'How charming the man is! Since I have been in prison, he has always been coming to see me; and at times he would talk to me, and was as good to me as could be, and now see how generously he sorrows on my account. We must do as he says . . . Let the cup be brought if the poison is prepared; if not, let the attendant prepare some.'

" 'But,' said Crito, 'the sun is still upon the hill-tops . . . Do not hurry—there is time enough.'

"Socrates said: 'I do not think, Crito, that I should gain anything by drinking the poison a little later; I should only be ridiculous in my own eyes for prolonging a life which is already forfeit. Please, therefore, let me have the cup now and not later.'

"Crito made a sign to the attendant, who went out and after a while returned with the cup of poison. Socrates said to him: 'You, my good friend, are experienced in such matters. Tell me how I am to proceed.' The attendant answered: 'You have only to walk about until your legs are heavy. Then you lie down, and the poison will act.' He then held out the cup to Socrates who, in the easiest and gentlest manner, took it in his hands, raised it to his lips and cheerfully drank the poison.

"Hitherto most of us had been able to control our sorrow; but now that we saw him emptying the cup, we could no longer forbear. Our tears were flowing fast—not because of Socrates, but because of our own calamity at the loss of such a friend. Socrates alone remained calm. 'What is this strange outcry?' he said. 'I sent away the women just to avoid such a scene; for I have been told that a man should die in peace. Be quiet, then, and have patience.'

"When we heard these words, we were ashamed, and restrained our tears. Socrates walked about until his legs began to fail, and then he lay on his back as he had been directed. The man who had given him the poison examined his feet and legs from time to time. After a while he pressed the foot hard and asked him if he could feel anything. And Socrates said, 'No.' And then the man pressed his leg, and so upwards and upwards and showed us that the body was growing cold and stiff . . . 'When the poison reaches the heart,' said the man, 'it will be the end.'

"And then Socrates uncovered his face (for he had covered himself up) and said: 'Crito, I must offer a cock to Asclepius. Will you remember to do it for me?'

"'It shall be done,' said Crito. 'Is there anything else?' There was no answer. A slight tremor—and Socrates was dead."

The philosopher's last words had been a request for a sacrifice to Asclepius, the god of healing—a thanks-offering for his deliverance from the fever of life.

CHAPTER VIII

Plato (427–347 B.C.)

SOCRATES had devoted his life to asking questions. Plato made it his business to find the answers.

In the words of Emerson, "Socrates and Plato are the double star which the most powerful instruments will not entirely separate." Plato wrote thirty dramatic dialogues in which he expounded his philosophy. But in all these dialogues Socrates is the leading character. Thus the principal ideas of Plato are conveyed through the mouth of Socrates. Indeed, it is hard to tell where the philosophy of Socrates ends and the philosophy of Plato begins. As a safe rule, however, we may regard Socrates as the great *seeker* and Plato as the great *seer*.

II

We have only a few scraps of information about Plato's external biography—the story of his life. But we have a complete picture of his internal biography—the story of his thought. So let us first glance at him as a citizen of ancient Athens, and then we shall try to understand him as the author of the philosophical bible of the world.

As we have already noted, Plato was one of the three pupils of Socrates who had offered to pay a fine for the liberation of their master. Plato could well afford his share of the fine. He came of a wealthy aristocratic family. And he was as handsome as he was rich. Tall and blond and athletic—*Plato* means "broad-shouldered"—he looked like Apollo, the god of light, descended from heaven. He had won two prizes for wrestling, and he had written a number of successful poems and plays.

He was therefore regarded as one of the rising young men of Athens. "I thank God," he said, "that I was born a Greek and not a barbarian, a freeman and not a slave, a man and not a woman; but above all, that I was born in the age of Socrates."

Yet it was his admiration for Socrates that almost proved his undoing. When his old teacher was condemned to death, Plato had to leave Athens for his own safety. He was twenty-eight at the time of his departure, and forty when he returned. During the intervening twelve years he traveled extensively in Europe and in Asia. He went to Italy where he joined the Pythagorean Society of True Friends; to Egypt, Persia, and possibly India, China and Judea, where he absorbed the oriental idea of one God and one universal law of justice for all; and to various other countries where he studied all sorts of governments under all kinds of social conditions and political creeds. He came back in the fullest sense a man of the world.

And then, at forty, he founded an Academy of Learning—the first university in the ancient world. The main purpose of Plato in opening this academy was to guide his pupils to national harmony through individual education. The leaders of the state, he declared along with Socrates, should be its best educated men.

He interrupted his teaching on two occasions to go to Sicily as adviser to a king—Dionysius II. In these attempts he was no more successful than Confucius had been a century earlier. Having offended the king with his insistence upon justice, Plato barely escaped with his life.

He was sixty-seven now; and he devoted his last thirteen years to his teaching and the publication of his *Dialogues*.

These dialogues are a sublime revelation of truth expressed in the language of beauty. "If Zeus came down to earth," wrote an ancient historian, "he would speak in the style of Plato."

The thirty dialogues of Plato embrace practically every

question that perplexed the people of his day—and continue to perplex the thoughtful people of our own day. Thus, he discusses immortality in the *Phaedo;* love in the *Symposium;* theology in the *Timaeus;* and dictatorship, democracy, socialism, communism, feminism, birth control, eugenics, education, morality, art, music, and psychiatry in his other books. Indeed, to quote Emerson again, "Plato is philosophy, and philosophy is Plato."

But most of Plato's ideas are summarized in his greatest work—*The Republic.* "Burn the libraries," declared Emerson, "for their value is in this one book."

We shall therefore examine *The Republic* in order to get at the heart of Plato's philosophy.

III

The scene of this dialogue is the house of Cephalus, a wealthy citizen of Athens. The characters are Thrasymachus, a sophist, or "professional teacher of wisdom"; Adeimantus and Glaucon, Plato's brothers; the aristocratic Cephalus and his son; and Socrates, who is the mouthpiece of Plato.

The discussion begins with the question, What is justice? Socrates, as usual, has posed the question. After several definitions which Socrates demolishes with his biting logic, Thrasymachus breaks in: "Why don't you enlighten us, Socrates, instead of confusing us? Anybody can ask, but only a few can answer."

But Socrates, unperturbed, asks another question: "Are you one of those who can give the answer?"

"Yes, I am."

"Well, then, let us hear it."

"Justice," exclaims the hot-headed Thrasymachus, "is the interest of the strong. In other words, might is right." And then this forerunner of Nietzsche continues: "The strong make the laws to protect themselves, and the weak call the laws unjust because they suffer under them." Morality, according to this sophist, is the code of the coward—the man who calls himself good because he lacks the courage to kick. The strong man does what he can, the weak man suffers what he must. "And this," concludes Thrasymachus, "is justice."

But, suggests Socrates, speaking for Plato, perhaps justice is not the protection of the strong against the weak, nor even the protection of the weak against the strong. Perhaps, rather, it is an adjustment between all members of society, an interdependent agreement between the individual and the state. Would it not, therefore, be a good idea to picture a just state in order that we may understand a just individual?

And then he launches into the picture of his ideal state, the Republic—the first great utopia in literature. This ideal state, declares Plato, is not a dictatorship, where only one is free and all the rest are slaves. It is not a plutocracy, where everybody tramples over everybody else in order to reach the pot of gold at the top. Nor is it a democracy, which is governed by those who are most popular and not by those who are most competent. "Democracy is mob-rule." Plato remembered the fate of Socrates at the hands of a democratic jury, "The people have no intelligence. They only repeat what they hear, and vote as they are told."

What, then, is the remedy for this sickness of unjust government? A more intelligent public. The first objective of our ideal state, therefore, is better education for all the citizens. The Republic of Plato is to be a state of wise men governed by the wisest of them all as their king. "Not until philosophers are kings or kings are philosophers, not until learning and leadership are centered in one man, will the human race be redeemed."

And so, declared Plato, let us begin with the education of the young. First of all, "let us send out into the country all the inhabitants [of our proposed Republic] who are more than ten years old, and let us take possession of the children, who will thus be protected from the bad habits of their parents."

Now that the parents are out of the way, we can go ahead with the training of the children. For the first ten years of their lives, we shall strengthen their bodies, for only a healthy body can shelter a healthy mind. The elementary school, therefore, will be a gymnasium and a playground.

At ten, the children are to add one other subject to their curriculum—music. To Plato, music meant harmony—the subject included mathematics, the science of harmonious numbers; history, the story of harmonious progress; and religion, the spirit of harmonious faith.

For the children of the ideal state must be taught the art of communion with one another. They must learn the lesson that all individuals are integral parts of the body of mankind, just as the head, the hands and the feet are integral parts of the individual body. Plato derived this idea from the oriental philosophers, and in turn handed it down to St. Paul and the Western world. "The children," said Plato, "must be trained to realize that all of us are members of one another."

And thus, all the children up to the age of twenty are to study gymnastics for the health of the body, and music for the harmony of the soul. Their training is to be coeducational. Boys and girls are to study together and play together. They are to strip when they take their exercise; and they must be taught to refrain from jeering at the sight of the human body. There is to be no false modesty in the ideal state, for the children must be trained to regard themselves as "sufficiently clad in the garment of virtue."

Moreover, they will be brought up as the children of one family—the state. This family feeling will be an actual fact rather than a philosophical theory. For the children born in the Republic will be the result of communal mating. The best men will be mated with the best women, the next best with the next best, and so on down the line. This idea, declares Plato, has been applied to produce superior cattle. It should also be applied to produce superior men.

In order to realize this idea, there are to be no individual marriages or private families in the Republic. All the adult citizens are to possess all the children in common. This community of children will have one great advantage—it will do away with parental rivalry. Nobody will be able to boast, "*My* children are better than *your* children." For all the children will belong to all the parents—a universal brotherhood of understanding and love.

This in brief is the idea to be implanted in the children up to the age of twenty. And then comes the great "weeding out." All the children are to be subjected to a severe physical, mental, and spiritual examination. Those who fail in the triple test will be relegated into the lowest class consisting of farmers, workers, and businessmen—"the baser metals of the state, such as brass and iron."

But those who pass the examination will be allowed to continue their schooling for another ten years. Their curriculum will consist mainly of the sciences—the measurement of the earth and the contemplation of the stars. At the end of this period, there will be another weeding out, considerably more severe than the first. All those who fail to pass this second examination will be assigned to the middle class of guardians, or military personnel. They will represent the "silver metal of the state."

Those who pass the second elimination are now thirty years old. They are the "gold metal" of the Republic. And they are to be trained as the potential rulers of the state—men and women alike, for Plato believed in the equal capacity and the equal right of women to leadership. The trainees for the highest positions are to enter upon a course of philosophy. This is to last over a period of five years, and the purpose of the course is to familiarize the students with the difference between the material world and the ideal world.

And this brings us to the gist of Plato's philosophy—his famous doctrine of ideas. Oceans of ink have been spilled in the discussions about this subject: "Just what did Plato mean by his world of ideas as compared with the world of things?" Let us see if we can explain the basic difference between the two worlds in a few short paragraphs.

Every temporal object in this world, said Plato, is the copy of an eternal idea that exists in the mind of God. Thus, you and I are human copies of the divine idea of Man. Every tree is a copy of the idea which governs the growth of all trees. Every good deed is a representation of the eternal idea of goodness. A person, a thing, a quality is created whenever the eternal pattern comes into contact with matter—the raw stuff out of which the Sculptor of the universe translates his permanent ideas into impermanent things.

To illustrate this point, let us regard the idea of manhood as a shining light surrounded by thousands of mirrors—some of them convex, some concave, some rough, some smooth, some broken, some sound. All these mirrors reflect the image of the selfsame central manhood. Yet no two reflections are identical, since every one of the images depends upon the nature of the reflecting surface. Hence different men, or images of manhood, are good or bad, strong or weak, straight or crooked, wise or stupid, speedy or slow. Moreover, all the reflected images are unreal. They are mere appearances—copies of the shining light, objects that seem real but are only shadows of the one perfect reality in the center.

And now suppose that one of the reflecting mirrors is smashed. The light in that mirror—or, as we say, the life of that man—has disappeared. "It is," as we are accustomed to think, "dead."

But no, it is only a *single reflection* of the eternal light that appears to have died. The material that temporarily shaped the reflection is gone. But the light which caused the reflection keeps shining on as gloriously as ever. This is but another expression of the belief of the Hindu philosophers that the individual soul is a fragmentary image of the World Soul.

We fail to realize this fact, declares Plato, because our senses deceive us. It is the intellect alone that can teach us to understand reality—that is, the realm of ideas which serve as the everlasting basis for all transitory appearances.

Plato then goes on to clarify this concept in one of his immortal similes. Those who rely upon the evidence of their senses, he tells us, are like men imprisoned in a cave which has a mouth open toward the light. But the prisoners cannot see the light. "For they have their legs and their necks chained with their faces turned away from the light, so that they are unable to move. Thus they can only see before them, being prevented by the chains from moving their heads either to the right or to the left . . . Behind and above them, at the mouth of the cave, there is a blazing fire, and in front of them there is a blank wall."

And between the fire at the mouth of the cave and the backs of the chained prisoners, there is an "endless procession of men carrying all sorts of objects . . . which cast a moving shadow upon the wall in front of their eyes." And the prisoners, condemned to keep their eyes fixed upon this wall, can see only the shadows of this moving traffic, but they cannot see the traffic that produces these shadows.

Indeed, they cannot even see their true selves. They can merely see their own shadows along with all the other shadows upon the wall. They regard these shadows as real for they do not know any better.

But now and then, asserts Plato, a philosopher escapes from the cavern of shadows and beholds, to his great delight, the outer world of things-in-themselves, the eternal world of ideas.

This, very briefly, is the substance of the philosophy that is to be taught to the advanced students in Plato's Republic. They are to learn the difference between the world of the senses and the world of sense. They are taught to understand the substance of eternity—the ideas of God—so inadequately translated into the temporary actions of men.

These ideas of God are woven into a harmony, like the notes of a song, which constitutes the pattern of life. And it is only the wisest among Plato's students in the Republic who can understand this pattern. They alone are fit to rule the state.

Yet even now their training is incomplete. They are to be taken down from the heights of philosophy and back into the cavern of competitive life. They are thirty-five years old now. For the next fifteen years they are to put their philosophy to the test—to beat their wings against the tempests of hatred and ambition and jealousy and aggressiveness and greed. They must learn to rise above the sordid struggle of their neighbors who are fighting to get ahead.

And the few who succeed in the final course of practical education are automatically chosen as the rulers of the state.

For Plato's Republic must be ruled by men and women with the sturdiest minds and the gentlest hearts. They alone will understand that the idea's the thing—especially the idea of justice. For justice is harmony—the law of moral and mathematical balance between part and part, and between the parts and the whole. The same delicate adjustment—Plato would call it the same spirit of justice—that prevails in the actions of a good man must also prevail in the guidance of a good nation and in the government of a good world. The same idea, the same law that impels the heavenly bodies to move together in a concerted unit—this same idea will ultimately impel the members of a city, a state, the entire human race to move together in a unit of concordant friendship. For men and the stars are akin in their music and their motions and their laws. All of them alike are the representations of the sublime idea of God.

IV

So much, then, for the education of the philosopher-kings and the philosopher-queens in Plato's Republic. These rulers will possess everything in common, and thus they will avoid the temptations arising from the desire for private gain.

As for the general public, they will be conditioned by their training and guided by their rulers to live in a world of adequate pay and fair play. Businessmen will abstain from amassing excessive profits. Workers will refrain from demanding unreasonable wages. Criminals will be treated like patients who are mentally sick. They will be sent to hospitals where they will be kept out of mischief until they are cured of their ills.

There will be no lawyers in the Republic, and only a handful of laws. "The more laws you enact," declared Plato, "the more temptations you offer for breaking them." The people will be taught to govern themselves without the restraint of the police. "In this way every man will have a right to mind his own business provided he does not interfere with the rights of other people.

And this, declares Plato, is the true definition of justice—a friendly interweaving of mutual interests instead of a hostile preparation for perpetual warfare.

Such was Plato's answer to his friends' question: What is justice? It is not the interest of the strong, but the harmony of *all mankind* in the orderly procession of the universe. And thus Plato adds one important element—harmony, or beauty—to the philosophy of the East. The world is built upon justice, virtue, love—and the creation of beautiful thoughts out of the idea of beauty in the mind of God.

"The Beautiful is the Good, and the Good is the Beautiful. By living a life of beauty we conquer death."

CHAPTER IX

Aristotle (384–322 B.C.)

ARISTOTLE was a pupil of Plato, just as Plato was a pupil of Socrates. Aristotle frequently disagreed with Plato, and Plato occasionally disagreed with Socrates; yet both pupils derived much of their greatness from their teachers. The stream of philosophy—the idea of the unity of life—flowed in a direct current from the oldest to the youngest of these three Greek thinkers.

It was the selfsame stream of thought, filtered through the minds of three different men. Socrates was a poor and blunt ascetic, Plato a rich and aristocratic poet, and Aristotle the son-in-law of a king and the tutor of a prince.

II

Aristotle lived at a most turbulent time—the first "world war" in history. And he was intimately acquainted with the leading character in that war. He served as the tutor of Alexander—the madman who accepted his master's idea about the unity of the world but who tried to keep it united in chains.

Aristotle was born at Stagira, a Greek colony about two hundred miles to the north of Athens. But he spent most of his boyhood at Pella, the capital of Macedonia on the Balkan Peninsula—the "Wild West" of the ancient world. His father had been appointed court physician to King Amyntas, the father of Philip and grandfather of Alexander.

Aristotle and Philip often played together as children. Philip displayed the arrogance of a prince and the ferocity of a wildcat. The young Stagirite learned to control his temper in order to preserve his life. The ability to hold yourself in check, he concluded, is the best protection against the violence of the world. This idea was to become a cardinal principle in his philosophy.

At eighteen he left Macedonia to enter Plato's academy in Athens. The other students looked rather askance at this young "fop of a foreigner." Suave, dapper, gentle, graceful, and polite, he dressed after the latest fashion and spoke with a lisp. "It might be a good idea," suggested Plato when he first saw him, "if you paid a little less attention to your clothes and a little more attention to your mind."

But within a few days after his matriculation, the young student demonstrated to Plato that he had one of the most richly endowed intellects in the world. He was open to every possible facet of knowledge—the science of the earlier philosophers, the speculations of Socrates, and the aspirations of Plato, in addition to such other branches of learning as politics, poetry, the drama, psychology, ethics, natural history, rhetoric, medicine, mathematics, and astronomy. In later years, Plato observed that his academy consisted of two parts—the body of his students and the brain of Aristotle.

The master and his favorite pupil had conceived a great affection for each other. But it was a union not without its lovers' quarrels. A philosophical dispute between understanding friends, they observed, arouses a pleasant warmth without stirring up a consuming fire. We shall find that in spite of their differences the two philosophers held many fundamental ideas in common.

Within a few years, Aristotle became a graduate instructor at the academy. But when the master died (347 B.C.), his disciple found Athens too unfriendly a place for a foreigner like himself. Philip, his boyhood playmate, now the king of Macedonia, had entered upon the subjugation of all the Greek states. Aristotle, though strictly neutral in the conflict, found himself suspect as an enemy alien. He was compelled to leave the city.

But he could not return to his native home. Stagira had been burned to the ground as one of the earliest victims of King Philip's ambition. Fortunately for the young philosopher, he received an invitation to visit Hermias, one of his former classmates, who was now the ruler of a province in Asia Minor.

The king and the philosopher got along very well. Hermias allowed Aristotle to marry his (adopted) daughter, and gave him a rich dowry as a wedding gift.

After three years of tranquil splendor at the court of Hermias, Aristotle received another invitation, this time to even greater splendor but not to tranquillity. King Philip asked him to become the tutor of his savage young whelp, Alexander.

Aristotle accepted the call. The teacher was now forty-one and the pupil thirteen. The royal household of Macedonia was like a jungle of snarling beasts. King Philip was a psychopath, his queen Olympias a tigress, and Alexander a monomaniac who believed that all men had been created to serve as slaves to his irrational whims. Again and again the philosopher tried to arbitrate the tempestuous quarrels of the palace, but in vain. Olympias kept taunting Philip that Alexander was not his son, but the illegitimate offspring of a god. Philip retaliated that he had plenty of other sons without her help. And Alexander treated both Philip and Olympias with indecent contempt.

Very often the royal quarrels took a violent turn. At one of the court debaucheries, the father and the son got into a physical brawl. The boy insulted the father, and the father tried to stab him. Philip was too intoxicated, however, to hit the mark. He fell to the ground as he lunged, and Alexander was saved for his future debaucheries and wars.

Such was the atmosphere in which the philosopher tried to teach the good life. He became convinced more than ever that the object of education was to tame the heart as well as to enlighten the mind. Men, he concluded, are the deadliest of animals, because they are able not only to think mischievous thoughts but to wield murderous tools.

And so he tried to impress his philosophy of gentleness upon the ungentle spirit of his pupil. And at times Alexander pretended to listen to his master's teaching. "I would rather excel in the knowledge of right," he said, "than in the extension of might."

But that was sheer hypocrisy. When Philip died—at the hands of an assassin hired by his queen—Alexander dismissed Aristotle as an "egghead" who merely hampered his own ambition. He succeeded to the throne and started out to conquer the world. One of his first royal acts was to hang Aristotle's nephew, Callisthenes, for his refusal to worship him, Alexander, as a god. Aristotle decided it was time for him to leave Macedonia.

III

He returned to the comparative safety of Athens with a disillusioned mind and a full purse—in addition to his dowry, he had received an enormous salary for his tutorial services. But he didn't pocket his money. Instead, he spent it all—the equivalent of about $5,000,000—upon his philosophical and scientific research.

And thus, at about the same time, the two outstanding personalities of the age embarked upon two diametrically opposed adventures—Alexander to kill and Aristotle to teach. While the warrior was mobilizing his ragtag army of murderers, the philosopher hired several hundred men, soldiers of science, to collect all sorts of living and non-living objects for a complete study of the world. And Aristotle organized the contributions of his co-workers into a comprehensive encyclopedia of universal knowledge.

He built a zoological garden and a museum of natural history and opened a new school of philosophy at Athens. This school, situated in a park, was nicknamed "Peripatetic," which means "walking about." The students listened to the lectures of their teacher as they strolled with him among the trees and the flowers of the campus.

Aristotle was about fifty at the time. His life lasted only another ten years. But within that single decade he produced a number of books and pamphlets, estimated at nearly a thousand, which rank to this day among the supreme achievements of the human intellect. These books cover almost the entire field of religion, science, and art. We have at present only a handful of these works; and in the opinion of many scholars they are the students' notations of Aristotle's ideas rather than the original ideas themselves. Yet even this fragmentary collection is so comprehensive in scope that it has been a dominant force upon the thought of the world throughout the centuries. Even today almost every philosopher is said to be either a Platonist or an Aristotelian.

Let us, therefore, examine the work of Aristotle as compared with the work of Plato—the "two supreme philosophers of the ages."

IV

Aristotle embraced a wider field of speculation than Plato; the Stagirite was a scientist as well as a philosopher. We shall briefly glance at his contribution to science before we take up his greater contribution to philosophy.

First of all, Aristotle founded a new science—logic, or the doctrine of correct thinking. Socrates and Plato had insisted upon defining their terms, and Aristotle devised a formula for arriving at all definitions. He called this formula "the system of syllogisms." A syllogism means an argument based upon logical thought. Such an argument consists of three propositions—a general premise or explanation, a specific premise or explanation, and a conclusion. For example:

General premise: Plato belongs to the class of *animals*.

But how is he different from other animals, such as a fox or a lion or a horse? This brings us to the

Specific premise: Plato is *rational*. Hence we come to the

Conclusion: Plato is a *rational animal*.

When we use a syllogism, however, we must be careful not to abuse it. We must have a general premise that applies to an entire class, and a specific premise that differentiates an individual from the rest of the class, in order to arrive at a correct conclusion. The following syllogism, for example, is ridiculous because it is based upon *two general* premises without any specific differentiation:

General premise: All men are animals.

General premise: All monkeys are animals.

Conclusion: All men are monkeys.

This is but one of the many ridiculous fallacies arising from the misuse of logic. Aristotle classified these fallacies in a scientific system of rules and diagrams which have guided the rational thinking of humanity down to the present day. "If you want to talk to me," said Voltaire, "learn to use the logic of Aristotle."

Not acceptable today, but regarded as sacred for almost two thousand years, was the astronomical theory of Aristotle. He believed that the earth was the unmoved center of the universe, and that the sun, together with all the other heavenly bodies, revolved around the earth like satellites around a royal throne. It was not until Copernicus published (in 1543) his famous theory of the earth's revolution around the sun that Aristotle's astronomical system began to be discarded. Many of his other scientific ideas—in biology, zoology, physics, and anthropology—though generally discarded today, represented in his own day the greatest advance in analytic thinking up to that time. We must remember that Aristotle had practically no apparatus to help him in his experiments; he relied mainly upon his own observation of the earth and the heavens. Yet he paved the way for a number of later scientific discoveries, such as the approximation between matter and energy, the gradual emergence of life out of non-living things, and the evolution of living organisms through the mastery of their environment.

All in all, however, Aristotle's rank in science is secondary to his stature in philosophy. Along with Plato, he is still inspiring some of our noblest thoughts about the nature of God and the Good Life.

V

Aristotle tried to refute all the thinkers who had come before him. "He believed he could not reign secure," observed Francis Bacon, "without putting all his brethren to death." That is, philosophically speaking. He tried to abolish even his beloved teacher. "Plato is dear to me, but the truth is dearer."

Yet Aristotle failed in his attempt to sacrifice Plato to the truth. Indeed, all he proved in his philosophy was that the teacher and the pupil saw the same truth, but from different angles. Our purpose in this book, as we have already noted, is to discover the circle of agreement uniting most of the great philosophical systems, instead of concentrating on the tangents of disagreement that lead us into infinite confusion. There is a great sphere of harmony, as we shall see, between Plato and Aristotle, and between the modern Platonists and Aristotelians.

Aristotle tried to emphasize his departure from Plato on three important subjects—the theory of ideas, the nature of God, and the duty of man. Yet when we compare the work of the teacher and the pupil in these three fields, we shall find very little difference in their thought.

1. *The Theory of Ideas.* Though Aristotle declared that he disagreed with the Platonic system of ideas, his disagreement was largely semantic—a quarrel about terms rather than thoughts. He substituted one word for another word, "form"

for "idea." While Plato's idea was an external pattern for men to copy, Aristotle's form was an internal stimulus for men to follow.

Thus, in the philosophy of Aristotle the adult person is the form—or the instinctive aim for growth—of which the child is the material; the child is the form of which the embryo is the material; the embryo is the form of which the sperm is the material; and so on. Everything has a compelling instinct—modern science would call it a natural function—for further growth.

And even with this distinction between idea and form, Aristotle agrees with Plato on one essential point: whether we copy an external standard (idea) or follow an internal prompting (form), we strive toward an ideal transformation of an inferior toward a superior world. Both philosophers believed that everything in the world is being constantly guided to become something better. And thus the real world is in the process of developing into an ideal world. Aristotle maintained that all life is impelled by an inner vision, while Plato had declared that all life is directed by an outer supervision, to a progressive march toward victory.

In other words, both Plato and Aristotle subscribed to a supreme driving power, or final cause, or God.

2. *The Nature of God.*   The Platonic God is the designer of the world's patterns, or ideas. The Aristotelian God is the mover of the world's actions, or transformations—that is, forms.

And here we find in Aristotle a unique idea which we have not seen in Plato. Plato's God is active, but Aristotle's God is inactive. Though he moves the whole world, he himself remains unmoved. "He guides the world," said Aristotle, "as the beloved object guides the lover." Let us suppose a beautiful woman sitting in a drawing room. She is completely absorbed in her own thoughts. She looks at nobody. But everybody looks at her. The presence of her beauty has turned all eyes, has moved all hearts into action, has stirred all minds into thought.

Such, according to Aristotle, is the nature of God. Without being moved himself, he "produces motion within us all by being loved."

Perhaps Aristotle arrived at this motionless and emotionless God through his incorrect astronomical theory. According to this theory, the earth is the unmoved mover of the universe. Situated in the center, our Queen of the Heavens is the final cause of the rotation of the planets and the stars. Aristotle's God appears to be the philosophical king to his scientific queen.

God, in the philosophy of Aristotle, is the magnetic power that animates the world. He is not a person but a force—a principle of pure energy—an uncreated but creative power that stimulates all matter into form and all life into growth. In short, he is a cold, impersonal, timeless, spaceless, and sexless mathematical formula.

Yet there were times when Aristotle forgot science and remembered Plato. And at such times, he was inconsistent with his own theory about an impersonal God. Here and there in his writings we see a conception of God as a self-conscious and world-conscious spirit. In these occasional revelations we see the familiar God of Plato and of the oriental philosophers.

"The divinity of man," observed Plato, "is but a copy of the divinity of God. He has lodged this idea within us to raise us from earth to heaven." And Aristotle, who, as we have seen, joined Plato in believing that everything in the world is being guided to something better, declared, "The spirit of God moves us to transform ourselves into God-like men"—that is, men who must learn to live more harmoniously together.

And this brings us to Aristotle's ethics as compared with the ethics of Plato.

3. *The Duties of Man.*   Here, too, the pupil began with a blast against his teacher and ended in almost total agreement with him.

The ethics of Plato, declared Aristotle, might apply to a race existing somewhere in heaven. What we need is a system

of morality that can work among the creatures of the earth.
For men are most closely allied not to the angels but to the
beasts. Together with the modern poet, Aristotle would say:

> How strange that man to heaven should aspire—
> A creature nine-tenths mud and one-tenth fire.

Plato's conception of brotherhood, declared Aristotle, may
apply to a family but cannot be extended to an entire community. If you try to make such an extension, you will turn a
close and warm relationship into something scattered and cold.
In like manner, the conception of public ownership cannot
work in a large society. If you share the total wealth among *all*
men, you weaken the personal responsibility of *every* man.

Moreover, objected Aristotle, the communal system of
Plato would rob our life of one of its greatest joys—privacy.
Everybody would live like a goldfish in the sight, and to the
disgust, of everybody else. Under such exposed conditions it
would be impossible to exercise the wisdom of justice, or even
the virtue of patience. Everybody would want to show off before everybody else. Let us, said Aristotle, forget the theoretical ethics of an imaginary utopia and concentrate upon the
practical morality of the world we live in. "We must assume
neither a standard of virtue which is above the attainment of
the average man, nor a system of education which is beyond
the reach of the average state. We must rather concern ourselves with the life which the majority of individuals can understand, and with the forms of government to which the
majority of states can attain."

To these objections Plato could have supplied a ready answer. "My Republic is not a blueprint for the perfect state of
today, but an aspiration for the better state of tomorrow. I agree
with everything you say, and I have therefore developed a
system of ethics for the commonplace region of men *as copied
from the superior morality to be found in the city of angels.*"

And Aristotle's code of ethics for the average man is very similar to that of Plato. The goal of every man's conduct, Aristotle said, is happiness through harmony. "We choose certain standards—such as honor, pleasure, knowledge—because we believe that these standards will make us happy."

But what is the nature of happiness? What is it that constitutes "the end and aim of our existence?" Aristotle defines this aim with a simple word—*eudaemonia*—which may be translated into the English word "well-being." But, said Aristotle, well-being is the result of well-doing. Happiness, in other words, is not a passive state but an active motion. We do not receive happiness; we must achieve it. The purpose of life, therefore, is to deserve happiness through the performance of good deeds "under the guidance of reason."

In order that we may thus act for our well-being, observes Aristotle, it is necessary first of all that we should possess a reasonable amount of material wealth. This adequate standard of living for each man is the duty of the state as well as the privilege of the individual. "It is difficult for a poor man to be either happy or good." And it is dangerous for the state to have men who are seething with discontent. Hence a fair distribution of private wealth leads to the greatest good of the commonwealth.

This idea about state-regulated private ownership was an elaboration of, rather than a departure from, the Platonic idea of the common ownership of all property. Plato advocated his communal system for the superior leaders only—the men and the women at the head of the state who, through their education and character, had proved their capacity for governing themselves as well as others. They alone could enjoy the advantages and avoid the dangers of common ownership. As for the masses in Plato's Republic, they would be allowed to accumulate private property, but under the direction of the state. Plato had devised his ethical system as an ideal for the few as well as for the many; and Aristotle tried to shape this ideal into a practical standard for all.

But let us continue with Aristotle's ethics. Having assured ourselves of our material welfare, he declared, we can now attend to our moral conduct—to transform our well-being into well-doing. And the road to this transformation is the middle way—the Golden Mean. We must strive to avoid the two extremes of human error as expressed in the fatal words *too much, too soon,* or *too little, too late.* We must always choose the rational course that lies midway between these extremes.

For example: When danger confronts us, we can meet it in one of three ways. We can resort to the extreme of rashness on the one hand, or of cowardice on the other hand; or we can choose the middle course of courage which is equally opposed to rashness and to cowardice. Every human action and every human characteristic, observed Aristotle, may be put to this threefold test of two opposite extremes and one Golden Mean. Thus, the mid-course between adulation and slander is truthfulness; between extravagance and stinginess, liberality; between arrogance and humility, self-respect; between drunkenness and abstemiousness, self-control.

Self-control, temperance, moderation in all things. This, according to Aristotle, is the highest virtue of man. And it is the safest road to happiness.

But this road must be used at all times. Self-control must become the habitual commerce between man and man. "A good character is *formed* by the daily *performance* of good deeds . . . A single swallow does not make a summer; and a single good action does not make a happy life."

The happy life, then, is a life of self-control guided by the practical application of the Golden Mean. We need wisdom to guide us along the right course. It is not always easy, as Aristotle points out, to distinguish between the mean and the extremes. Every man subconsciously thinks that he is at the center and that everybody else, whether to the right or to the left of him, is on the wrong side. Thus, "the courageous man is called *rash* by the cowardly, and *cowardly* by the rash." (In modern politics, the liberal is called a communist by the reactionaries, and a reactionary by the communists.)

To avoid this confusion between the mean and the extremes, we need better education. The good life, in other words, is based not only upon right action but also upon correct knowledge. And here again Aristotle agrees with Plato, in spite of his effort to disagree. Both the teacher and the pupil assert, though in somewhat different terms, that unhappiness is the result of bad conduct, which in turn is the result of ignorance. Happiness, on the other hand, is the result of good conduct, which in turn is the result of knowledge. We must be educated to control ourselves, declares Aristotle, to moderate our personal desires and our actions toward our fellow men. This is but another way of expressing Plato's assertion that we must be educated to adjust ourselves, to modulate our conflicting desires and our relationships with our fellow men. Both philosophers express the selfsame idea, Aristotle in the language of the scientist, and Plato in the style of the poet.

Indeed, Aristotle speaks almost like Plato in his summary of ethics: "He alone is completely happy who, sufficiently equipped with health and wealth and friendship, is active *in accordance with his knowledge of complete and harmonious virtue throughout a complete and harmonious life* . . . He will act at the right times, with reference to the right objects, towards the right people, with the right motive and in the right way." This is a pretty good picture of Plato's Just Man, Isaiah's Righteous Man, and Confucius's Superior Man. There is no interruption in the central current of the stream of wisdom, whatever the landscape through which it flows. The philosophy of Aristotle is but a continuation of the essential unity in all philosophy. "The *completely happy man* is the *completely gentle man.*"

"The complete *gentleman,*" said Aristotle, "takes joy in *doing* favors, but feels shame in *receiving* favors . . . He does not speak evil of others, even of his enemies, unless it be to themselves. But always his words are stamped with the truth and with a kindly sympathy." He is a cementer of friendships. "When you see two friends," observed Aristotle, "you see two bodies with a single soul." The complete gentleman is generous because he is wise. "His concern for others is but a reflection of his concern for himself." For he knows that every man is a part of the body of mankind.

VI

Aristotle's picture of the complete gentleman is the picture of Aristotle himself. He retained his composure amidst the worldwide conquests of Alexander. This former pupil of Aristotle's had failed to learn his lesson. He had yielded completely to his lust for power. The refugees who arrived from the devastated countries told amazing stories about this Macedonian madman. His life was a furious whirlwind of caprices. He would donate a kingdom to a friend and then dash out the recipient's brains in a drunken fit. One of his officers died because of his refusal to follow the physician's orders. Alexander crucified the physician for his failure to save the officer's life. And then, as an "atonement" for his own injustice, he slaughtered the inhabitants of an entire city. Once, when a dancing girl who had entertained him asked for a torch to light her way home, Alexander set fire to the palace of the Persian king. "This, my dear, will give you plenty of light," he said.

Such were the stories Aristotle heard about Alexander, who wept, it was reported, because there was only one world for him to conquer. "It's a pity," remarked Aristotle, "that he hasn't learned to conquer his own greed."

These words reached the ears of Alexander. His teacher, he felt, was subversive. Aristotle had dared to criticize his dictatorial attitude toward the world. "Of all governments," Aristotle had observed, "dictatorships are the worst." This statement, believed Alexander, was meant as a direct stab against himself. He declared his determination to "dispose of Aristotle" as soon as he got through with his conquests.

Aristotle was spared from this danger when Alexander died suddenly (323 B.C.) in a drunken debauch. But now the philosopher was faced with another danger. The Athenians accused him of sending secret information to Alexander's successor, Antipater. They prepared to arrest him, like Socrates, for "blasphemy against the gods and treason against the state."

Aristotle eluded the arrest just in the nick of time. "I will not give Athens," he declared, "a second chance to sin against philosophy."

He escaped to Euboea, an island in the Aegean Sea, where he died a few months later, of a self-administered cup of hemlock, it was believed. "When I can no longer teach," he said, "I no longer care to live."

Just before he died, he wrote perhaps his greatest work—a will in which he liberated his slaves. This Emancipation Proclamation antedated Abraham Lincoln's by about twenty-two hundred years.

CHAPTER X

Diogenes (about 412–323 B.C.)

DIOGENES said, regarding Plato's completely just man and Aristotle's completely happy man, that such a man rarely if ever exists.

Like Plato and Aristotle, Diogenes was a product of the Socratic school of philosophy. He was a pupil of Antisthenes, who had been a pupil of Socrates. Unlike Plato and Aristotle, however, Antisthenes and Diogenes were Cynics, or "canine" philosophers. They "barked" at the world because it contained "ninety-nine scoundrels for every decent man."

Diogenes lived in an era of disillusion resulting from a century of wars. Philosophy, to quote Professor C. F. Angus in his *Cambridge Ancient History*, was "no longer the pillar of fire going before a few intrepid seekers after truth." It was rather "an ambulance following in the wake of the struggle for existence and picking up the weak and wounded." But Diogenes didn't even join the ambulance force to help the victims of the wreckage. He merely watched the tragedy and vented his bitterness at a world that allowed itself to be wrecked.

He saw no valid reason for an existence the principal job of which was plunder and ultimate goal death. He had no respect for conquerors or their conquests. One day, so goes the story, Alexander the Great came to visit this philosopher who had made his home in a tub. "What," asked Diogenes, "is your greatest desire at present?"

"To subjugate Greece," replied Alexander.

"And after that?"

"To subjugate Asia."

"And after that?"

"To subjugate the world."

"And after that?"

"To relax and enjoy myself."

"Then why don't you relax and enjoy yourself right now?"

Alexander is said to have thanked Diogenes for his advice. "Is there anything I can do for you?" he asked.

"Yes," said the philosopher. "You can remove your shadow that stands between me and the sun. I, too, desire to relax and enjoy myself."

The king laughed and said: "If I were not Alexander, I would rather be Diogenes than any other man."

"And if I were not Diogenes," retorted the Cynic, "I would rather be any other man than Alexander."

Diogenes was so fearless because he had nothing to lose but his life. "And my life has been forfeit from the day I was born. It makes no difference whether I pay the debt now or later on."

II

It was the desire of Diogenes to bring about a transvaluation of values—a better understanding of the difference between the worth of a thing and its price. He wanted to see happiness, but not at the cost of aggression; justice without the surtax of vengeance; contentment measured not by the accumulation of silver or gold, but by the possession of a serene mind. He aimed to establish, to quote his own expression, a "reminting of the coin." Throw out the false coinage, bring in the true. Mint your thoughts and your deeds out of the superior metal of a better character.

Diogenes was sensitive on the subject of counterfeit coinage. His father, a banker, had been imprisoned for stamping coins out of inferior metal. And Diogenes himself, in his youth, had been exiled from his native city of Sinope, on the Black Sea, as a suspected accessory in the crime.

The suspicion was probably groundless, for Diogenes looked upon money, and upon the comforts it could buy, with the utmost contempt. But he was not sorry to leave his home town. When the judges condemned him to depart from Sinope, he retorted: "And I condemn you to remain in Sinope."

He went to Athens and applied for admission to the philosophical school of Antisthenes. The manner of his application was rather sensational. The master was lecturing to his class when the ragged and unkempt vagabond stomped into the room and insisted on taking his place among the students. He was greeted with shouts of anger and derision. "Get out, you mangy dog!" "No beggars allowed here!" "Back to the gutter, where you belong!"

Antisthenes tried, gently but firmly, to dismiss the intruder. "Perhaps if you go home and tidy up a bit——"

"I have no home, and insist on staying here the way I am! They call me a dog. Very well. I've got a dog's grip on philosophy. And I'm going to hold on!"

Some of the more violent students began to beat him. "Go ahead," he cried, "hit me as much as you like. There's no fist hard enough to drive me away!"

So they allowed him to stay on. And before long, their contempt for Diogenes became tempered with a measure of respect. They couldn't help admiring a young man who refused to follow the conventions because he tried to pursue the right.

III

There was much in common between Socrates, Antisthenes, and Diogenes. All three of them believed in the doctrine that the beginning of all knowledge is self-knowledge. But Antisthenes went a step beyond Socrates; and Diogenes went several steps beyond Antisthenes.

Socrates had said, "Know thyself." And Antisthenes declared, "Advance from *self-knowledge* to *self-mastery*." An aristocrat up to the time of Socrates's death, Antisthenes then decided to dedicate himself to a life of simple goodness. He had become disgusted with the injustice of the judges. Socrates, through his submission to the death penalty, had declared his faith in the man-made laws of Athens. Antisthenes tried to determine whether or not the man-made laws of Athens were in agreement with the God-made laws of the universe.

And he found that there were times when the two sets of laws were in conflict. He therefore decided to renounce the social conventions of his country, and to return to the guidance of Nature, to establish, in other words, a sort of Platonic utopia of his own—the Kingdom of Heaven on earth.

This Christian philosophy four centuries before Christ insisted upon the rejection of material wealth and the acceptance of spiritual wisdom. Like Pythagoras, Antisthenes declared that nothing should be owned in private. He believed in a community of possessions and a communion of souls. He advocated the abolition of slavery. He maintained that there must be no luxury for the masters, no hunger for the masses, and no laws that favored the strong at the expense of the weak.

His pupil Diogenes was even more radical than the master. He not only objected to private property but rejected all property. He lived by begging and paid for his alms with "the most precious of coins—philosophy." He called himself a brother of all mankind and of all living things. He became a vagabond citizen of the world. Divesting himself of all goods, he found the greatest gift—freedom from fear of the world's thievery, because he had nothing worth stealing. He regarded himself as completely independent. "Aristotle," he said, "eats when it pleases the king; Diogenes, when it pleases Diogenes."

Yet there were times when the vagabond philosopher went hungry. Some of the people he asked for bread replied with stones. One day he was seen begging from a statue. To those who wanted to know the reason for his peculiar behavior, he said: "I am taking lessons in the art of being refused."

Humble as a beggar, proud as a king—this, in a few words, is a summary of Diogenes's character. His topsy-turvy outlook on the world revealed many a truth under a new light. Once, in the course of his wanderings, he was captured by pirates. When he was put up for sale at the slave market, he greeted his prospective purchasers with the words: "Slaves, come buy a master!"

He was always ready to act, as well as to teach, his philosophy. Catching a boy who had committed an act of vandalism, he took the culprit to his home and slapped his father. "I put the blame for the misdeed not upon the son who has learned no better, but upon the father who has taught no better."

And thus he walked about in his shabby cloak, encountering many blows, a little respect and the peace that came through a clear understanding of the vanity of life. "When I meet a man who is elegantly dressed," he said, "it is not his eyes but mine that get the richer feast. For I see his splendor, and he sees my rags." One night he observed a mouse running around with no need of a lodging or fear of the dark. "The mouse and I," he observed, "are congenial spirits. He sleeps in his hole and I in my tub; and until both of us are caught in the trap of fate, we are content to scurry unhampered over the world."

He was free from all care because he was devoid of all property. He carried his few necessities in a knapsack slung over his shoulder, curled himself up in his tub when the weather was inclement, and stretched himself under the open sky when the weather was good. "What softer pillow than a bundle of rushes, and what richer furniture than the flowers and the trees?"

He traveled constantly—on foot—from place to place, but made his headquarters at Athens. Here he lectured, like Socrates, to people in the streets. Most of them scoffed, a few of them guffawed at his jests, which were not always of the parlor variety, but now and then a listener came away with a richer mind and a gentler heart.

For the ragged clothes and cynical tongue of Diogenes concealed one of the warmest hearts in the ancient world.

IV

Diogenes was so bitter against folly because he was so tender toward the fools. He wanted all men to find greater happiness through superior wisdom. A life lived under the guidance of wisdom, he said, will result in simplicity, liberty and security.

1. *Simplicity:*   Happiness, he declared, lies in the fulfillment of desire. And the simpler your desires, the more easily they can be fulfilled. "The greatest pleasure," he said, "is to despise all pleasure." You can gain the world by renouncing the world. The source of all evil is to desire too much. God punished Prometheus, the legendary hero who discovered the use of fire, because "the gift of fire is the road to luxury and laziness and all the other woes of civilized life." When someone argued that men, unlike beasts, were tender and naked and needed artificial warmth, Diogenes retorted that frogs, who had less hair than men, could live comfortably in the coldest water. "It is all a matter of habit," he said.

The shortest way to contentment, declared Diogenes, is to avoid luxury. When asked to summarize the secret of the good life, he replied: "I can do it in three words—*fortitude without fortune.*"

On one occasion he joined a crowd of people on their way to an athletic contest. "Are you, too, going as a spectator?" asked someone.

"No, I am going as a contestant."

"What sort of contestant?" jeered the stranger.

"A runner and a wrestler," said Diogenes. "I am the speediest runner away from pleasure, and the strongest wrestler against pain."

Like Henry Thoreau, his Yankee disciple, Diogenes came to his hardihood through his hardship. "This saintly Cynic," observed the Stoic philosopher, Epictetus, "found himself happiest under the discipline of privation . . . His utter simplicity was not a pose; it was the practical teaching of a man so gentle and philanthropic that he cheerfully took poverty upon himself for the common good of mankind."

Blessed are the poor, for they shall inherit the earth. One of the stories told about Diogenes sounds almost like a parable out of the New Testament. "I weighed the gifts of those who offered me bread," said Diogenes, "and from those who profited by my instruction I accepted, while the others I refused. For I thought it unfair to receive from those to whom I was unable to give . . . Once I went to the house of a very rich young man, and was ushered into a room hung all over with pictures and decked out with gold. I showed him, by my demeanor, that I respected neither his person nor his possessions . . . 'Your attitude,' he said, 'seems to indicate that I am an uneducated boor; but you shall not have a chance to upbraid me again. Henceforth I shall be at your side.' And in fact, on the very next day, he disposed of all his property to his family, put on the Cynic's knapsack and followed me."

And for the first time in his life, added Diogenes, his new disciple experienced true peace of mind. Having risen from riches to rags, he renounced the tyranny of possession and found freedom.

2. *From simplicity to liberty.* Diogenes's contempt for the counterfeit values of life enabled him to become "the one complete master in a world of slaves." A forerunner of St. Paul, he declared that God "has made foolish the pretended wisdom of man." He went about with a lighted lamp one day; and

when asked why he did it, he said: "I am looking for a man who is honest, wise and free."

Freedom, he said, is the fruit of self-sufficiency. When a friend asked him what was the proper time for marriage, he replied: "When you are young, it is too early to marry; when you are older, it is too late. A bachelor himself, he was opposed to marriage because a family man, he said, is a slave to fortune. He would have welcomed race suicide as the supreme liberation from pain—a final serene sleep after a nightmare of brutality, hatred, injustice, and hunger for rank, honor, and wealth. But since race suicide was impossible, Diogenes accepted the next best thing—the liberation of the individual from the feverish pursuits that produced the nightmare of the conventional life.

In order to be free, declared Diogenes, cast away the shackles of your ambitions and fears. Don't become a slave to your anxiety about the future or regret about the past. What has been has been; what will be will be. Assert your independence, in the face of your fate and in the presence of all men.

It was his own independence that gave Diogenes his liberty. Even during his servitude as a captive among the pirates, he remained by his own definition a free man. "I am free from self-inflicted suffering. All suffering is merely a state of mind. It is not your misfortune but your self-pity that produces your pain." The voluntary death of Socrates, in the opinion of Diogenes, was an act of slavery. Socrates submitted to an unjust law. But unlike Socrates, Diogenes regarded himself as absolutely free. "For I refuse to be enslaved by stupid conventions or unfair laws." He had attained the highest mastery of all—the complete mastery of himself. "Self-mastery," he said, "is the only liberty worth while."

3. *From liberty to security.* Diogenes considered himself free because he was simple, and secure because he was free. "You can lighten the blows of fate," he said, "by preparing yourself in advance." The less you expect of life, the fewer the

disappointments. The smaller your possessions, the lighter your losses. If you own nothing, you have nothing to lose or fear. Real security consists not in acquiring but in rejecting possessions. Ask much, and your hunger will never be stilled. Ask nothing, and you get a free and tranquil soul. In this philosophy, Diogenes is at one with the writers of the Old Testament. "He possesses the most who is satisfied with the least." As Diogenes expressed this idea, "If you cannot have what you want, be content with what you have."

Contentment, maintained Diogenes, is the shortest way to security. And discontent is the long and winding way that has no ending. The goal keeps always receding just beyond your reach. "One more bend of the road," you say, "and I will be there." But when you have turned the corner, you find still another bend, and another. They lure you on and on you are always agitated and hungry and fearful, never satisfied or secure.

"So let us stop pursuing the impossible and adapt ourselves to things as they are. Even our misfortunes. Let us suffer as actors in the tragedy of life; but let us learn, as spectators, to laugh at our own suffering. "If we meet our hardships with a courageous heart, we can stand secure amidst a falling world."

V

The philosophy of Diogenes—based upon simplicity, liberty, and security—was an attempt to find inner peace amidst the turmoil of a war-torn world. He had become an optimist through an excess of pessimism. Expecting the worst, he had built a shield of cynicism against all blows. And behind the shield he had found the safety of a bitter humor. He laughed to keep himself from crying.

For at his best he was a lover of mankind. "As befits a servant of God," to quote Epictetus, "Diogenes had the care of the world always in mind." He went through life as a physician of the soul. Sometimes his remedies were painful. But they were always meant to heal. "See how I myself have found peace of mind," he said. "Accept my medicine and you, too, shall have peace."

Buddha and Lao-tse would have found in Diogenes a companion after their own hearts. And some of the early bishops of the Church, like Athanasius and Gregory, acclaimed him as a kindred spirit. In the over-all summary of the world's great thought, Diogenes may be ranked as a disciple of the oriental philosophers and a teacher of the Christian saints.

CHAPTER XI

Epicurus (342–270 B.C.)

DIOGENES had sought tranquillity in his contempt for worldly goods. Opposed to his Cynical school was the philosophy of the Skeptics—a group of thinkers who doubted even the existence of their worldly goods. And the Skeptics sought felicity in their doubt.

The founder of this school was Pyrrho, an officer in Alexander's army. Like Socrates, Pyrrho declared: "I know only this that I know nothing." Pyrrho believed that we are aware of the world only through our senses, and our senses are deceptive. No two people see the same things; moreover, nobody ever sees the same things on two different occasions or from two different angles. What appears as ice today may appear as water tomorrow. What appears as an elevation from a valley may appear as a valley from a mountain. Hence we cannot trust our knowledge and must question all our beliefs, even our belief in the existence of God.

And since we know nothing, let us be serene in our ignorance. The Skeptic, as Paul Elmer More has put it, had "a genial indifference to fate." Why worry about the future? It may never come; and even if it does come, it may be entirely different from what we expect it to be. So why spoil today by speculation about tomorrow?

The Skeptics quarreled bitterly with the Cynics. Yet the quarrel, as in most other philosophical controversies, was concerned with words rather than with thoughts. At bottom the Cynics and the Skeptics were in complete agreement. The "barking" followers of Diogenes looked for tranquillity, and the "doubting" disciples of Pyrrho aimed at felicity—two different words with a very similar meaning.

In addition to the Cynics and the Skeptics, who tried to find peace in a warlike world, there was a group of philosophers —the Pessimists—who believed that the easiest way to end the turmoil of life was to put an end to life itself. The leader of this group, Hegesias, taught his pupils that the best thing for a young man to do was to commit suicide. He himself, it is interesting to note, died a natural death at the age of eighty. When asked to explain the reason why he refused to practice what he preached, he replied that it was necessary for him to submit to the misery of living in order that he might teach others the happiness of dying.

II

In the midst of this battleground of philosophical creeds came a young man who showed still another way to felicity. This young man, Epicurus, founded the Hedonist school—so-called from the Greek word *hedone,* which means pleasure. The Hedonist philosophy advocated a life devoted to pleasure as the best way out of our troubles and tribulations.

Epicurus was born on the Aegean island of Samos, fourteen years after the birth of Alexander. His father was an Athenian teacher whose salary was so meager that his wife had to help support the family through the peddling of religious charms and fake medicines. She was a quack doctor of the soul. Epicurus was often obliged, after school hours, to assist her in the sale of her pious frauds, and in this way he acquired an early and hearty contempt for religious superstition.

He showed, even as a youngster, a great interest in mental gymnastics. One day, when he was about twelve years old, his teacher told him that the world was created out of chaos.

"Yes," said Epicurus, "but who created chaos?"

"God."

"And who created God?"

"I don't know," replied his teacher. "Only a philosopher can give you the answer to that question."

Right then and there Epicurus decided to study philosophy and to find out who it was that created God, who in turn created chaos, out of which the world was created.

When he was a little older, he perplexed another of his teachers with his questions. "Tell me," he asked, "does God control everything?"

"Yes, everything."

"Then he is responsible for our pains as well as for our pleasures?"

"No," said his teacher. "God is not responsible for our pains."

"In that case," insisted Epicurus, "does God have power to give us our pleasures but no power to take away our pains?"

"I guess so," said his teacher.

"What, then, does God do when we are in pain?"

"He turns away his eyes, I suppose."

"Does this mean that God can neither do all things, nor see all things, nor care for all people at all times?"

"I really don't know," said his teacher in perplexity. "You'll have to ask the philosophers to answer these questions."

Epicurus became more determined than ever to search for his answers in the various schools of philosophy. At eighteen he went to Athens where he dipped into the teachings of the Greek thinkers and found few of them to his taste. Too much fighting about their differences, too little effort to arrive at a basic agreement. From Athens he set sail for the East and for a number of years he traveled from country to country, an eager prospector for the nuggets of oriental wisdom. Enriched with his findings, he returned to Athens at thirty-five, bought a house and garden in one of the suburbs, and set up an outdoor academy for the teaching of his philosophy. The academy was open to men and women, rich and poor, masters and slaves.

For, as Epicurus explained, there are no sex or class distinctions in the realm of learning. And the philosophy he taught at the academy was designed to bring about an ideal world—not an impossible utopia like Plato's, but a society of friendly people devoted to the promotion of pleasure and the abolition of pain.

First of all, he declared his disbelief in a future existence. "Today we are alive, and this is all the certainty we have. So let us make the best of our present existence."

With this simple creed of "plucking the flowers of today," he became the most popular philosopher in Greece. Those who were unable to attend his lectures bought his books, of which no fewer than three hundred were published.

Most of his work has been lost. Fortunately, however, we have a complete outline of his philosophy in Lucretius's epic poem *De Rerum Natura*, "On the Nature of Things." Lucretius was an Epicurean philosopher who lived in Rome about 250 years after Epicurus. His poem on the nature of things is one of the strangest compositions in the history of literature. It is a plea for cold logic, and yet it is written in a white heat of passion. It is the work of an infidel who believes that nothing in the world is divine except human happiness. It is one of the great bibles of the world—a testament for unbelievers.

Let us invite Lucretius to visit us for a few minutes and to outline for us the main features of the philosophy of Epicurus.

III

The purpose of living, according to Epicurus, is to enjoy life. We have no other business, and no other duty, in this world. We are not the children of a benevolent God, but the stepchildren of an indifferent Nature. Life is an accident in a mechanical universe; but we can make it, if we will, a happy or at least an interesting accident.

So let us at the outset recognize the fact that we must

depend upon ourselves, and not upon an external power, for our own happiness. The universe is not the handiwork of the gods. It is the fortuitous outcome of the movement of atoms through infinite space.

This brings us to the atomic theory of Epicurus. He borrowed this theory from the earlier Greek philosopher, Democritus, who had anticipated, by his mechanistic interpretation of the origin of the world, one of the most important discoveries in modern physics.

Epicurus, adopting the atomic theory of Democritus, made it the foundation upon which he built the superstructure of his own philosophy. We are, he said, nothing but combinations of atoms whirled out of chaos into the world and almost immediately whirled back into chaos. These atoms, of which all things are composed, move eternally downward in the infinite void. Now and then they swerve to one side or another and come into collision, like the motes in a sunbeam. They are of different sizes and different shapes, and in their continual deflections and collisions they become gradually kneaded into the substance of stars and earths and moons and suns and universes.

Our universe, declared Epicurus, is not the only one in existence. There are others equally vast and equally wonderful. They, too, have their earths, with their mountains and oceans, and their races of men and generations of wild beasts. We are not the only pebbles on the beach of the infinite oceans of space, for the atoms come into the same sorts of combinations under the same kinds of conditions over and over again as they whirl forever downwards through the infinite aisles of space.

All this movement of the atoms, according to Epicurus, is spontaneous. There is no divine hand to guide it. Even the gods are the product of the atomic swirl. They are made out of a finer, more subtle structure of atoms than those that go into the making of men. But the gods, too, are perishable. They live in the vast spaces between the universes, utterly indifferent to our human existence. They roam over the heavens, just as we roam over the earth, waiting for their final dissolution into the separate atoms out of which they came. Since the atoms are in continual motion, breaking away from one body after another, it follows that the world is gradually wearing out, and that the earth will in the end become nothing but a cold cinder floating aimlessly down to the rubbish heap of burnt-out universes.

IV

It is not quite clear where the gods fit into the Epicurean scheme of things. Epicurus had a definite belief in the gods as a race of aloof and superior beings. We are, it seems, of no interest to them, and consequently they should be of no interest to us. Yet perhaps Epicurus thought the human race needed them as models to follow—patterns of that supreme felicity in heaven which we on earth should try to attain. The gods of Epicurus are very similar to the Platonic ideas of perfect men. "They have no troublesome business themselves and they bring no trouble upon one another." They enjoy uninterrupted bliss in a round of mutual pleasure. The example of their happy divine life, declared Epicurus, should act as a spur to our own human quest for happiness. He tried to turn his Epicurean garden into a facsimile of paradise.

And thus Epicurus admitted the existence of the gods as the ideals for men to follow. Yet he denied that they had anything to do either with the creation or with the guidance of this world of ours. Life, he said, is too crazy a farce to have originated in a divine mind. No sane God would order a temple to be built in his honor and then strike it down with his lightning. No benevolent Providence would bring a young boy through a dangerous illness only to send him to a worse death on the battlefield. So let the gods look out for themselves and let us try to imitate them without, however, calling upon them for help. Our salvation lies within ourselves. For we live in a

world that has been self-generated through the accidental con-
fluence of atoms, particles of matter which move in an infinite
variety but without any design.

Yet how does it happen that the gathering together of the
unguided particles of matter should have resulted in a world
of trees and flowers, of birds and beasts and men? Through
what process have the atoms succeeded in producing a scientist
like Democritus or a philosopher like Epicurus? Through the
blind process of trial and error, replied Epicurus; through the
gradual development of matter from cruder to finer forms;
through the natural elimination of the unfit and the survival
of the fittest. In short, through the process of evolution.

Epicurus advanced the theory of evolution twenty-two
hundred years before Darwin. But we have already noted even
earlier hints of this theory in the Egyptian philosophy of Ptah-
hotep and in the Chinese philosophy of Confucius. The idea
of evolution, therefore, may be traced back not only to Epicurus, but to the oriental philosophers who lived many centuries before his day. As King Solomon observed, there is
nothing new under the sun.

V

But let us return to the Epicurean theory of evolution as
represented in the poem of Lucretius. The atoms in their eternal whirl, declares Epicurus, underwent all sorts of combinations and dissolutions until they finally became united into what
we call "the world." At first our earth was a lifeless lump of
clay; but gradually it began to put forth grass and shrubs and
flowers. Animal life came next. Birds began to fly and make
music in the air, and beasts prowled over the forests and filled
them with their bellowings. Some of these species were adapted
to their environment and were enabled, either through their
courage or their cunning, to survive. Others were born with
insufficient sight or hearing or means of locomotion. They were

the freaks of nature, the victims of a blind experiment in a planless world, and they became extinct. Man, the leading actor in this play without a plot, was the last to arrive upon the scene. Hardy and savage and naked, he roamed over the earth like the other animals, living upon herbs and fruits and acorns, and sleeping in the open fields at night.

Attacked by the more ferocious beasts, he was compelled after a time to seek refuge in caves. The herding together of many beast-men into a single cave for mutual protection resulted in the gradual development of speech and pity and the first crude feelings of friendship. Seeing strange forms in their dreams, they endowed these forms with superior powers and everlasting life and began to worship them as gods.

Little by little, as they learned to stand upright and to transform their forelegs into arms, they discovered the use of metal for the making of better tools and weapons. And thus they became more able to protect themselves and to kill their enemies. Some of the groups began to interchange goods and ideas—and blows—with other groups; and thus, little by little, they learned the arts of barter, commerce, navigation, agriculture, poetry, music, architecture, politics, diplomacy, litigation, and war. In short, all civilization is nothing but an evolutionary process which enables man to adapt himself to an inhospitable world and to survive for a brief space in the eternal struggle for existence. For all life is a continual warfare, and there is no truce for any of us except in death.

VI

And thus we come back from the science of Epicurus to his philosophy. The earth we live on, he declared, is rented to us for a little while; and when the time comes for us to move on, we are dispossessed without a moment's notice.

But if we cannot conquer death, let us at least overcome the fear of death. Let us not grieve at the brevity of human life. Instead, let us rejoice in it. For there is no consciousness after death. "The dead have rest from pain." There is no punishment in hell for any mistakes we may have made during our stay on earth. The white hand of Death soothes us into a sweet and dreamless sleep. Death is the friendly warden who signs the papers of our release from the madhouse of the world. He is the gentle physician who cures us of the most dreadful of all diseases—life.

Yet even if some of us have found life to be a continual feast of blessings, is it desirable to keep on gorging ourselves indefinitely? Is it not much better to leave the table before we are overfilled, and to retire smilingly, like a tired but happy banqueter, to a pleasant sleep? One fatal day, you lament, will rob you of all the prizes of life. But you forget to add that this same fatal day will also free you from the craving to possess these prizes.

You will have no desires in the sleep that awaits you. And no fears. But what of the great terror that haunts you while you are still alive? This present thought of your future annihilation, the presentiment of sinking into an "abyss of nothingness," isn't this in itself a cause for your greatest distress?

Not in the least, declared Epicurus. "Why feel distress over a dead body which can feel nothing at all?" You are not terrified at your non-existence before you were born. Why then be terrified at your non-existence after you die? Your life is the dream of a moment between a sleep and a sleep. And the dreamless sleep is far sweeter than the dream.

Moreover, even the longest sleep is but a moment in duration. Have you ever awakened after a sound sleep of several hours with the feeling that you have just barely closed your eyes? In the sleep of death, this fleeting moment of insensibility is the measurement of a million years as well as of a single night.

And in this eternal instant of death, you will not even be aware of your identity. That which has no personal awareness is nothing to you. Your dead self will be no relation to your living self. It will have no concern for your former desires, and no regrets over your unfulfilled hopes.

So enjoy your present life as a fascinating day-dance between two eternities of the sweetest sleep. Join the careless dance of the atoms over the infinitude of space.

VII

This was the goal of the Epicurean philosophy. A dance of pleasure in a friendly embrace. This Epicurean philosophy has been often misunderstood. Epicurus has been depicted as a devil of debauchery. The adjective "epicurean" is synonymous with "sensual," "licentious," "unrestrained." The early Church Fathers condemned the philosophy of Epicurus as "an invitation to the pigsty." Among the pious Jews a follower of Epicurus—or an Epikoiros—is an atheist, a scoundrel, and a clown. And even among many of his adherents today, the pleasure philosophy of Epicurus is confounded with the belly-lusts of the material world.

Yet this is far from the meaning which the gentle philosopher attached to his own idea of pleasure. What Epicurus aimed to attain was a state of *ataraxia*—a word which, translated into English, means imperturbability. "Let your mind, like our academy, be an island of peace amidst the turbulence of the world." His school of philosophy was a sequestered garden of friendship in an unfriendly world. His definition of pleasure was a reciprocal exchange of good will—a "kindly comradeship" serving as a shield against the onslaughts of life.

Above all, Epicurus was opposed to the grosser indulgences of the body. "The pleasure of a moment," he said, "may result in the suffering of a lifetime." But the purpose of the Epicurean type of pleasure was to abolish suffering and to establish a happy life. "A quiet state of continued happiness is more important than the boisterous excitement of transitory delights."

And thus he taught a new kind of joy—the joy of an unruffled mind as it watches from a distance the troubles and the turmoils of the world. To be sure, our life is a bitter gift—so bitter, indeed, that we enter and leave it with a cry of pain. Yet we can turn even our pain into a source of pleasure. For one of our greatest pleasures is the recovery from pain.

So let us cultivate our garden of simple joys. Let us live quietly, eat and drink moderately, and enjoy the company of those who have joined us in our tranquil life. "It is more important to know *with whom* you are to eat and drink than *what* you are to eat and drink."

Epicurus himself was the simplest of men. A meal of barley bread was sufficient for him, if only he could break it in the presence of a friend. He had a genius for friendship. "Cultivate this greatest of all our blessings. Make a religion of it. Worship it. For friendship is a sweet and beautiful and holy thing. The sympathy of true friendship is the only certain gift we possess in this world of doubtful values. If the sufferings of life can reconcile us to death, the joys of friendship can reconcile us to life."

And thus the Epicurean philosophy of "secluded pleasure shared with congenial friends" was not merely a self-centered escape from the world. It was rather a concerted effort to calm the world's fever and to lessen the world's pain. Epicurus often spoke of his school as "our holy company." The members of this school were dedicated to the holiness of shared sympathy and the continual rejoicing in one another's joy.

Epicurus spent much of his time writing letters to his friends, and especially to their children. He wanted the children to grow up in a world of "enlightened selfishness"—of giving their compassion that they might be repaid with gratitude. His own life was a long series of gentle words and generous deeds. His was the supreme pleasure of giving and receiving in kind.

The knowledge that he was surrounded with kindness sustained him through all his suffering. Poverty, bereavement and disease had transformed the "dream of his life" into a nightmare. Yet just before his death he wrote to one of his friends: "I am now passing through this last day of my life. Strangury (a painful obstruction of the bladder) has laid hold of me; and I am wracked with torments which the body can no longer endure. But over against all this, I set my joy in the recollection of our thoughts and words in the past."

Joyful thoughts of the past, and no fear for the future. After a lifelong banquet of simple food and tender affection, he was ready to depart quietly to a night of untroubled sleep. Was it not better to sleep forever than to awake to the pain of another day?

This philosophy of Epicurus—an effort to escape from pain (through our acceptance of a material universe) to an emancipation from the fear of death—this serene agnosticism influenced some of our leading modern thinkers, including Kant, Shelley, Mill, Schopenhauer, and Bertrand Russell. And it prompted even the Catholic philosopher, Santayana, to the observation that Epicurus proclaimed "perhaps the greatest thought that mankind has ever hit upon."

CHAPTER XII

Epictetus (about 60–120 A.D.) *and*
Marcus Aurelius (121–180 A.D.)

UP TO THIS POINT we find most of the philosophers, from Ptah-hotep to Epicurus, united in a common belief: "Only the wise are happy." The Stoics accepted this idea, with one qualifica-tion: "Only the wise are happy, but only the brave are wise."

The founder of the Stoic school, Zeno (340–260 B.C.) taught his disciples in a colonnade called the Stoa Poikilé—the Painted Porch. Hence the name Stoic, to designate the "phi-losophy of the Porch."

The two leading exponents of the Stoic philosophy were a slave and a king. Epictetus, the slave, was chained to his servitude; and Aurelius, the king, was bound to his throne. Yet both of them tried to rise above their handicaps to the courage of a free soul.

II

Epictetus was the more fortunate of the two. For he found it easier to maintain a free soul in the slavery of his body. Along with Diogenes, he declared: "I have nothing to lose but my life." And he valued his life less than Aurelius valued his throne.

We know very little about the life of Epictetus. But we do know that he was a cripple in addition to being a slave. Yet in spite of these handicaps, he was one of the happiest of men. For he had learned to follow the guidance of his reason rather than the goading of his flesh. "If you cannot raise your achievement to the level of your ambition, lower your ambition to the level of your achievement." In other words, learn to be content.

And so he accepted his lowly station with a shrug and a smile. He served under a cruel master who delighted in tormenting his slaves. One day his owner subjected him to physical torture. "You had better stop," said Epictetus, "or you will break my leg."

The owner continued the torture and broke the leg. "I told you so," remarked the philosopher. "Now you will suffer the pain of paying for my medical care."

In spite of his calmness, Epictetus met with misfortune after misfortune. Freed from his slavery after his owner's death, he tried to teach philosophy in Rome. But Domitian, the Roman emperor, expelled him from the city as "a danger to the state because he made people think."

Epictetus then opened a school in Greece where he was allowed to remain as "a poor and harmless madman." But he accepted his poverty, as he had accepted his torture, with stoic indifference.

One day his lamp was stolen; but when the thief was arrested, the philosopher refused to press charges against him. "He has already paid for it much more than I. The lamp has cost me only a few pennies. It has cost him his soul."

The freedom of the soul was to Epictetus the greatest possession in the world. "You can chain my body, you can starve it, you can even kill it, but you cannot harm the essential part of me—that is, my immortal self." In order to maintain the independence of his soul, Epictetus never married.

Yet he refused to live by himself. He had adopted a child when its parents, unable to support it, were about to put it to death. And he hired a nurse to live in his house and to take care of the child. He treated both the child and the nurse with frugal generosity, supplying their every need without ever encouraging their greed.

And thus the "lame old man," as he called himself, took care of the orphaned child and taught his pupils that all of them were the children of God. He impressed upon them the nature of our existence—a school for learning through sympathy, which means sharing one another's suffering, that we are the members of one human family. Our business, he said, is to live in harmony in a united world brotherhood—to bring ourselves, as far as possible, into a likeness with God, our Father.

God, declared Epictetus, is all-powerful, all-wise, all-good. The pain that we suffer in this life—here Epictetus echoes the oriental philosophers—is merely a hurdle to strengthen our souls. In one of the supreme passages of literature, Epictetus gave the following expression to his philosophical credo: "Since most of us are walking in darkness, should there not be some one to sing the praises to God for all? And what else can a lame old man like me do but chant the praise of God? If indeed I were a nightingale, I should sing as a nightingale; if a swan, as a swan; but as I am a rational creature, I must praise God. This is my task; I do it, and I will not abandon this duty so long as it is given me. And I invite you all to join in this same song."

This Stoic philosopher was a practitioner of Christianity although he had never heard of Christ. "The truth," he said, "reaches us like the sunlight through many windows—at different times, in different places, by different words. But the meaning is always the same—the Fatherhood of God, the Brotherhood of man, and the universal commandment to give and forgive. Give unstintingly of yourself, and forgive those who are unable to do likewise."

Above all, Epictetus was a man of peace. "Life is a battle-ground," he said, "not, however, against an enemy but against the spirit of enmity." The best way to destroy an enemy is to turn him into a friend. To illustrate this idea, he told an interesting story about Lycurgus, the famous lawgiver of Sparta.

Lycurgus, he said, was attacked during an uprising of the mob and blinded in one eye. The assailant was captured and handed over to him for appropriate punishment. Lycurgus, however, spared the young man and accepted him as a pupil. Several months later he took him to the theater. When the Spartans expressed their amazement, Lycurgus said: "My punishment for this young man has been logical and just. I have received him from you as a ruffian; I return him to you as a gentleman."

This characteristic story about Lycurgus is in keeping with the character of Epictetus himself. He repaid his ill-treatment at the hands of the world's hoodlums by trying to convert them into gentle men.

III

Marcus Aurelius, though unlike Epictetus in station, was very like him in thought. The only difference between them was that the slave arrived at his Stoic philosophy through his optimism, while the king came to it through his pessimism.

Aurelius was condemned to a career for which he had no taste. An emperor who hated war, he ruled over a nation that made a business of it. From early boyhood he had wanted to be a philosopher instead of a soldier. Fired by the example of Socrates and the Cynics—those intrepid thinkers who preferred righteousness to riches—he had dressed himself in a shabby cloak and slept on a hard bench. He had been happy in his poverty. But at eighteen it was his misfortune—or so he considered it—to be raised from a pauper to a prince. Torn away from his philosophy, he was compelled to become the adopted heir of his uncle, the Roman emperor Antoninus. When the emperor died (161 A.D.), Aurelius inherited unwanted riches and an unrighteous war.

He was honest enough to detest his fortune, but not courageous enough to reject it. Dragged into a series of wars through the aggressiveness of his country, he made the saddle his throne and the soldier's tent his palace. It was here during his military campaigns, by the wind-blown flicker of a torch, that he wrote his philosophical *Meditations* on life and death. Dazzling flashes of wisdom, amidst the dark plans for the next day's slaughter. "All life," he wrote from his own bitter experience, "is a warfare in a strange land."

He was the unhappy victim of his own ambition. Yet like a faithful Stoic, he submitted to his dignity as an emperor and to his cruelty as a soldier. To do so, he said, was his duty as a man. A most distasteful duty, he confessed. For at bottom he was simple and honest and kind.

This better side of his nature is reflected in the pages of his book, where he looks away from the world and into his own heart. And here he finds serenity amidst the crowd of gladiators, cutthroats and thieves that make up the bulk of his army. "The time of a man's life is as a point . . . and fame after life is no better than oblivion. What is it, then, that will persevere? Only one thing, philosophy. And philosophy consists in this—for a man to preserve the soul that is within him from all manner of arrogance and hatred, and especially from pain and pleasure; never to do anything rashly or falsely or hypocritically, to embrace contentedly all things that happen to him as coming from Him from whom he himself also came . . .

"The end and object of a rational creature is to do nothing rashly, to be kindly affected toward other men, to be altogether indifferent toward his own fate, and in all things willingly to submit unto God . . ."

Philosophy, in short, should bring you to a magnanimous tranquillity of mind. Don't feel elated over your successes or dejected over your failures. "Remember that at best, as Epictetus reminds us, you are a carcass carried by your soul through the pilgrimage of life. But at worst you are a soul which, in spite of the corruption of your body, remains divine."

So live in accordance with the divine nature of your soul. Act as a peaceful sailor in a stormy sea. Some of the more aggressive Romans, realizing that Aurelius had no heart for his conquests, made an attempt to overthrow him. They started a revolt, with one of his own generals, Avidius Cassius, at the head. "Avidius," it was said facetiously, "is avid to replace Aurelius on the throne."

"As well as in his bed," added some of the more outspoken gossips.

The ugly rumors had finally reached the emperor's ears. A tottering throne, an unfaithful wife. To add to the confusion, the conspirators had spread the falsehood that the emperor was dead, and many of the legions were ready to enthrone Avidius in his place.

But Aurelius reacted to this crisis like a true Stoic. "Accept your fate," his teachers had advised him as a young man. "Follow the pattern of your life; be true to your nature." Very well, he knew the pattern of his own life—to meet every emergency like a king. With foresight and firmness, but without malice or hate. "The best kind of revenge for an evil deed," he had written in his *Meditations*, "is not to become like the evil doer." He called his soldiers together and addressed them as follows:

"Men, I am told that my best friend is plotting to overthrow me. I am therefore compelled to take the field against him . . . There is only one thing I fear: Avidius Cassius may kill himself in a moment of shame, or someone else may kill him in a moment of rashness. In either case, I shall be robbed of the greatest triumph possible to any conqueror—to forgive the man who has wronged me, to remain a friend to him who has broken his friendship with me."

Just as he had feared, Aurelius was robbed of his triumph. One of his hot-headed followers assassinated his rival, Avidius. The emperor's soldiers were ready to throw themselves upon all the other conspirators. But Aurelius nipped the plan in the bud. "Let the banished come home. Let the dispossessed take back their property. I wish that I could recall from the dead the poor victims who have already suffered the penalty."

He set out, together with his wife, on a personal visit to the seditious provinces. He was anxious to pour the oil of mercy upon the turbulence of rebellion. It was in the course of this mission that he suffered one of his deepest sorrows, the death of his wife.

In spite of the rumors about her infidelity—and he had reason to believe these rumors—he had loved Faustina devotedly throughout their married life. And this devotion persisted even after her death. He built a golden statue in her likeness, and he took it along with him on his campaigns. He founded a home for destitute women in her memory, and he offered a daily prayer to her image.

Yet, true to his Stoicism, he tried to master his own grief. "Let us remain indifferent to pain and pleasure, and unperturbed by the scandals of the wicked and the gossip of the fools."

As for Faustina, "she is happier now that she has awakened from the misty dream of her life."

And so he went back to his battles, and tried to find a meaning to his own misty dream, and killed innocent strangers for his kingdom, and felt a great pity for those he killed. "Soldiers," he wrote, "are like spiders or wild beasts. What do they do for the most part but hunt after prey?"

In his strange nightmare of a philosopher condemned to be a king, he uttered wisdom and perpetrated folly with the illogical sequence of a mind trying to stir itself out of a deep sleep. "All of us," he said, "are brothers in sorrow. I cannot be angry with my brothers, or sever myself from them. For we are made by the pattern of nature—or if you will, by the Providence of God—to help one another like brothers." Yet he failed to recognize the Christian members of his brotherhood. These Christians believed in a "strange Kingdom of Heaven"—a dangerous challenge, Aurelius thought, to the Roman kingdom on earth. In the progress of this new doctrine, Aurelius foresaw a struggle between Christian idealism and Roman imperialism. And in his own soul he sensed a similar struggle. His Stoic simplicity was on the side of the Christians; his royal ambition, on the side of Rome.

And the promptings of his ambition decided him against his better self. He ordered the Christian leaders to be crucified.

This was the darkest stain on his character, and the greatest tragedy of his life. It was just as hard for the royal soldier as for the rich man to enter into the Kingdom of Heaven.

IV

And thus Epictetus and Aurelius arrived at Stoicism by different roads and saw it from different points of view. The philosophy of the slave was positive: Rejoice in the few things you possess. And the philosophy of the king was negative: Don't grieve about the many things you do not possess. Epictetus said: "All of us are kings in the freedom of our souls." But Aurelius declared: "All of us are slaves in the subjection to the lusts of our bodies." Epictetus accepted evil as a necessary part of life: "It is only by contrast to the bitter that the sweet is so good. It is the emergence out of the darkness that makes the sunrise so beautiful." But Aurelius tried to shut his eyes to the evils of the world. "Is the cucumber bitter? Throw it away. Are there briars in your path? Turn aside from them. Do not ask, 'And why were such things ever created?' Just ignore them."

This different approach toward Stoicism appears throughout the philosophy of Epictetus and Marcus Aurelius. Epictetus, having had his fill of misery, heartens us with the hope of something better to come. "Be content. What God has chosen for you is greater than what you choose for yourself. Rest assured that tomorrow, like today, He will give you what is best for your soul." But Aurelius, having emptied his cup of glory, cautions us against the dregs at the bottom. "Camillus, Scipio, Cato, Caesar, Augustus, Hadrian, Antoninus—all are forgotten. All things hasten to an end, shall speedily seem old fables, to be mouthed for an instant and then to be buried in oblivion." Both of them teach the importance of an undisturbed mind— Epictetus because life at its worst is so good and Aurelius because life at its best is so bad.

The Stoic philosophy, therefore, has a double appeal. It fortifies the humility of the poor, and it tempers the arrogance of the rich. It enables all of us to find a middle ground of reliance upon the natural pattern of the universe. Whatever is, is right. All of us are created equal—with a death-bound body but an ever living soul.

When Walt Whitman proposed to "inaugurate a religion," he merely re-echoed the religion of the Stoics: "Me imperturbe, standing at ease in nature , . self-balanced for contingencies, to confront night, storms, hunger, ridicule, accidents and rebuffs . . . with serene aplomb."

In their insistence upon an equal destiny for all, the Stoics were the first democratic philosophers in history. For all men belong to the "divine average" of God's plan. Rich or poor, emperor or slave, famous or obscure, you are no better than the average—but no worse. For the average is divine. So accept your fate with absolute trust in Nature and with perfect peace of mind.

Accept your fate. Know that whatever this fate may be, it will be good. "I rest content in this thought," writes Epictetus, "that God has given my soul to myself and has put my will in obedience to my own divine power." And Marcus Aurelius, in a similar vein, declares: "Take me up and cast me where you will. I shall have serene within me my own divinity."

In other words, you can possess within yourself your best friend or your worst enemy. It is up to you. So refuse to be a little soul trying to carry a big body. The strain may be too much for your spiritual strength. Live in accordance with your capacity. "We are born," said Epictetus, "with two ears and one tongue, in order that we may hear twice as much as we talk." Be temperate in your talk, your actions, your emotions, your thoughts. Avoid too much ambition; it is dangerous, like too much wine. The first cup—of ambition or of wine—leads to pleasure, the second to intoxication, the third to violence.

Retain a firm grip upon yourself. Accept whatever comes to you, whether it seems good or bad, with a courageous soul. Rest assured that your Father knows best. Rely upon the judgment and the goodness and the parental love of God. Whatever happens to you, even your death, is for the best. To quote the Stoic Walt Whitman again: "Has any one supposed it is lucky to be born? I hasten to inform him or her that it is just as lucky to die." For birth and death are the parts assigned to you in the sublime drama of your life. And your entrance and exit cues—make no mistake about it—have been accurately and intelligently timed.

And your role upon the stage is that of an interrelated actor. Learn to speak your lines and to perform your actions in harmony with your fellow men. Act as a courageous, helpful and hopeful member of your society, the society of the human race. "Live in accordance with reason," said Epictetus, "not merely as a member of your family, your city, or your state, but as a compatriot of all mankind." And Aurelius, echoing this idea, wrote: "So far as I am an emperor, my city is Rome. But so far as I am a man, my country is the world."

For only thus, maintained the Stoics, can you live in accordance with your nature and in harmony with God, transforming your passion into compassion and your lust into love.

Both Epictetus and Aurelius insisted upon our universal collaboration to a common end. In summarizing their philosophy, the two Stoics employed the selfsame figure of speech. They compared the organized human body to the organization of mankind. "Consider nothing as if it were detached from the community and belonged to you alone. Act as your hand or foot would act, if they had reason to understand their relationship to your head and your heart."

Significantly enough, we find this simile of Epictetus and Aurelius translated into the Christian doctrine of St. Paul. "Many as we are," writes the Apostle, "we are members of one universal body . . . and we are interrelated parts of one another." The light of truth, an oriental poet has observed, is variously reflected in the thoughts of different men. The reflections are many, the light is one.

PART

3

The Philosophy of Christianity

CHAPTER XIII

St. Paul (3–68 A.D.)

CHRISTIANITY, as a philosophy distinct from Judaism, began not with Jesus but with Paul—a student of the pagan sages and the Hebrew prophets. Before the advent of Paul, the followers of Jesus had regarded him as the Jewish Messiah who had come to reaffirm the teachings of the Old Testament. "I am here not to destroy but to fulfill the Law." But Paul added pagan learning to Jewish law and paved the way from the Old Testament to the New. It was he who proclaimed Jesus not merely as the Messiah of the Jews but as the Saviour of mankind.

II

He was born at Tarsus, the capital of Cilicia in Asia Minor. This flourishing city on the Mediterranean served as an ideological and commercial link between the East and the West. As a child, Paul imbibed not only the sacred history of his own religion but the secular pageantry of the Greeks and the Romans. Tarsus had been a center of Stoic philosophy, the site of Cicero's administration as the Roman governor of Cilicia, and the scene of Antony's and Cleopatra's excursion on the Cydnus in a gilded barge propelled by silver oars. There was much in the lore of this city to stir the imagination of a lively youngster like Paul.

At birth he was named Saul. But his Gentile playmates called him Paul, a Latin nickname which meant "little fellow." He was a puny child with a superior mind. His father was a pious Jew who enjoyed the rights of Roman citizenship under the rule of the Roman governors. He encouraged his child to absorb the pagan as well as the Hebrew culture of his native city.

Paul wanted to be a teacher. But the ancient rabbis believed in the education of the three H's—the Head, the Hand, and the Heart. "Learn with your Head, earn with your Hands, and serve with your Heart." The greatest Hebrew scholars engaged in manual trades such as cobbling or carpentry for a living, but received no pay for teaching people how to live. Among the Hebrews it was considered vulgar to exchange wisdom for worldly goods. Following the advice of the rabbis, Paul apprenticed himself to a tentmaker.

At fifteen he went to Jerusalem. Here, in the Temple courts, he sat at the feet of Gamaliel for advanced instruction in the Torah—"the inspiration of the prophets of the past, and the hope of the Messiah to come." In his spare time, he visited the various sects and studied their different interpretations of the Bible. He was especially interested in the Essenes, a peculiar group of Jewish hermits who had fled from the turmoil of society to find peace of mind in solitude. They held their goods in common, spurned material success, denounced oppression, persecution and bloodshed, and looked forward to "the Kingdom that is not of this world." They were the pre-Christian communists of Palestine. They took their meals together, referring to the custom as a Holy Communion. And they symbolized the cleansing of their souls by means of daily baths—a custom adopted by the Christians as the rite of baptism. Paul found in this fraternity a peculiar blend of pagan stoicism and Hebrew mysticism. His contact with the Essenes was one of the springboards for the philosophical structure of Christianity which he was later on to develop.

It is possible that as a young student in Jerusalem, Paul heard about a little boy of Nazareth who had confounded the rabbis of the Temple with his questions. But Jesus and Paul never met in the flesh.

After a few years in Palestine, Paul returned to his secular studies at the university of Tarsus. And then, his education completed, he settled down to what he then regarded as his life's work. He wanted to be a free-lance teacher without pay. His equipment for this job was an undersized body subject to the "thorns" of disease, but a mind like a crystal prism that reflected the sunlight from many angles, and a heart overflowing "like a volcano" with devotion to God.

At first his devotion took a fanatical turn. He joined the reactionaries among the Jews who persecuted the Nazarenes, as the followers of Jesus were then called. This new sect held many beliefs in common with the Essenes. But there was one essential difference which aroused the fury of Paul: the Nazarenes believed that Jesus was the true Messiah. Paul was a member of the Pharisees, a Jewish sect which looked upon the Messianic claims of Jesus as a dangerous heresy. To them Jesus was but another of the false Messiahs who were constantly springing up to contaminate the stream of their religious faith.

In common with the other Pharisees, Paul believed that the heresy of the Nazarenes must be crushed. He was present at the martyrdom of Stephen, one of their early spiritual leaders. The executioners asked Paul to watch their cloaks while they were stoning the martyr to death. He heard Stephen's dying words: "Master, lay not this sin against them."

Paul left the place of the stoning with mingled emotions: pity for the martyr's suffering, admiration for his forgiveness, but hatred for his "stubborn belief in a false Messiah." Paul's hatred, fed by his fanaticism, stifled all his other emotions for the moment. He decided to throw himself more passionately than ever into the persecution of the new sect.

Yet it was the very conflict in his own soul that drove him into his crusade against the Nazarenes. They taught a false doctrine, he felt; hence they must be destroyed. But what was there about them that made them so utterly resigned to die, so passionately eager to forgive? Could falsehood breed such gentleness in the human heart? The more he thought about this, the more perplexed he became and the more enraged against his perplexity. And thus he tried to castigate his own conscience by whipping the followers of Christ.

This was his state of mind when he set out for Damascus, one of the principal centers of the new sect. He took along a number of men to help him in his savage but, as he believed, essential job of stamping out the "heresy" of the Nazarenes. He was doing this work, he felt convinced, in obedience to the commandment of the Lord.

And then, just before the gates of Damascus, he lost his eyesight and began to see.

III

The story of Paul's vision is one of the great dramas of history. Together with the other fanatical persecutors of the Nazarenes, he had made a long and exhausting journey from Jerusalem to Damascus. They had traveled most of the way on foot. Their eyes were inflamed from the sandstorms of the desert. As they approached Damascus, the noonday sun flared down upon their heads. Paul, the weakest man in the group, was exhausted almost to the point of death. He had suffered several attacks of malaria on the way. His body was ready to succumb to the fever and the sweat and the lashing of the sand. His eyes, his nostrils, his mouth, his very lungs were choked with dust.

Yet his spirit kept driving him on. He was bent upon a holy mission—to free his country from the "blasphemy" of the Nazarene creed.

And so he persevered through the tortures of his journey until he reached the walls of Damascus. This spot at the edge of the desert was one of the most enchanting regions of Asia—

the fabled Garden of Eden, the world's first meeting place between man and God.

And here, suddenly, a great darkness fell upon Paul. He dropped to the ground. His companions bent over him in alarm. His sightless eyes were wide open, and his lips moved as if in earnest but silent conversation with someone.

For several minutes he remained in this trance; and then he whispered to his companions: "I have seen him."

"Seen whom?"

"The Messiah."

"The false one?"

"No, the true one. Jesus of Nazareth."

They shrugged their shoulders but made no reply. Their leader, they thought, must have gone crazy with the heat.

And Paul said nothing more to them at the time. If he had described his entire vision, they probably wouldn't have believed him. Indeed, he could hardly believe it himself. At first, total blindness. And then, a great light out of the darkness—and in the midst of the light, a Rabbi dressed in a white robe as for the Sabbath. A radiant face with compassionate eyes. And the Rabbi had stretched out his hands toward him. "Saul, Saul," he had said, "why dost thou persecute me?"

"Who art thou?"

"I am Jesus of Nazareth, the crucified Son of God."

"And what am I to do?"

"Go into the city, and there it shall be revealed to thee what thou must do . . ."

Paul's companions, still convinced that he was suffering from delirium, brought him into the city. There he lay blind and helpless for several days. He was nursed back to health by the very Nazarenes he had come to slay. "Why are you so kind to me?" he asked.

"Jesus has taught us to return good for evil."

During his convalescence, Saul gave a great deal of thought to these words. "To return good for evil." This was also the teaching of the Jewish rabbis, Gamaliel and Hillel. One day he spoke to his Nazarene physician, Ananias. "Perhaps I have been chosen to spread the Gospel of Jesus as a continuation of the teaching of the rabbis?"

Ananias nodded. "You are right, my son. You have come here trying to hurt us. We have received and healed you. You can repay our services to you by offering yourself as a servant to the Lord."

IV

After his dramatic conversion, Paul spent three years in the desert where he attempted, like Moses, to decipher the will of God. And then he returned to the world as the ambassador of Christ—the word Christ is the Greek translation of the Hebrew word Messiah.

His missionary adventures for Christ carried Paul over tens of thousands of miles, and plunged him into almost incredible hardships. On five different occasions he was scourged with leather thongs. Three times he was beaten with rods. Once he was stoned and left for dead. Four times he was shipwrecked. During one of these shipwrecks he remained in the water, clinging to a plank, for over twenty-four hours. Again and again, he writes, he found himself "in perils from waters, in perils of robbers, in perils by mine own countrymen, in perils by the heathen, in perils in the city, in perils in the wilderness, in perils in the sea, in perils among false brethren." Yet he endured all this suffering as a "labor of love"—the wages of his love for God. For he had enlisted as a soldier of Christ in a lifelong battle of peace.

His crusade after his return from the desert began at the scene of his conversion, in Damascus. On his arrival, he was compelled to hide in order to escape from the Pharisees. They had set up a watch at all the gates; but he finally escaped in a basket lowered at night from the city wall.

From Damascus he went to Antioch, where the Nazarenes first called themselves Christians. And then on to Cyprus, where he began to preach Christianity as a religion embracing the Gentiles—a word which means "the nations of the world" —no less than the Jews.

He then went to Lystra, where the people started to worship him as a pagan god and ended by stoning him when he told them that he was only a man; to Ephesus, where the silversmiths who sold models of the statue of Diana organized a riot against him for spoiling their business through his denunciation of idolatry; to many other cities of Asia and the Mediterranean islands; and then on to spread the Gospel of Jesus to Europe as well. And everywhere he carried bread for the body and comfort for the soul. Again and again he was thwarted by his illness and hooted down when he tried to speak. Yet little by little he compelled even his enemies to listen to him.

For there was a most amazing magnetism in the "balding, bow-legged little man"—I am quoting from *The Acts of Paul and Thecla*, a work of the second century A.D.—"with his converging eyebrows and somewhat hooked nose; a fellow full of grace who sometimes appeared like a man and sometimes had the face of an angel."

And thus he went on, spreading the Gospel through the world, meeting with a little respect and many blows, and finally transforming the old philosophies into a new creed. He cared little for personal triumph. He insisted upon preaching without pay, and expected no thanks for his charity. He was completely dedicated to his work. When he could spare the time, he attended to his tentmaking for his simple needs. To his followers who asked him how he could endure his sufferings, he replied: "They are but a drop in the ocean as compared to the sufferings of Christ."

V

Often, when he was unable to come to the Christians in person, he sent them letters of faith and comfort and hope. At times he scolded them for their quarrels, but always he softened his scolding with words that brought tranquillity to their souls.

These epistles of Paul—his beautiful poems of pity—explain the basic philosophy of Christianity. This philosophy, a blending of the profoundest thought of the East and the West, is founded upon three ideas united into one—the Father, the Son, and the Holy Ghost. Translated into popular terms, the three ideas represent (1) the fatherhood of God and the brotherhood of man, (2) the transcendent power of love, and (3) the immortality of the soul.

1. *The fatherhood of God and the brotherhood of man.* This idea, as we have seen, originated in the philosophy of Ikhnaton, fertilized the thought of Zoroaster, and permeated the wisdom of the Stoics. "God is our Father in Heaven, and all of us are Brothers in the Universal City of God which is the World." The Hebrews had narrowed this idea, regarding themselves alone as the children of God. But Paul widened the family once more to include the entire human race in the divine relationship. Paul was among the first internationalists in history. In his Epistle to the Romans he writes: "Is he the God of the Jews only? Is he not also the God of the Gentiles?" All of us, Jew and Gentile, black and white, master and slave, "are the joint heirs of God."

To facilitate the entrance of the Gentiles into the "covenant with the Lord," Paul developed Christianity into a simpler form of Judaism. He abolished circumcision and some of the other more difficult of the Old Testament rituals. But he insisted upon retaining the central idea of righteousness. Let no man act unrighteously toward his fellow men. In common

with the Hebrew prophets as well as with the pagan philosophers—Paul is said to have corresponded with the Roman
Stoic, Seneca—he declared that we are members of one body.
We have been brought into this world—like the eyes, the ears,
the hands, the feet—to perform our different functions in the
common business of life. We need every organ, every function,
every man for the healthy existence of the body of mankind.
The Hebrew prophets had referred to this idea as social justice;
the Greek philosophers had called it harmony; Paul translated
it into the ideal of human brotherhood. "Be kindly affectioned
to one another like the brothers of a single family." And between brothers, "it is more blessed to give than to receive."
Those of us who are strong should bear the infirmities of the
weak. Let us, therefore, be slow to inflict but quick to forget
an injury. For thus, and thus only, can we "follow after the
things which make for peace."

2. *The transcendent power of love.* The road to harmony
is through tolerance, the way to peace is through love. This
was the common doctrine of the great philosophers of Egypt,
Persia, India, China, Israel, and Greece; and it became one of
the cornerstones in the trinity of Paul's philosophy. His Canticle
to Love—Chapter 13 of his First Epistle to the Corinthians—
is one of the high peaks in the literature of the world:

"Though I speak with the tongues of men and of angels,
and have not love, I am become as sounding brass, or a tinkling
cymbal.

"And though I have the gift of prophecy, and understand
all mysteries, and all knowledge; and though I have all faith
so that I could move mountains, and have not love, I am
nothing.

"And though I bestow all my goods to feed the poor, and
though I give my body to be burned, and have not love, it
profiteth me nothing."

The word "love" in this chapter has often been translated
as charity. But in the Pauline philosophy, love is more than

charity. It means not only giving, but forgiving. It denotes gentleness, courage, understanding, humility, compassion—complete forgetfulness of self in the devotion to serve others. The rest of the chapter shows clearly that Paul had this wider meaning in mind when he wrote:

"Love suffereth long, and is kind; love envieth not; love boasteth not, is not puffed up, doth not behave itself unseemly, seeketh not her own, is not easily provoked, thinketh no evil . . .

"Beareth all things, believeth all things, hopeth all things, endureth all things . . ."

And this brings us to the climax of the chapter—the quintessence of the Apostle's philosophy:

"And now abideth [the Gospel of] Faith, Hope, Love, these three; but the greatest of these is Love."

3. *The immortality of the soul.* Love, declared Paul, is our common heritage as the immortal children of God. In the single family of mankind, there is no high or low, no rich or poor, no master or slave. All of us, regardless of our race, caste, or station in life, possess the equal gift of an immortal soul.

Here again, Paul based his Christian philosophy upon the beliefs of the Egyptian, Persian, Hindu, Chinese, Greek, and Hebrew teachers. Each of us, he said, is not only a physical member of the universal body of mankind, but a spiritual member of the universal soul of mankind.

To disbelieve in immortality, according to Paul, is to take a worm's-eye view of the world. A worm, burrowing under the earth, sees a seed rotting in the darkness. This, concludes the worm, is the end of the seed's life. The worm has no conception of the new life of the seed—the bud, the stem, the flower —that grows out of the "dead" body under the surface of the earth. "Some men will ask, 'How are the dead raised up? And with what body will they come?'

"Thou fool, that which thou sowest is not quickened unless it die . . . So also is the resurrection of the dead. It is sown in corruption, it is raised in incorruption; it is sown in dishonor, it is raised in glory; it is sown in weakness, it is raised in power; it is sown in a physical body, it is raised in a spiritual body . . .

"The first body is of the earth, earthy; the second is from heaven . . . And as we have borne the image of the earthy, we shall also bear the image of the heavenly . . .

"Behold, I show you a mystery. We shall not sleep, but we shall be changed . . . For this corruptible must put on incorruption, and this mortal must put on immortality . . ."

Have no fear, then, about your last day on earth. The death-day of your life is the birth-day of your immortality. Your final journey is but a passage through a tunnel of darkness into a greater light.

And thus life is triumphant, eternal, assured. It is the loving heritage of all God's children on earth. "O death, where is thy sting? O grave, where is thy victory?"

This idea of immortality was, in the philosophy of Paul, not a mere speculation. It was the mature conviction of a man who not only had steeped himself in the best thought of the East and the West, but who had himself experienced a great deal of learning through suffering.

"When I was a child, I spoke as a child, I understood as a child, I thought as a child. But when I became a man, I put away childish things." And therefore, he declares, he knows what he is talking about. "Now, in this life, we see through a glass, darkly; but then, in the life to come, we shall see face to face. Now I know in part; but then I shall know even as I am known."

VI

And what is the sum and substance of what we know in part? The promise of eternal life in the loving communion of all mankind, under the universal fatherhood of God.

Buttressed by this faith and love and hope, the Apostle continued through his almost unendurable hardships to the end. Arrested in Jerusalem and handed over to the Roman governor of Judea, he appealed as a Roman citizen to be sent to the emperor.

In so doing, Paul passed from the frying pan into the fire. The Roman emperor was Nero, still young at the time and somewhat under the influence of his tutor, the Stoic philosopher, Seneca. The savage had not as yet emerged from under Nero's civilized mask. He posed as a patron of art and student of philosophy and religion. For a few years he allowed Paul, under "protective custody," to preach the Gospel in Rome.

And then Nero unmasked himself. Like several of the other Roman emperors, he was hopelessly insane. He ordered his mother to be strangled, kicked his pregnant wife to death, compelled his tutor Seneca to take his own life, and finally perpetrated one of the most atrocious crimes in history. Having deluded himself into the belief that he was a great poet, he set fire to Rome in order to get the material for an epic "more sublime than Homer's burning of Troy."

But he had to find a scapegoat for the fire; and so he pinned the crime upon the Christians. He declared a Roman holiday for their wholesale execution. He fed many of them to the lions in the arena, while the audience shouted "Hail Caesar!" and the victims sang the Psalm, "The Lord is my shepherd, I shall not want." And then Nero crucified some of the surviving Christians and lighted them as torches for his triumphal procession through the Roman streets. "Behold my poem of Fire," he gloated, "a masterpiece such as the world has never seen!"

Paul had noted the growing madness of Nero. He realized that his own days were numbered. But he was not afraid. "I have fought the good fight," he wrote, "I have finished the course, I have kept the faith."

As a concession to his Roman citizenship, Nero treated

Paul with "special mercy." He saved him from the lions and the cross—he merely ordered his head to be cut off.

"This," exulted Nero, "is an end to Christianity!" But the ending of Paul's life was the beginning of the Christian Church.

CHAPTER XIV

St. Augustine (354–430 A.D.)

THE PHILOSOPHY of St. Augustine is a blending of the Judaeo-Christian conception of God, the Stoic translation of divine law into human duty, and the Platonic idea of a better world. Every one of us, declared Augustine, is a part of God. Led by our destiny, we are bound to follow his will—that is, to direct our gaze from the shadow-world of appearances to the substantial world of ideas, from the confusion of the earth to the Kingdom of Heaven.

But it was the long road of perplexity that led Augustine to the end of his philosophical quest.

II

He started life as a juvenile delinquent. Born in the Roman province of Numidia (modern Algeria) of a pagan father and a Christian mother, he was from the outset subjected to conflicting influences. His father urged him to be a teacher; his mother, a priest. As for himself, he just wanted to enjoy life, to lose himself—as he wrote in his *Confessions* many years later —"in a multiplicity of sins." As an adolescent, he tells us, he was "a liar, a bully, and a cheat." It seems, however, that his deviltry was not nearly so black as he painted it. He exaggerated his vices because he suffered from an oversensitive conscience, smarting under the puritanical tongue-lashings of his mother.

Following his father's advice, he prepared himself as a teacher of rhetoric—"the science that praises falsehood in ele-

gant words." But he indulged in extracurricular activities of
the flesh, "wallowing through the mire of Babylon," cohabiting
with a woman out of wedlock and begetting an illegitimate
son. His own father had died when Augustine was seventeen.
His mother scolded him and prayed for him, but in vain. "Her
scoldings and her prayers failed to reach my heart."

And so he continued "to commit fornication, to defile other
men's wives, and to look forward to chastity and continence—
ultimately, but not yet." He hated himself for enjoying the for-
bidden fruits, but he was loath to give them up. He called
himself "a soul astray in a sea of mud," and found himself unable to struggle to the shore. For several years he taught rhetoric in his native Africa; and then he went to Rome and Milan,
in quest of "promotion, profit and praise." Yet again and again
he asked himself, "To what end?"

And then came his "first vision of the truth." He had just
delivered a public eulogy on the Roman emperor. The oration,
"full of lies, was applauded by those who knew I lied." Elated
over his triumph, he was swaggering with some of his friends
over the streets of Milan. They were accosted by a beggar who,
"enjoying a full belly at the moment," greeted them with a jest
and a ribald song.

The chance meeting left a deep impression upon Augustine. "The beggar was intoxicated by his food; I was intoxicated
by my fame. What he had obtained by his unearned pennies,
I was trying to obtain by my unearned praise. The beggar rejoiced in his drunkenness, and I rejoiced in my glory. What
difference was there between us?"

Augustine decided that he would no longer be a beggar
for glory. The only prize worth possessing was spiritual rather
than material success. A man's happiness depended not upon
the pleasure of his flesh but upon the ecstasy of his faith.

Faith in the goodness of God, and hope for the salvation
of the soul. He recalled a prayer of Cleanthes, one of the Stoic
philosophers:

> Lead me, O Zeus, and thou, O Destiny,
> Lead thou me on.
> To whatsoever task thou sendest me,
> Lead thou me on.
> I follow fearless, or, if in mistrust
> I lag and will not, follow still I must.

This prayer was very like the biblical hymns that Augustine's mother had read to him when he was a boy. "Lead thou me on!" He would renew his acquaintance with the Bible and, under the guidance of God, he would try to adopt a new philosophy from now on.

III

But the end of his road was not yet in sight. "I had overcome my pride, but I was still pursued by my lust." He organized a communist society, after the custom of the earlier Christians, and invited his friends to join him in rejecting "the struggles of ambition and the turbulence of life." They moved into a single household and united their possessions into a common fund. But the women became jealous of one another, and the community broke up.

Augustine was still entangled in the fetters of the flesh. "I delayed to turn completely to the Lord . . . because I thought I would be too miserable unless folded in a woman's arms." His mother, in an effort to moderate his passion, urged him to get married. He became engaged to a young girl selected by his mother, and dismissed his mistress. "At our parting," he writes, "my heart was torn and bleeding." But the marriage, owing to the youth of his betrothed, had to be postponed for two years, and so he took another mistress. Again, as in the past, he enjoyed his courtesan's embraces and castigated himself for his joy.

He never married his betrothed because he became fully

converted during his engagement and adopted celibacy for the rest of his life. At the time of his conversion, Augustine was thirty-two years old.

IV

His final conversion was the result of his mother's determination to turn him "fromward Satan and toward God."

He described his "renunciation of the flesh for the discipline of the Soul" in one of the most touching passages of his *Confessions*. He was sitting in his garden together with an intimate friend. They were talking about Ambrose, a devout Christian they had met in Milan. At the thought of this "holiest and best of men," Augustine became unusually agitated. "I found myself poised on the threshold of decision. Two conflicting wills were struggling for the possession of my soul"—the boisterous call of the flesh, and the still small voice of God. His friend, seeing his perturbation, said nothing for fear of distracting his thought.

Finally Augustine burst into tears. "Ashamed to be seen weeping like a woman," he excused himself and went into a secluded corner of the garden. And there, under the shelter of a tree, he cast himself on the ground and gave vent to his emotion.

He stayed there for some time, just as Buddha had stayed under his fig tree, searching his soul for the truth.

And it came to him in a voice, as of a child, chanting the words: "Take up and read, take up and read." Regarding this as a command from Heaven, he took the Bible which he carried in a fold of his cloak and opened it at random to "a passage of the Apostle—St. Paul."

This is what he read: "Not in rioting and drunkenness, not in lechery and wantonness, not in strife and envy, but in the Lord is thy trust."

He had no need to read any further, he tells us. "For instantly, at the end of this sentence, by a serene light infused into my heart, as it were, all the darkness of doubt vanished away."

It was not only, however, the sudden revelation he received from St. Paul but also his long study of the Platonists that resulted in the ultimate conversion of Augustine. Plato, like Paul, had insisted that "to begin its ascent to God, the soul must purge itself from the desires of the flesh."

He was baptized on Easter Day, and he returned to North Africa where he became (in 396) bishop of Hippo, a city not far from Carthage. He served in that office until his death. His life was now dedicated to the "glory of the City of God as against the frippery in the cities of men."

V

While Augustine was writing about *The City of God*, Rome—the city of man—was sacked by the Goths. His philosophy, therefore, had a practical application for the people of his day. The city of man, he said, is a transitory copy of the City of God (just as Athens was a transitory copy of Plato's ideal Republic).

We are visitors, said Augustine, in the city of man, but citizens in the City of God. The city of man may be destroyed by an enemy as Rome was destroyed by the Goths. But the City of God—that is, the Kingdom of Heaven—remains eternally unassailed. Let no one grieve over the destruction of his temporary home. For his permanent home, if only he leads a virtuous life, is ready and waiting for his arrival. There is no expiration to the good man's lease on heaven. Have you lost your goods, your savings, your life? Never mind—here we find an echo of the Stoic philosophy—you have not lost your soul. For that is indestructible. Has your virgin daughter, in the capture of your city, submitted to the coercion of rape? God will forgive her, provided she has not also submitted to the pleasure of being raped. For compulsory sin unenjoyed is no sin at all.

In any event, and under all conditions, rely upon the guidance of God. Try to submerge the material part of yourself in order that the spiritual part may emerge. Purify your body for the salvation of your soul. For your soul is ever trying to return to the divine from which it came.

This idea, originating with the oriental philosophers, came down through Plato to the Judaeo-Christian philosophers Paul and Augustine.

The human soul, said Augustine, is a part of God—an idea developed centuries later by Spinoza. The soul exists in the body for the purpose of establishing on earth a copy of the perfection which it vaguely recalls from its pre-existence in Heaven.

For the soul has lived before our earthly life and will continue to live after it. This Augustinian belief in the immortality of the soul is beautifully expressed in Wordsworth's "Ode on Immortality."

> Our birth is but a sleep and a forgetting:
> The soul that rises with us, our life's Star,
>   Hath had elsewhere its setting
>   And cometh from afar:
>   Not in entire forgetfulness,
>   And not in utter nakedness,
> But trailing clouds of glory do we come
> From God, who is our home:
>
>   .   .   .
>
>   Hence in a season of calm weather
>   Though inland far we be,
>   Our Souls have sight of that immortal sea
>   Which brought us hither . . .

To use a figure borrowed from music, the soul is like a composer who has caught the vision of a great symphony. This

vision will not let him rest until he has translated his divine
idea into human sound. The ceaseless effort of the soul is to
create a world that shall approximate the vision which has en-
tranced it—to make the material as sublime as the ideal.

The material, explained Augustine, exists in time; the
ideal, in eternity. And this brings us to one of the most interesting phases of Augustine's philosophy—his discussion of the
meaning of time. In this discussion Augustine anticipated Einstein's theory of relativity. Your concepton of Time, said Augustine, is relative to your position in the universe.

This may sound obscure, but it can be made clear in a
few words:

Time, as understood on earth, is measured in hours, days,
months, years, and so on. This measurement is due to the constant changing of our position with respect to the sun and the
moon. Other celestial bodies would have other measurements.
A year on earth may be but a minute in the motion of a distant
star.

In other words, declared Augustine, time is subjective
rather than objective. It exists *within*, and not *outside of*, the
human mind. Actually, time is not a matter of duration but a
momentary sensation. We can sense only the present instant.
What we call yesterday and tomorrow are really parts of today. Yesterday is today's memory of the past; tomorrow is today's expectation of the future. The human mind, because of
its relative limitations, has developed a threefold conception
of the present. We talk of the past and the present and the
future. What we really mean, said Augustine, is that *all these
three points of time are present.* "There is a present of things
past, a present of things present, and a present of things future."

In order to clarify this idea still further, let us compare
the observer of time to a man riding in an airplane between,
let us say, Washington and New York. At this moment the
rider is over Baltimore, which represents the present. Behind

him is Washington, the past. Before him is New York, the future. It is wrong to say that Washington *was*, Baltimore *is*, and New York *will be*. All three of them at this moment *are*, even though the rider has left Washington, is sailing over Baltimore, and has not yet arrived in New York.

Time, therefore, is *a finite mental image of an infinite eternity*. And the human world is a temporary mental image of the eternal divine world.

The eternal world of the eternal God. In him there is no past or future, but only an everlasting present. The word "time" has no meaning as applied to the existence of God. For God created time—or rather, different conceptions of time for different places—when he created the world. God exists out of time, just as he exists out of space. He has enrolled our souls as pupils for a time in the school of eternity. He has provided us with the entire universe for our textbook, and with all the objects of the earth, including our mortal clay, as the instruments of our learning. When this state of our instruction is over, we shall put aside the textbook and the tools of our present life, for our souls will no longer need them; and we shall be ready to re-enter, educated and purified, from the cities of men to the City of God.

VI

Augustine lived in an age of violence, aggression, and hate. Added to the universal turmoil was his personal loss—the death of his son to whom he was passionately devoted. But in spite of his own suffering, he directed his fellow sufferers to the heights from which they could see the idea of eternity over the mists of time. "What though the whole world is threatened with death? Go on with thy business in meekness and hope, so shalt thou be beloved by men and acceptable in the eyes of God."

CHAPTER XV

St. Thomas Aquinas (1227–1274)

THE PHILOSOPHY of Aquinas, like that of Augustine, is a blending of Judaeo-Christian ethics and Greek metaphysics. But while Augustine bases his ethics upon the Platonic theory of ideas, Aquinas bases his upon the Aristotelian doctrine of forms.

Let me explain. Both Augustine and Aquinas believe that the highest good of man is to strive toward the perfection of God. But they trace somewhat different paths that lead to this perfection. Augustine maintains, with Plato, that the good man copies the idea of goodness which exists in heaven for all of us to emulate. And Aquinas declares, with Aristotle, that the good man develops according to the form of goodness which exists in everything and is helped to its further growth through our good actions.

Let us, for example, take the planting of an acorn. To Plato (and to Augustine), this planting is an effort to copy the oak-tree idea that exists in the mind of God. Every oak tree on earth is an imperfect copy of that perfect oak tree in heaven. But to Aristotle (and to Aquinas), the act of the planting is an attempt to develop out of the acorn the oak tree whose form resides within that acorn.

All this, however, is but semantic quibbling—a quarrel about words. Actually, both Plato and Aristotle, both Augustine and Aquinas, mean the same thing. When the acorn is planted and dies, the oak tree is born. Both the idea and the form of the tree reside within the acorn. So, too, when the man dies, the angel is born. In other words, every man has within him the urge, the form, the makings of an angel. In this respect, both the Platonic Augustine and the Aristotelian Aquinas agree.

And they also agree in their insistence upon the Judaeo-Christian ethic of the good life, a life of righteousness, as a means toward the attainment of the ideal form of divine goodness, divine beauty, divine love.

Here again we find the same philosophic thought that has flowed like a stream of living waters from the earliest oriental thinkers down to Aquinas. The good is the end at which all nature aims. And this end is the essential harmony that embraces the apparent diversity of the world.

But let us look a little more closely at Aquinas who, among the Catholic churchmen, is regarded as *the* philosopher down to the present day.

II

Born in Italy of a noble family of soldiers, Aquinas refused to follow in their footsteps—he preferred to live as a Dominican friar. From early childhood he was "consumed with wonder" at the mystery of the world. At the age of five he asked, "What is God?" And he spent all his life in an effort to find the answer.

His father, who was related to the Roman emperor, strenuously objected to the boy's preoccupation with theology. Thomas's brothers had served in battle with distinction. His grandfather, after whom he was named, had been the commander of the imperial forces. But Thomas, though he lived in a century of turmoil, insisted upon a life of peaceful meditation.

And, thought his father, it was a great pity. Even as a boy, Thomas was a mountain of strength. Huge body, huge head, and arms that could hold you as in a vise. What a soldier he would have made for Emperor Frederick! But the boy wouldn't

listen to his father's advice. Instead, he sat at the feet of the
mendicant friars who came to his father's castle at Aquino. He
heard their stories about the inner world of the spirit as opposed to the outer world of the flesh. He rarely spoke—"The
boy," said his companions, "is as dumb as an ox"—but he absorbed everything he heard and wondered about the sanctity
of God and the savagery of men. Why so much oppression and
war in a world that promises so much beauty and peace? This
was the problem he would make every effort to understand.

And the only place to acquire such understanding, he felt,
was a monastic retreat.

At last his father yielded to his son's pleas. He had him
enrolled at the University of Naples. Here, hoped the Count of
Aquino, Thomas would be trained to become the abbot of
Monte Cassino. From that position he might rise to the rank of
bishop, perhaps cardinal, and—who knows—maybe even Pope?

But once again, Thomas disobeyed his father. "I don't want
the dignity of high office. I just ask for the humility of a simple
monk."

To free him from his "madness," his parents locked him
up in a tower of their castle. Here they brought him spicy
food and romantic books, but he left his physical and mental
appetizers untouched. He had caught the vision of St. Francis
—"God's beloved fool." He wanted to resemble as closely as
possible this "court jester of heaven" who, it was said, could
understand the language of birds because they, like himself,
knew but a single song—the song of universal love.

Once, in an effort to bring Thomas back to his senses, his
parents brought a beautiful courtesan to his tower. It was a
cold night when she was ushered into his room. A fire was blazing in the fireplace. He saw her in the firelight—her red-gold
hair was enough to stir the blood of any man. But Thomas
snatched a burning log and lunged toward her. She fled from
the room.

He closed the door behind her and with the flaming torch burned a cross upon the wall of his prison cell.

The "dumb ox" had passion in his soul. He was consumed with love for God.

With the help of some of his friends, he escaped from his tower and left for Cologne. There he continued his studies in theology and philosophy under the Dominican professor, Albertus Magnus. "This amazing teacher," observed the scholars of the day, "carries the whole universe in his head." Albertus had written books on zoology, botany, mineralogy, physics, alchemy, and astronomy. He advanced unorthodox theories about the roundness and the gravitation of the earth, and about the cluster of the distant stars which appeared as a luminous cloud across the sky and which today is known as the Milky Way. Many of his contemporaries regarded Albertus as a magician. But Thomas came to revere him as a great and holy man.

And Albertus came to recognize Thomas as his profoundest pupil. Behind the enormous dome of this young student's forehead, mighty thoughts were being formed and analyzed and digested in silence. But when Thomas was ready to speak, his teacher prophesied, the whole world would listen to him.

Yet to his fellow students, Thomas still appeared as a fellow of slow motion, hesitant speech and sluggish thought. "A dim-wit," they called him. They made him the constant butt of their jokes. And he retaliated upon only one occasion. As he was sitting in his study, a number of his classmates shouted up to him from the campus: "Look, Brother Thomas! Come and look! A flying ox!" He rushed to the window and looked, only to be greeted with howls of derision. "He believed it, the fool! He actually believed it!" Thomas faced the students unperturbed: "I'd rather believe that an ox can fly than that a Dominican can lie."

III

When his studies were completed, Thomas became a priest. His ambition was to build a cathedral—not of stone, but of thought. A structure that would embrace the mystery of God and the meaning of life.

The *truth* about life. "What," his teacher Albertus had once asked him, "is the most important faculty of the mind?"

"The faculty to recognize the truth," Thomas had replied.

"But there are those who assert that man can never recognize the truth."

"Those who make this assertion are only contradicting themselves. For they state *as a truth* the postulate that they do not *understand the truth*."

"You've got a keen mind that can pierce to the heart of a subject," his teacher had said with a smile. "Use this mind to enlighten your fellow men."

Thomas adopted this advice as the shining goal of his life. He took the black and white garb of the Dominican Order, and dedicated himself to the teaching and the writing of philosophy. At thirty-three he was appointed professor of theology at the University of Paris. And he proceeded to build his cathedral of thought in a series of books whose arguments form a majestic structure reaching from earth to heaven.

At the foundation of this structure lies this Thomistic formula: "Our faith must not be based upon our reason, but our reason must be based upon our faith." Belief cannot come out of knowledge, but knowledge can come out of belief. Start with a basic belief in the goodness of God, and from this basis you can prove the harmony of the universe and the salvation of your soul.

This formula may be graphically represented by a pyramid with faith established at the base, reason carrying the mind upward along the sides, toward the truth at the apex:

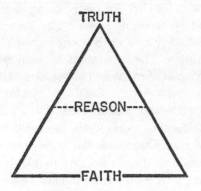

And the truth, as St. Thomas sees it, enables you to understand that your soul is engaged upon a Godward journey in the vessel of your body. To use the Aristotelian phraseology, your soul is the form and your body is the substance of your true self. Your soul, the divine part of you, exists within your body. It is the Word made flesh and it is ready to flower into its potential glory, just as the tree exists within the seed, waiting to rise into its potential growth.

And so, declares Aquinas, believe, that you may understand. Seek and you shall find. God has created you in order that you may grow toward him, that you may realize the purpose of your life, that you may recognize the divine image which constitutes the pattern of your existence.

The goal of our existence is God. But this goal is not offered to us as a gift. It must be attained through persistent effort. Nature is a compound of imperfect matter and perfect form. It takes a struggle to transform the matter into something closer to perfection. The plant must struggle through the soil before the seed can sprout into leaves and flowers.

And this brings us to Aquinas's discussion of suffering and evil in a world which, he maintains, is fundamentally good. Goodness, he tells us, is not a negative state, but a positive achievement. It is a battle against evil. When we ask, why does God allow evil, what we really mean is this: Why does God allow what we condemn as evil? The answer is that in the sight of God, infinitely clearer than our human sight, evil is the result of separation. The separation of man from God. And goodness is the result of reunion. The reunion between man and God.

And thus evil cannot stand alone. It is an imperfection of the good, a shadow that blots out the sunlight. It is a challenge to the spirit of man. Overcome the imperfection, remove the obstacle that produces the shadow. An evil body is a sick body, and the suffering that results from the sickness is the pain of a sundered soul. When we overcome evil, we make ourselves whole again.

Holiness, therefore, is but another word for wholeness. And goodness is another term for godliness. But the question still remains: Why does God make it necessary for us to be sundered in order to be reunited, to fall sick in order to become well again? In other words, what is the purpose of suffering and pain? The answer is that without suffering and pain the world as we know it would be meaningless. Imagine a state of continual health, incessant sunlight, eternal bliss. This would be a state of everlasting and intolerable boredom. It is contrast that makes our lives worth living. We prize our successes because we know the suffering of our failures. Our greatest pleasure is the feeling of recovery from pain.

And so our supreme good lies in our continual struggle against evil. Our life is a journey from the pain of separation toward the happiness of reunion.

But this reunion with God, declares Aquinas, can never be fully accomplished on earth. It must await the next stage of our journey beyond this world. Our life on earth contains only a part of our experience, but it determines all the rest of our experience in the life to come.

IV

It is the contrast between the different parts of the world that makes for the unity of the whole. It takes pleasure and pain to produce happiness, hope and disappointment to engender compassion, life and death to achieve immortality.

These contrasts are the ingredients out of which the world is being created. The act of creation was not an isolated incident of the past; it is a continuous process of all time. However, to the omniscient mind of God who lives *outside* of time, all time is an eternal present—here we have an echo of St. Augustine. God therefore knows all that ever was, all that ever is, all that ever will be. Just as the statue exists in the mind of the sculptor before it is embodied in marble, so do the generations of men exist in the mind of the Creator before they are embodied in flesh.

And God creates all things because he loves all things. This idea of the creation of the world through the love of God is Platonic rather than Aristotelian. Aquinas was a warmer personality than Aristotle. Hence the God of Aquinas is a more sympathetic Being than the God of Aristotle. All philosophers represent God after their own image. While the God of Aristotle is the unmoved mover, the God of Aquinas (and of Plato) is the creative Lover. God keeps creating not only man but the entire world after his own image. And all things in the world are trying to become as like him as possible.

Life, then, is a continual striving toward perfection. And all mortal creation is an instinctive imitation of the divine. For God wills it so, and His will is the beginning and the end of existence. All the contrasting parts of the world—which we see as pain, pleasure, sickness, health, envy, compassion, vengeance, forgiveness, death, and life—are like the different colors of a prism. Blended together, they melt into the white radiance of God's Goodness, Intelligence, Love.

Hence all that is good comes from God, all that comes from God is good, and evil is but a challenge to turn our life's journey into a zestful and meaningful crusade.

V

And thus Aquinas kept building his cathedral of faith supported by reason. "There is much in my faith," he said, "that surpasses my reason, but nothing that contradicts it." In his various books—especially the *Summa Theologica*—he gave a new voice to the old Christian belief in the humanity of God and the divinity of man.

And this was but a restatement of the still older philosophic beliefs of the Egyptians, the Hindus, the Chinese, the Persians, the Hebrews, and the Greeks. "God," the Egyptian sages had declared, "sits within the heart of every man." And the Hindus, elaborating this idea, had said: "God is the Universal Self." The Persians, taking up this thread of philosophy, had asserted that "all suffering is a cleansing of the Soul to make it more Godlike." The Hebrews, translating theology into ethics, had proclaimed social service as the highest form of religious service. "Since man is the essence of God, to do good to our fellow men is to do good in the eyes of God."

St. Thomas Aquinas, therefore, was the spiritual descendant of St. Ikhnaton, St. Buddha, St. Confucius, St. Zoroaster, St. Isaiah and St. Plato as well as of St. Augustine and St. Paul.

And like the other holy men of wisdom, he exchanged worldly success for a peaceful soul. He was only forty-seven when he died. But he had no regrets about the brevity of his life. "God has given me what I have asked of Him. If He has made me wise at an earlier age than others, it was because He meant to shorten my exile and to bring me sooner into His glory."

PART

4

The "Rebirth" of Philosophy

CHAPTER XVI

Francis Bacon (1561–1626)

THE THREE CENTURIES following Aquinas were, philosophically speaking, dark centuries. The entire era produced only a few thinkers of the first rank. People were too busy quarreling about politics or fighting about religion to devote themselves to the pursuit of wisdom. Christians were killing Moslems in the name of Jesus, the Prince of Peace; Moslems were killing Christians in the name of Allah, the Lord of Mercy; and in the tumult of the slaughter the voice of philosophy was drowned out.

In such an atmosphere the weeds of pseudo-intellectualism had stifled the healthy growth of the intellect. Even the so-called educated people busied themselves with astrology, the belief in the stars as the agents of our fate; alchemy, the effort to turn baser metals into gold; demonology, the speculation about devils and angels; and superstition, the credulity based upon irrational fears.

And then came the Renaissance—the reawakening of the human mind. Astrology gave way to astronomy, alchemy stepped aside for chemistry, demonology became transformed into anthropology, and superstition retreated under the flood-light of science. Columbus had discovered a new world across the sea, and Copernicus had traced a new way across the heavens to the stars.

At that period of general enlightenment, philosophy found a new voice in Francis Bacon, "the most powerful mind in modern times."

II

In their efforts to discover the meaning of life, Aquinas and Bacon adopted methods that were directly opposite. Aquinas had moved from faith to reason; Bacon proceeded from reason to faith. Aquinas, the churchman, had said: "My mind must prove only what my heart believes." But Bacon, the statesman, replied: "My heart must believe only what my mind can prove."

Yet the two philosophers arrived in their different ways at practically the same conclusion. The paths to the truth are many; the truth is one.

III

From his very birth (in England on January 22, 1561) Bacon was destined for a public career. His father, Sir Nicholas Bacon, was the Keeper of the Royal Seal under Queen Elizabeth I. His mother, Lady Anne Cooke, was the sister-in-law of Sir William Cecil, the queen's Lord Treasurer. Francis spent his boyhood in the glamor of the palace. And in the glory of the Elizabethan Era—one of the supreme ages in the history of man. At twelve he entered Trinity College; and at sixteen he left college to accept a post on the staff of the English ambassador to France. He was interested in philosophy even at that early age; and for a time he couldn't decide between philosophy and politics as his life's work. Years later he described his mental perplexity as a young man: "I believed myself born for the service of mankind . . . I therefore asked myself how I could most advantage mankind . . . I found in my own nature a special adaptation for the contemplation of truth . . .

"But my birth, my rearing and education had all pointed not toward philosophy but toward politics. I had been, as it

were, imbued in politics from childhood . . . I also thought
that my duty toward my country had special claims upon me
. . . Lastly, I conceived the hope that, if I held some honorable
office in the state, I might have secure supports to aid my
labors, with a view to the accomplishment of my destined
task. With these motives I applied myself to politics."

And thus he chose politics as a vocation, to help him in
the pursuit of philosophy as an avocation. He decided to apply
himself to the good of his country in order to learn how to serve
the good of mankind.

It must be noted that he had another motive for his decision to choose politics over philosophy. He loved the concrete
coin of the realm as much as, perhaps even more than, the
abstract coin of truth. His effort to serve both God and Mam-
mon, as we shall see, was to bring about his undoing.

Perhaps, however, there was some excuse for his excessive
devotion to money. His father, who had provided for his five
older sons, was preparing to make provision for his youngest
when he suddenly died (in 1579). Francis became terrified
when he found himself penniless at eighteen. Having lived in
luxury up to this point, he couldn't bear the thought of facing
poverty for the rest of his life. He was determined to become
rich at whatever cost. In his effort to keep up with the gilded
tradition of his family, he succumbed to an obsession that even
a philosopher could hardly overcome.

For Francis was a philosopher, and not a saint.

He applied for a position at the royal court; and he asked
his uncle, Sir William Cecil, to advance his cause. But Cecil had
a son of his own who needed to be advanced. He turned a deaf
ear to his nephew.

Francis decided, though not too patiently, to study law for
a while. Upon his graduation from Gray's Inn, he tried once
more to gain a foothold at the court. This time he sought the
sponsorship of the young and dashing Earl of Essex whose heart
he had won with his eloquent flattery. But Essex, though the

queen's favorite at the moment, was unable to extend her favor to his "dearest friend."

To assuage his friend's disappointment, however, Essex presented him with a costly estate. In return for this munificent gift, Bacon helped to bring about his benefactor's death. His hunger for future success was greater than his gratitude for past favors. When Essex had incurred the enmity of the queen, she ordered his arrest on the charge of treason. And—of all ironies—she selected Bacon as her attorney to prepare the case against his own best friend. Bacon did the job so well that Essex was sent to the block. "My ambition," declared Bacon, "is like the sun which passes through pollutions yet remains as pure as before."

It was over the body of Essex that "the wisest and meanest of mankind"—to quote Alexander Pope—took his first step toward the heights of society.

IV

Bacon received more than thirty pieces of silver for his treachery. The actual amount was twelve hundred pounds— a considerable sum in those days. Yet he complained that it was not enough—throughout his life his expenses ran far ahead of his income.

And his hunger for power kept pace with his passion for money. His rise after the Essex betrayal was steady. Yet he was too much of a philosopher to be too greatly elated over his success. His perfidy toward Essex had won him many political enemies. They were just waiting for the opportunity to trip him up. As for his political friends, he realized that they were but a pack of dogs snarling after the same bone—preferment at the court.

Yet in spite of his enemies and even of his friends, he advanced step by step, and—to paraphrase his own words—rose by his indignities to all his dignities. He had a simple formula

for success: "Truckle to the powers above you; and treat everybody as does the bee, with honey that contains a sting." At
forty-five he married—for money and not for love. "Great spirits," he observed cynically, "keep out this weak sentiment [of
love]." He kept building his house upon a shaky foundation and
surrounded himself with every luxury save the most important
of them all—contentment.

Once, in his failure to meet his expenses, he was arrested
for debt. But he returned from the debtor's prison and went
right ahead with his ambition. First under Queen Elizabeth,
and then under King James, he begged and pushed and flat-
tered his way to the successive positions of Prosecutor of the
Realm, Solicitor General, Attorney General, and finally Lord
Chancellor. This was the highest office in England next to the
king.

Bacon was now the greatest and perhaps the richest man
in England. He owned several estates in the city and in the
country. The acres surrounding one of his palatial mansions
contained a lake studded with a number of islands. On the larg-
est of these islands he had built a pretentious summer house
with a marble colonnade and a gallery for musicians. Here he
entertained hundreds of friends with the choicest meals and
drinks served by dozens of liveried retainers. It was quite a
setting for the beruffled little popinjay who stalked among his
guests with his pompous airs and grandiose dreams. The Viscount St. Albans—this was now his official title—had reached
the summit of his ambition.

And then came the fall. Bacon was celebrating his sixtieth
birthday. His London residence, York House, was crowded
with guests. The poet Ben Jonson recited an ode he had written
in honor of the occasion. A troupe of actors presented a pageant
extolling the glory of the viscount. At the end of the pageant,
a guest proposed a toast to the "most honored, most fortunate
subject of the King."

As the other guests were drinking the toast, one of Bacon's

retainers whispered something in his ear. An ominous message from Parliament. They had decided to investigate his conduct as the highest judicial officer of the Crown.

The charge on which he was to be tried was bribery. It was alleged that as a judge he had extorted money from a suitor by means of promises and threats. This sort of thing was a common practice at the time. But Bacon knew that his enemies would make the most of their opportunity to crush him.

Yet at first he tried to brazen it out. "Your Lordships," he wrote, "I know I have clean hands and a clean heart . . . But Job himself may for a time seem foul, especially when greatness is the mark and accusation is the game."

Later on, however, he admitted the charge and begged for the king's pardon. "Your Majesty's heart, which is an abyss of goodness as I am an abyss of misery, will judge me . . . with the honor of your mercy."

And then, with amazing frankness, he offered to "repay" the king for his pardon. "Because he that hath *taken* bribes is apt to *give* bribes, I will present your Majesty with a bribe. If your Majesty give me peace and leisure, and God give me life, I will present your Majesty with a good history of England, and a better digest of your laws."

King James refused to interfere in the trial. Bacon was imprisoned in the Tower and fined forty thousand pounds. His prison term was ended after two days and his fine was remitted. But his pride was broken. "I was the justest judge in England these fifty years," he said, "but this"—referring to his condemnation—"was the justest judgment in Parliament these two hundred years."

V

He retired to the country and lived the last five years of his life in peaceful poverty. And now out of the muck of his disastrous ambition came the full flower of his philosophy. He regretted that he had given too much of his time to the pursuit of folly and too little to the cultivation of wisdom. Yet his work, though fragmentary in his own eyes, represents perhaps the greatest achievement of the human intellect from the time of Aristotle to his own day. "His philosophy," to quote Macaulay, "moved the minds that moved the world." His works, over a score in number, cover and illumine almost the entire field of literature, science, and art. "I have taken all knowledge to be my province," he wrote. And his aim was to make men know in order to make them free. "The greatest happiness," he wrote, "is for a man's mind to be raised above the confusion of things," where he may understand the order of nature and the errors of men.

And the greatest of errors is to seek too much—a truth Aristotle had discovered almost two thousand years earlier. "The desire of power in excess," observed Bacon, "caused the angels to fall."

The desire for excessive power, due to inadequate knowledge. This thought lies at the foundation of Bacon's philosophy. His philosophy contradicted his own life. But let us not judge him too hastily. This fallen angel had felt that he was riding his ambition to his own ruin. Yet he recklessly went ahead. His mind was a mind of the ages, but his ambition was the ambition of the age. Bribery among high officials was the rule rather than the exception in Elizabethan England. The trouble with Bacon, as he himself realized, was his too great insistence upon worldly success. He was selfish, to be sure, but so were all his competitors for royal favors and public applause. Unfortunately for him, this self-love turned out to be self-hatred in the end.

Though he disregarded his selfishness in his actions, Bacon sensed it in his philosophy. "In philosophy we converse with the wise, as in actions with fools." He had tried to emulate the fools and to surround himself with the trappings of glory. Yet later on he wrote: "Virtue is like a rich stone—best plain set."

He had subordinated everything, even his philosophy, to his scramble for money. Yet he knew, even before his downfall, that an unfair distribution of wealth may lead to revolution and war. And therefore he observed that "money is like muck, not good unless it be spread" among as many people as possible. Having emptied the cup of luxury to the bitter dregs, he realized that what we need is not more luxury but more light.

More light! Greater knowledge to a serener faith. Learn in order that you may believe. This was the ultimate aim of his encyclopedic writing and philosophical quest. Less blundering, through greater understanding. Fewer opinions, more facts. Investigate as much as you can, about as many subjects as you can, and base your faith upon what you have learned. "It is knowledge alone that clears the mind of all perplexity."

And so, if you dedicate your life to learning, you will find a reason for your life. You will free yourself from "the clouds of error that turn into the storms of perturbations." Raise your mind above the confusion of things. Therein lies your salvation and true delight.

Purge your intellect of its counterfeit values. Destroy the false images—Bacon calls them mental "Idols"—that give you a distorted picture of life.

VI

An Idol, as Bacon defines it, is a shadow taken for a substance, a picture mistaken for an original.

There are, declares Bacon, four kinds of Idols or false images: *Idols of the Tribe, Idols of the Cave, Idols of the Market Place,* and *Idols of the Theater.*

1. *Idols of the Tribe.* This class includes the fallacies—such as the superstitions, dreams, and omens—that are common to all mankind, "the entire human tribe."

It is commonly believed that things are as they appear to the human mind. "On the contrary," argues Bacon, "the human mind resembles those uneven mirrors which impart their own properties to different objects . . . and distort and disfigure them." We misrepresent these distortions as realities and translate our prejudices into creeds. We believe not what *is* true, but what we had rather *were* true. Our picture of the world is thus the product of our imperfect vision. We see but fragments of the real world; and these fragments appear all out of proportion to one another. The human mind jumps too easily from faulty observations to false conclusions. It must learn to take pains and to be patient. "It must not be supplied with wings, but rather hung with weights to keep it from leaping and flying." The imagination should be not the capricious master but the obedient servant of the intellect. For this is the only way in which the human mind can be cleansed of the Idols of the Tribe.

2. *Idols of the Cave.*   These are the errors that belong not to the tribe but to the individual. "Every one . . . has a cave or den of his own, which refracts and discolors the light of nature." Some minds are analytic—they see the trees and not the forest; others are synthetic—they see the forest and not the trees. Thus we have the unphilosophical scientist on the one hand, and the unscientific philosopher on the other.

Moreover, every individual has a personal bias as a result of his heredity and training. Every man sees the world through the colored glasses of his nation, his business, his family, his political party and his church. Thus the world presents different views to the Englishman and the Russian, the manufacturer and the laborer, the bridegroom and the bachelor, the Christian and the Jew. The true scientist, the true philosopher, will recognize the limitations of his own point of view and he will therefore try to correlate it with as many other viewpoints as possible.

So get out of the cavern of your little self. Step into the daylight and examine the surrounding vista as an object of universal rather than individual interest. The Idols of the Cave will be abolished, and the millennium will be close at hand, when the poet can see the world with the eyes of the scientist, and the scientist can view it with the heart of the poet.

3. *Idols of the Market Place.*   These errors arise from the association of men with one another in the business of living. "Men communicate by means of language; but words are imposed according to the understanding of the crowd; and there arises, from a bad and inapt formation of words, a wonderful obstruction to the mind." Men use their words too loosely, with the result that they tend to conceal rather than to reveal their thoughts. For example, they talk about cause and effect. But who knows the exact meaning of these two words? What was the first cause of anything? What will be the last effect? A hen, observed a wit, is merely the egg's ingenious way of creating another egg. What is Aristotle's—or anybody else's—meaning when he speaks of God as the unmoved mover, or causeless cause, or uncreated creator, of the universe? Words, quibbles, subtleties, lies. It is of the utmost importance, insisted Bacon, to drive out from the language of philosophy such vague and misleading expressions as the above. We must be merciless with our words if we want them to express exactly what we mean. Like Socrates, Bacon declared that the Idols of the Market Place—the errors of our speech in the common business of living—must give way to a greater precision in the use of our language. The beginning of philosophy is the accurate employment of words. We must learn to speak truly in our search for the truth.

4. *Idols of the Theater.*   "In my judgment," declared Bacon, "all the received systems of philosophy are but so many stage plays . . . And in the plays of this philosophic theater you may observe the same thing which is found in the stage plays of the dramatists." Indeed, all life is a play upon the stage of the world. And most of us commit the error of making this play "more compact and elegant, more as we wish it to be" than it actually is. Too often the mystic, like the man in the

street, conceives a fairy world of his heart's desire, and then tries to prove that it is the actual world in which he exists.

But in order to ascertain the nature of the real world, argued Bacon, we must scrap our false definitions and our unfounded dogmas. We must work not from propositions to observations, not from faith to reason, but from observations to propositions, from reason to faith. "If a man will begin with certainties, he shall end in doubts; but if he be content to begin in doubts, he shall end in certainties."

VII

And thus Bacon introduced the scientific method into the study of philosophy. This method is the way of *experimentation* . . . "It first lights the candle and then, by means of the candle, shows the way."

And the end of the way, as lighted by the candle of reason, is faith. "A little philosophy," he declared, "inclineth a man's mind to atheism; but depth in philosophy bringeth men's minds about to religion." For there is "a Great Mind above, which guides our little minds below." The more we delve into philosophy, the more clearly we realize that "men are not animals erect but immortal gods." Philosophy enables us to find a divine pattern in the universe. "While the mind of man looketh upon scattered causes (in nature), it may sometimes rest in them and go no further; but when it beholdeth the chain of them . . . linked together, it must needs fly to Providence and Deity." Nothing in the world is accidental; everything is preordained —that is, the result of an originally planned order. "*Chance* is the name of a thing that does not exist."

Our greatest aim in life, therefore, is to discover the patterned order of the universe and to adapt our ambitions to this pattern. There are three ways in which we can do this: the first two are wrong and the third is right.

The first wrong way is to extend our individual power as

against all other individuals. The second wrong way is to extend our national power as against all other nations. But the one right way is to extend the power of the entire human race over the forces of nature.

Just before he died, Bacon wrote a brief account of a utopia—*The New Atlantis*—in which he pictured a race of men dedicated to the co-operative conquest of nature. H. G. Wells has called this work "Bacon's greatest contribution to philosophy." The inhabitants of the New Atlantis, writes Bacon, have reached a stage of superior happiness through superior intelligence. Here is no scrambling for office through flatteries and bribes, but honest selection on the basis of fitness and character; no selfish exploitation by bankers and businessmen, but unselfish service by philosophers and scientists; no individual struggle of man against man, but a united effort of every man for the good of all mankind.

But the most interesting features of these utopians is the character of their international trade. "We maintain a trade, not of gold, silver or jewels, nor for silks, nor for spices, nor for any other commodity or matter; but only for God's first creature, which was Light." For this purpose, the utopians maintain a class of businessmen called "Merchants of Light"—philosophers and scientists who travel throughout the world for the international exchange of new ideas and fair play.

The final quest of Bacon—of all great philosophers. Greater harmony through more light.

VIII

It was in the search for more light that Bacon ended his life. He died as the result of a scientific experiment. On a cold March day in 1626, while traveling over the countryside, he thought about a new method for preserving meat from putrefaction. To use snow instead of salt.

He dismounted from his carriage, purchased a fowl, killed it, and stuffed it with snow.

Right after the experiment, he suffered a chill which developed into pneumonia. A few days later he was dead.

His last will was a mixture of humility and pride. "I bequeath my body to be buried obscurely . . . my soul to God . . . my name to the nations and the ages." And he might have added, "my philosophy to the establishment of a united world."

CHAPTER XVII

René Descartes (1596–1650)

AQUINAS had advanced from faith to reason, and Bacon from reason to faith. But Descartes took neither of these two starting points in his quest for the truth. He began by doubting everything. Yet his doubt, like Aquinas's faith and Bacon's reason, led him finally to God.

II

René entered life with a handicap. His mother died of tuberculosis shortly after his birth. The doctors warned his father that René, too, was threatened with the disease. The child was put into the hands of a nurse who coddled him into an effeminate delicacy. Most of his early adventures were mental rather than physical. His father, a well-to-do member of the French Parliament, encouraged him in his intellectual gymnastics. He proudly referred to him as "my little philosopher."

At eight the "little philosopher" entered the Jesuit college of La Flèche, where his teachers allowed him to "rest his body while he exercised his mind." He studied in bed till a late hour while the other students recited their lessons in the classroom. As a result of this extra leisure, René was always at the head of the class.

At sixteen René left the Jesuit college and went to Paris. Here, in the company of other well-to-do youngsters, he gave up his austere thinking for riotous living. He became an expert gambler—winning most of his bets, as his friends remarked, because of his "uncanny knowledge of mathematical probabilities."

But before long he grew tired of his boisterous friends and enlisted in the Dutch army "in order to find peace." Since Holland was not engaged in war at the time, he enjoyed two years of quiet meditation. He even took pleasure in his military drill —having completely outgrown his tubercular taint, he was delighted to find that he had a vigorous body to shelter his brilliant mind.

Indeed, his body clamored for action after its long period of incubation. He left the Dutch army to enlist with the Bavarian troops. The Thirty Years' War had just broken out, and Descartes was now eager to engage in actual combat.

Yet he still found plenty of time for meditation between battles. In one of his books—*Discourse on the Method of Reasoning*—he tells us about one of his meditations. It was in the winter of 1619–20. The weather was extremely cold, and Descartes, to keep himself warm, crept into a brick oven where he stayed all day. "When I came out of that oven," he said, "my philosophy was more than half baked. It needed but a little extra heat to make it crisp and complete."

Socrates, it seems, could think best when he was cold, Descartes when he was warm.

Ten years of travel after his resignation from the army; and then one night he was visited by a dream. "I heard a clap of thunder," he said . . . "It was the spirit of Truth descending to take possession of me." He wrote a book—*Le Monde* [The World]—in which he expressed some of his ideas about what he regarded as the Truth. He agreed with Copernicus and Galileo that the earth was in motion.

People began to spread rumors about his unorthodox beliefs, and Descartes found it prudent to get beyond the reach of persecution. He went to Holland, the haven of free thought in the seventeenth century. (It was in Holland that the philosophers Spinoza and Locke were to find refuge later on.)

Here Descartes lived for thirty years, 1620 to 1649, trying "in silence and solitude to arrange his thoughts into a consistent whole."

III

Even in Holland Descartes was not entirely free from attack as an "atheist." The authorities of the University of Leyden forbade their students to mention his name, and they took steps to have him arrested. But the ruler of the Netherlands saved him from actual persecution. He told the university professors "not to be silly in your hounding of a wise man." Descartes was allowed to pursue his philosophy in comparative peace.

In order to train himself for his philosophical studies, he decided to adopt a simple code of morals consisting of three principles:

"The *first* was to obey the laws and customs of my country . . .

"The *second* was to be as firm and resolute in my thoughts as I was able . . .

"The *third* was to endeavor always to conquer myself rather than my fortune, and to change my own desires rather than the system of the universe . . ."

And then, having subjected himself to this rigorous mental diet, he started upon his journey to the summit of wisdom. "I gradually rooted out from my mind all the errors which had hitherto crept into it." The first result of this uprooting was a state of absolute doubt about the world as observed through his senses. "Can I doubt, for example, that I am sitting here by the fire in a dressing gown? Yes, indeed; for sometimes I have dreamt that I was here in a dressing gown when actually I was naked in bed."

Here we find an echo of the ancient Chinese philosopher who couldn't decide whether he was a man dreaming that he was a butterfly or a butterfly dreaming that he was a man. But, unlike the Chinese philosopher, Descartes refused to remain content in his skepticism. He felt rather like "a traveler who, when he has lost his way in a forest, refuses to stay in one place, but proceeds constantly in as straight a line as possible. For in this way," continues Descartes, "if he does not exactly reach the point he desires, he will come at least in the end to some place that may be better than the middle of a forest."

And so Descartes used his doubt not as a passive end but as an active beginning. In all his uncertain opinions, he found one certain truth: he was able to *think*. The entire physical world, including his own body, might be a delusion; but his thought was a fact. "While I wanted to think everything false, it must necessarily be that I who thought was something; and remarking that this truth, *I think, therefore I am*, was so solid and so certain that all the most extravagant suppositions of the Skeptics were incapable of upsetting it, I judged that I could receive it without scruple as the first principle of the philosophy that I sought."

Cogito, ergo sum—"I think, therefore I am." This is the first positive step that Descartes took out of the jungle of his doubts. The only certain thing in the world is the *thinking mind*. The person known as "I"—that is to say, the mind by which I am what I am, "is wholly distinct from my body . . . and is such, that although the body were not, the mind would still continue to be all that it is."

In order to think, therefore, it is necessary for the mind to exist. I may doubt that I am a body or that there is a material world in which I live. But I cannot doubt that I am a mind which is able to think, even to doubt. "Hence I know that I am a being whose entire nature is to think and for whose existence there is no need of any place, nor does it depend on any material thing for its existence."

The mind or soul, therefore, is distinct from the body; it is recognized more easily than the body; and it would be able to think even without a body.

In other words, the fact that I can think proves that I exist as a living soul. This is our first step out of the wilderness of doubt toward the light of philosophy.

The next step brings us to a consideration of the body as the *material* substance, just as the soul is the *thinking* substance of our being. And it is the thinking of the soul that gives us our knowledge about the body. The soul is the mechanic, and the body is the machine.

This Cartesian philosophy (named after Descartes) is known as a *dualistic* system—that is, a system that divides the world into two parallel but independent entities, matter and spirit. Descartes is therefore the father of two divergent schools of modern thought—materialism and idealism. The materialists assert that the mind is but a part of the body, that the mechanic is only a wheel in the machine, and that the world is therefore a body without a soul. The idealists, on the other hand, maintain that the body is a part of the mind, that there is no matter but only spirit, and that the world is therefore a soul without a body. This philosophic quarrel, however, is fortunately coming to an end. For modern science has demonstrated that the body and the soul, matter and energy, are not different things but different aspects of the selfsame entity.

But to return to Descartes. Starting from doubt, he proved —at least to his own satisfaction—that each of us has (1) a thinking soul, and (2) a material body revealed by the thoughts of the soul. He then goes ahead to prove a third fact, the existence of God.

"My idea of God," he said, "stemmed from the search of my imperfect mind for something more perfect than myself. I realized that my mind was imperfect because I had doubts. To doubt implies less perfection than to know." And having pondered over this idea for a long time, Descartes tells us, "I was led to think of something more perfect than myself; and I clearly recognized that I must hold this notion from some Nature which in reality was more perfect than mine." This superior Nature, he concluded, possessed within itself all the perfections of which the human mind could form any idea. All these perfections, summarized in a single word, spell out God.

The Cartesian God, therefore, is the sum of all perfection, the creator of all minds, and the guide of all thoughts and actions toward a better and more intelligent life. He is "infinite, eternal, immutable, omniscient, omnipotent and, in short, the possessor of all the perfections which my mind can possibly conceive." Such imperfections as doubt, inconstancy, anger, revenge, and the like cannot be found in the nature of God.

In brief, our faith in God results from our knowledge of our own shortcomings and from our instinctive effort to eliminate these shortcomings. God is the shining light which reveals to us our little selves and guides us in the direction of his own greatness. Whatever we possess that is beautiful or true proceeds from the infinite source of beauty and truth. To express the thought in Platonic terms, God is the perfect idea, and man is the imperfect copy of this idea.

This, then, is Descartes's philosophical picture of man—a material body, a thinking soul groping toward the light, and the spirit of God guiding and sustaining us all.

IV

Descartes was fortunate enough to follow a path of tranquil contemplation in his adventure toward the light. At his father's death, he inherited a sufficient income to save him from the competitive struggle for existence. He was able to live in comfort if not in luxury. He never married. He ate well and slept well; he generally stayed in bed till late in the morning. Now and then he took a trip abroad, but for the most part he did his traveling in books and in "conversation" with his foreign friends through the medium of correspondence.

And thus he spent his uneventful but thoughtful days, "loving life," as he wrote, "but not fearing death." He experienced one great sorrow, however. He lost his only child, Francine, at the age of five. Though the little girl was illegitimate,

Descartes was deeply attached to her. Yet he shook off his tragedy and went ahead with his leisurely life—arraying himself (unlike a philosopher) in the latest fashion and dangling a sword at his side. He wrote mathematical and scientific as well as philosophical books. He worked in an octagonal study with windows looking out upon a picturesque garden with a distant view of the sea. He was a dapper little fellow with a huge head and pale face, a shock of black hair growing almost down to his eyebrows, a dark brown mustache over his narrow upper lip, and under his lower lip a tuft of hair trimmed after the French fashion to resemble an inverted mustache instead of a beard. When he went out of the house, he put a wig on his head, and drew heavy woolen stockings over his hose. Owing to "the inherited weakness" of his chest, he dreaded the slightest drop in temperature or the mildest breeze.

And it was a drop in temperature that proved his undoing. He had started a correspondence with Queen Christina of Sweden. A stocky little sovereign measuring about five feet of intellectual curiosity and having an inordinate desire to pick the brains of the great, she "invited" Descartes to become her teacher in philosophy. For a time he refused to accept her invitation. But the queen was determined to have her way. "I will not let you escape!" she wrote playfully; and finally Descartes agreed to become her "willing prisoner."

She sent her warship to fetch the celebrated philosopher to her "land of bears between rocks and ice." It was in the fall of 1649 that Descartes set out for Sweden.

And his doom. The queen demanded daily lessons, and at the "unearthly" hour of five in the morning. This pre-Sunrise Semester in the rigorous blasts of the Scandinavian winter was too much for his delicate constitution. "In this country," he complained, "a man's blood freezes up like a river." Within a few weeks after his arrival at the palace he caught a heavy chest cold. A few days later, on February 11, 1650, he died.

"But my thinking soul," he whispered, "will live on."

CHAPTER XVIII

Baruch Spinoza (1632–1677)

THERE WAS much in common between Spinoza and Descartes. Both of them found in Holland a measure of tolerance toward the expression of their thought. Both were determined to doubt whatever they were unable to prove. Both were excoriated as atheists because of their unorthodox ideas about God. And both arrived at a picture of God as the sum of all perfection in the universe.

But at this point Descartes stopped, and Spinoza went ahead. Descartes saw the world as a philosophical trinity—a material body, a thinking soul, and an all-pervasive God. Spinoza, however, beheld it as a unity—"the Body, the Soul and God are One."

And thus the philosophy of Spinoza is known as pantheism —from the Greek *pan* (everything) plus *theos* (God). It declares that God is in every one of us, and that every one of us is a part of God.

II

Spinoza was only eight when he witnessed a scene that spurred him to philosophical speculation. It was at the Amsterdam synagogue. The members of the congregation were trampling over a man who was lying across the threshold.

"What is this man's name?" Spinoza asked his father.

"Uriel Acosta."

"What did he do to deserve this punishment?"

"He is a freethinker, Baruch." And then his father explained how Acosta had been expelled from the Jewish congregation because he had questioned their religion; and how the members of the congregation were now "stamping" the sins out of him before his readmission into the synagogue.

Little Spinoza went home in a thoughtful mood. That afternoon, as he was playing in the street, he tried to express his sympathy for the victim; but one of his playmates struck him in the face.

The next day, the Acosta tragedy came to a head. Unable to endure his public disgrace, the young freethinker shot himself to death.

A strange world of foolish people, thought little Spinoza. Everybody was trying to hurt everybody else, it seemed. Baruch was wise beyond his years. Along with the rest of his family, he had been driven out of Spain because the Christians hated the Jews. And now the Spinozas lived in Holland where the Jews hated their own kind. What was the meaning of all this? "When I grow up," he said to his father, "I'll try to find a way to stop people from hating one another."

III

As Spinoza grew older, he learned more and more about man's inhumanity to man. The Jews, he noticed, were being scourged from country to country—the victims of the very people to whom they had given a Bible and a God. Drifting about like so many bits of wreckage, some of the refugees had gone to Africa where they were murdered for the jewels they were reported to have swallowed. Others had tried to get into Italy, only to be ordered to move on. Still others had settled in Poland and in Russia, to be herded like animals within the confines of the ghetto. The Spinozas, however, were among the few who had met with a friendly reception in Holland.

Yet even in Holland Spinoza found his heritage of misfortune not only as a Jew but as a human being. He studied Latin

under a Dutch scholar, Van den Enden, and fell in love with
his teacher's pretty daughter. He proposed to her; but she preferred a prosperous businessman to an impecunious philosopher. Spinoza remained single for the rest of his life.

But disappointment followed disappointment. When his
father died, his sister tried to cheat him of his inheritance. He
sued her for his share, won his case—and tore up the verdict
in his favor. He gave the entire inheritance to his sister. "I de-
plore her greed," he said, "but I sympathize with her need."

He required very little money for himself—his tastes were
simple. The elders of the synagogue offered him five hundred
dollars a year—not to teach them wisdom, but to hold his
tongue. They were afraid of his unorthodox views. But he refused their offer. He was content, he said, to live with an empty
pocket and a free soul.

The elders of the synagogue, however, wouldn't allow him
to enjoy his freedom. On July 27, 1656, they excommunicated
him, just as they had excommunicated Acosta sixteen years earlier.

The scene of the excommunication was one of savage so-
lemnity. The decree was proclaimed amidst the wailing of the
congregation and the sounding of the ram's horn. The candle-
lights, which had burned brightly at the beginning, were
snuffed out one by one until at the end the synagogue was left
in utter darkness—a symbol of the dark and dismal life to which
they condemned Spinoza. He was a man accursed among
his fellow men. "We pronounce against him the malediction
wherewith Elisha cursed the children . . . Let him be accursed
by day, and accursed by night; accursed in his sleep and accursed in his waking; accursed in going out and accursed in
coming in. May the wrath of the Lord never pardon him; may
it blot out his name from under the sky . . ."

And then the leader of the congregation commanded all
the Jews to banish him from their homes and their hearts.
"Let no one do him any service, let no one abide under the

same roof with him, let no one approach within four cubits length of him, and let no one read any document dictated by him, or written by his hand."

Spinoza listened to this excommunication and felt no rancor against his persecutors. "It is my business not to criticize, to execrate, or to condemn," he wrote, "but to understand." He realized that the elders of the synagogue believed themselves desperately in the right. For the Jews, tormented on every side, found their only stronghold in their faith. They believed that any attack against this stronghold threatened the very existence of their people. Hence they looked upon Spinoza as a traitor. They were anxious to prove to the entire world that they were a people united in their determination to survive. Spinoza threatened their survival, as they thought, and therefore he must be expelled from the community of the Jews.

But Spinoza felt equally convinced of his own right. He saw the world "under the aspect of eternity," while his judges saw it only under the aspect of the moment. He decided to stay in Amsterdam, alone with his thoughts and his books—a stranger among his people but "a constant companion of God."

His people, however, refused to leave him in peace. One night a fanatic tried to kill him with a dagger. Spinoza escaped with a minor cut, but decided to move into the gentile neighborhood of Ouwerkerk, a suburb of Amsterdam. He changed his first name from Baruch, which is the Hebrew for "blessed," to its Latin equivalent, Benedict. He took lodging in an attic and turned to lens grinding for a livelihood. Though unorthodox in his belief, he still adhered to the Jewish doctrine that every scholar should learn a trade. "Use your hands," the ancient rabbis had advised, "for worldly goods; your head, for heavenly thoughts."

He now lived among the Christians, but he joined none of their sects. "The different religions divide people, but it is my desire to unite them."

His Christian host and hostess found him so gentle that

they persuaded him (in 1660) to go along with them when they moved to Rijnsburg, near the city of Leyden. Here he shut himself "like a silkworm in his cocoon," going out only for an occasional stroll or to buy his simple food of milk and corn bread and a handful of raisins. His chief interest was to watch the battles of the spiders in his attic.

There was so much in common between spiders and men, he observed. Such amazing ingenuity in the weaving of their webs and the building of their homes, and such utter stupidity in the wanton destruction of their handiwork!

Spinoza was twenty-eight at this time. He met practically no people from the outside world; but sometimes he came down from his attic to converse with his host and his hostess. He spoke to them on their own level of understanding; but now and then a phrase would open the very heavens for them, as they expressed it. "This Jew," said his host, "is the only man who talks like Christ."

His appearance, like his manner, was unimposing. Medium height, swarthy skin, dark curly hair, long black eyebrows, and eyes burning with the fever of chronic tuberculosis. He dressed rather shabbily—"a mediocre article should not be put into a costly wrapper." He earned little, but managed to live within his means. "I am like a snake who forms a circle with his tail in his mouth," he said. "My outgo just meets my income, and I have nothing left at the year's end."

And so he sat in his attic, weaving the pattern of his philosophy and trying his utmost to finish his work in his feverish race with death. In this effort he was not wholly successful. He was unable to complete the last and perhaps best of his books—*A Treatise on Politics*. And he declared that his other books—*A Treatise on Religion, On the Improvement of the Mind,* and *Ethics*—contained but a "fragment of the truth." For even the greatest philosopher, he said, looks upon the world like a prisoner through a chink in the wall of his body, which is his lifelong cell.

Yet this vision, however narrow, is a hint of the true vision if we see it *in the framework of eternity*. These three words—*sub specie aeternitatis*—represent the substance of Spinoza's philosophy. The battles of the spiders, the struggles of the nations, the tortures on the rack, the excommunications from the synagogue, the misunderstandings and hatreds and plots between individuals and families and states—these are but the darker threads in the eternal weaving of the pattern of life. In common with many of the other great philosophers from Zoroaster down to his own day, Spinoza believed that the darker as well as the brighter threads are necessary in the weaving of the complete pattern. Evil is only our partial view of the whole. "All's well that ends well." And in the end—or, as Spinoza expressed it, in the over-all picture—the world is good.

And thus we must learn to see the world as God sees it. Nothing is isolated. Our joys, our sorrows, disasters, fires, floods, even wars—all these are but the fragmentary glimpses of the eternal landscape of the universe. Just as we can forget our past misfortunes, let us try to see in perspective our future calamities. They do not concern us, if only we look upon them as incidental threads in the ultimate pattern of life.

And what is the meaning of this pattern? *The divine unity of the world.* Imprisoned as we are within the physical cell of our senses, we catch only occasional segments of the divine whole. Yet, to Spinoza, these illuminating glimpses are enough to demonstrate that every one of us is a definite part of God —a cell in His body, a thought in His mind, a syllable in His poem of life. A half-blind person can distinguish only a few indistinct colors. Our senses are color-blind to the manifold attributes of God and of our own selves. A worm, burrowing in the ground, can have but an infinitesimal notion of the vast world of which he is a part. We possess only a worm's-eye view of the world. The greatest philosopher, maintains Spinoza—and here he echoes the thought of Ikhnaton—is but an infant in his understanding of the pantheistic nature of God.

But the philosopher has caught a glimpse of the vision. And he knows that he must not confuse his own puny intelligence with the infinite intelligence of God. The world is governed not in accordance with our individual desires, but in accordance with God's comprehensive design. "Not my will but Thine be done." The story which God has woven into the drama of our human lives is beyond our understanding. It is enough for us to know that it is an essential scene in the drama of eternal life. It is not for us to pass judgment upon it, since it has not been written for the fulfillment of our selfish human plans. And our human mind is not able to understand the entire play.

All things, to be sure, partake of the intelligence of God —just as a dog partakes of the intelligence of a man. In other words, the world contains many different grades of intelligence. The mind of a tree, for example, is far below the mind of an animal; the mind of an animal is far below the mind of a man; and the mind of the average man is far below the mind of a great poet. But even the mind of a Shakespeare, as compared to God's, is like the mind of a tree as compared to Shakespeare's.

Thus far, however, the pantheistic philosophy of Spinoza is somewhat negative. It assures us that we are parts of God, but rather insignificant parts as seen under the aspect of eternity. The entire earth, as a cynical Spinozist has remarked, is but a troublesome pebble caught between the toes of God.

And yet there is a heartening phase to Spinoza's philosophy. Our destiny, he declares, is greater than we think. Each of us, though a small part of God, is an equally important part. Under the eternal aspect of existence, there is no such thing as smaller or greater. Our present life, as the Spinozist Walt Whitman has observed, is but a stage in our ultimate development. All of us—from the vagabond in the gutter to the king on his throne—are interrelated pupils in the classroom of eternity. At this moment we happen to be in different grades, depending upon our present mental and spiritual development. All of us are taught in accordance with our capacity to learn. But in the long run, whatever our grade or degree of knowledge at this stage of our learning, every one of us will reach the senior class of the elect.

For the present, therefore, let us be friendly schoolmates in the Alma Mater of the universe. Let us look up to those who are ahead, and help those who are behind. This doctrine in the philosophy of Spinoza is the essence of democracy. For it advances the principle that every one of us is an equally favored pupil in the school of life. And the purpose of our education in this school is to become inspired with an "intellectual love of God"—that is, with an intelligent affection toward our fellow men. "For all of us partake of God." There is a bond of infinite love, declares Spinoza, which exists between our better, or divine, selves. And "he who clearly and distinctly understands his divine nature" will surrender himself to this infinite love which emanates from God and embraces all living things.

This all-divine idea of the universe has prompted Ernest Renan to observe that Spinoza had "perhaps the truest vision ever conceived of God."

IV

If only we follow our divine nature, wrote Spinoza, we shall reach the ultimate objective in life—supreme happiness. "A man's happiness consists in this, that his power—his zest for living—is increased." And this increased power—for living, for working, for noble effort—can come about only through "the love of self." Let us not, however, misunderstand the meaning of the word "self" in the Spinozist philosophy. The self-love of Spinoza is not the narrow egotism of the aggressor, the schemer, the man of hatred, envy or strife. It is rather the enlightened, all-inclusive selfishness of the humanitarian, the conciliator, the lover of mankind.

For the entire world consists of one God, one Body, one Soul, one universal Self. In the words of St. Paul, one of the men who most deeply inspired Spinoza, "we are parts of one another."

The entire human race, believed Spinoza, is an organic unit of life. When you hurt another, you are hurting yourself—"the divine essence of your better self." It was no mere bravado that induced Spinoza to give his inheritance to his sister. Having secured justice, he set it aside for mercy. "He who wishes to revenge injuries by reciprocal injuries will always be unhappy." For he will live—as the world is living today—in a perpetual atmosphere of suspicion and retaliation and war. Spinoza recognized only one kind of aggression as being always and everywhere just. A universal aggressiveness for peace. "The greatest victories," he maintained, "are to be won not by force of arms but by nobility of soul."

This nobility of soul is "the strength of the wise man." The truly wise man, in other words, is "the man who is aware of his social soul." He gives himself to others because he knows that all of us are children of eternity. He enjoys the only freedoms worth while. Freedom from hatred: "The greatest injury you can do me is to plant hatred in my soul." Freedom from fear: "A free man fears nothing, not even death." Freedom from envy: "When you and I are free, why should we envy each other?" Freedom from tyranny and slavery: "A free man is master of himself and servant of none." Freedom from ignorance, prejudice, and spite: "Wisdom leads to forbearance, and forbearance to further wisdom."

Hence the completely free man—that is, the completely wise man—"will desire nothing for himself which he will not also desire for the rest of mankind."

V

When Spinoza gave his philosophy to the world, he was assailed in orthodox circles as "the most impious atheist that ever lived." Here and there, however, he heard an approving voice. One of his admirers, Simon de Vries, a rich merchant of Amsterdam, offered him a gift of $1000. Spinoza refused it. An even more flattering offer came from King Louis XIV. The Sun King of France, anxious to buy the greatest brains of his generation, promised Spinoza a generous income for life. There was only one condition: Spinoza must dedicate his next book to the king. Again the philosopher refused the offer.

And then, in 1673, he received still another offer: a professorship of philosophy at the University of Heidelberg. "You will have complete freedom of speech in your classes," the regent of Germany assured him, "provided you refrain from criticizing the established religion of our state." Once again Spinoza politely declined. "A free man is master of himself, servant of none." He was determined to speak his mind without orders or favors from the outside.

And so he sat alone in his garret, sending out his lenses to improve the sight and his ideas to illumine the vision of his fellow men. He was equally impervious to censure, flattery, and even threats. On one occasion he was almost lynched by an infuriated mob. He had received an invitation for a philosophical chat with Prince de Condé, who had invaded Holland at the time. On his way home from the camp, Spinoza was assailed with stones and angry shouts: "Renegade!" "Atheist!" "Traitor!" He had a hard time convincing the mob that he was merely a philosopher and not a spy. The conflicts of men had no greater concern for him than the battles of spiders. He was not a nationalist; he subscribed only to the international brotherhood of free and fearless men.

And it was in fearless freedom that "the holy and excommunicated philosopher" met his death. It came on a Sunday afternoon (February 29, 1677). Spinoza was forty-four at the time. His host and his hostess had gone to church. The only person who remained with him was Dr. Meyer, his physician and friend. Spinoza died calmly in Dr. Meyer's arms. "A free man," he had written, "thinks of nothing less than of death; and his wisdom is a meditation not on death, but on life."

CHAPTER XIX

John Locke (1632–1704)

ONE OF THE rare visitors to Spinoza's attic was Baron Gott-fried Wilhelm von Leibniz. This German scholar had heard of the "God-intoxicated philosopher" and was anxious to get his ideas at first hand. He stayed a month with Spinoza and came away with the conviction that a world which could produce so noble a soul was the best of all possible worlds. He wrote a book in which he developed this idea—an optimistic outlook on life which has been widely accepted to this day.

Yet a number of philosophers objected to the excessive optimism of Leibniz. "Yes," observed F. H. Bradley sarcasti-cally, "this is the best of all possible worlds, and everything in it is a necessary evil." And Voltaire, in his *Candide,* caricatured Leibniz as Doctor Pangloss, to whom every human misfortune is a blessing in disguise.

But there was one philosopher who accepted Leibniz with an important qualification: This *can* be the best of all possible worlds, provided we strive to make it better than it is today.

The name of this philosopher who aimed at a better world was an Englishman named John Locke.

II

Locke was an idealist who tried to replace the "divine right of royalty" with the divine royalty of right. He was one of the leading actors in the historic drama of transition from mon-archy to democracy. He was the apostle of the British Revolution of 1688, and the prophet of the American Revolution of 1776.

He was born (1632) in the midst of a thunderstorm. And he grew up in a hurricane of oppression, dictatorship and civil war. He was ten years old when the British people rebelled against their king, the tyrannical Charles I. Locke's father, a country lawyer, joined the people's army of Oliver Cromwell against King Charles. And Locke was seventeen when the king was captured, tried for treason, and beheaded.

This historic event—the successful uprising of the sheep against the wolf—helped to mold the dynamic thought of John Locke. And the events that followed the death of King Charles gave final form to his thought. The dictatorship of Oliver Cromwell had replaced the tyranny of King Charles. Those who had been oppressed under the king became the oppressors under the dictator. The sheep were no better than the wolves.

The death of Cromwell (1658) was followed by a period of spiritual anarchy. "Let us eat, drink and be merry. For life is cheap, and joy is fleeting. Tomorrow we may be called upon to die." The new king, Charles II, had plunged into a perpetual spree, and all Merrie England had followed him. When the Dutch sailed up the Thames (1667) and burned the British fleet almost under the walls of the palace, the people were too intoxicated with pleasure to fight back. For they had no leader. Their king, we read in Pepys's *Diary*, "did sup with my Lady Castlemaine, and they were all mad, hunting a poor moth."

Such were the moth-chasing scenes that surrounded the education of John Locke.

III

Locke found little pleasure in his studies. "I received no light to my understanding," he remarked. His teachers at Christ's College, Oxford, recited the poetry of ancient Greece and ignored the politics of modern England. Shortly after his graduation, he was appointed instructor of Greek at Christ's College. But he rebelled against his intellectual strait jacket. He devoted his leisure time to the study of medicine and government. And especially philosophy, not as an abstract theory but as a practical way of life.

And life, as he learned when he had reached his middle twenties, is a process of adjustment from sorrow to serenity. He had lost his mother, his father, and his only brother. And he himself was threatened with the family disease, tuberculosis.

But he paid little attention to this threat of sickness. He was more concerned with the greater sickness of his country. This concern, he found, was shared by one of his college friends, Lord Ashley. Like Locke himself, Ashley was disgusted with the frivolity of the public and the debauchery of the king. Together the two young men threw themselves into the struggle to bring sanity into an insane age. Locke the philosopher became the mind and the voice of Ashley the statesman.

And he also became the tutor of Ashley's children, and their family physician. He had never received a medical degree or practical training in surgery. Yet he served as the obstetrician when Ashley's daughter-in-law was delivered of a child, and he successfully removed a tumor from Ashley's breast. Referring to the medical judgment and skill of this unlicensed practitioner, one of the leading surgeons of the day, Dr. Sydenham, wrote to a friend: "I thoroughly rely upon John Locke's methods for curing disease." In those days, we must remember, it was not a crime for a man to practice medicine without a college degree. In Locke's case, it was a distinct blessing to humanity.

Locke's interests were almost as versatile as those of his earlier compatriot, Francis Bacon. But his character was far above that of the Elizabethan philosopher. Locke was a man completely dedicated to the service of his fellow men. Like Bacon, he went into politics; but unlike Bacon, he was an honest politician. Through the recommendation of Ashley, who had become Lord Chancellor, he secured a post on the board that administered the affairs of the crown colony of Carolina. He helped to draft a liberal constitution for the colony, emphasizing a program of political, social, and religious tolerance.

And then came a series of blows. In his late thirties he developed the symptoms of his family disease. For over thirty years he was racked with a cough that gradually sapped his strength. But not his sense of duty. He worked faithfully, under the aegis of Ashley, until the chancellor fell into disfavor with his king. Ashley, now known as the Earl of Shaftesbury, had been one of the prime factors in the evolution of the British government from autocracy toward democracy. The merchants had begun to encroach upon the power of the monarch. Shaftesbury was head of the mercantile party called the Whigs as against the king's party, known as the Tories.

The king, having become suspicious of Shaftesbury's influence with the liberal faction, removed the chancellor from his office and threw him into the Tower. Locke, an active worker among the liberals, escaped to France just in time to avoid a similar fate.

Shaftesbury was finally released from the Tower, and Locke was allowed to return from his exile. But both of them were marked men. Shaftesbury lived on for a while, only to die in disgrace; and Locke, who had resumed his teaching at Oxford, found himself surrounded by spies on every side. Word had reached the king that Locke was the author of a pamphlet advocating rebellion against tyranny. The spies, posing as students of his philosophy, tried to goad him into arguments that would betray his "disloyalty."

The philosopher, to avoid further trouble in England, escaped once more to the Continent. This time he went to Holland, the refuge of free thought. The spies reported to the king that Locke had "vanished into thin air." Actually he was concealed in the house of a friendly physician at Amsterdam. Here he lived unmolested, like Spinoza, while he elaborated his blueprint for a better world.

IV

The keynote of Locke's philosophy may be summarized in a few words—the conquest of prejudice through common sense. What the world needs above everything else, he said, is the ability to think clearly. We must submit logic to reason. We must make our words express clearly what we think. Take, for example, the word "hole." "To make a gun," said an Irishman, "procure a hole and pour metal around it." But this absurdity is the result of false logic, poor reasoning, a shabby misuse of our language. The word "hole" may mean a number of things; a hollow place in a solid body, an excavation, a figurative flaw (I put a hole into his argument), a predicament (I got myself into a fine hole), a narrow channel, a deep place in a river (they bathed in a swimming hole), and so on. Be careful, said Locke, in the use of your language. Like Socrates, he declared that the right thoughts can come only through the right usage of words. "The ill use of words," he observed, "results in errors and obscurity, mistakes and confusion . . . There is some reason to doubt whether language, as it has been employed, has contributed more to the improvement or hindrance of reason . . ."

And reason, said Locke, consists of two parts: first, an inquiry as to what things we *know;* second, an investigation as to those things that we *believe.* The first part deals with certainties; the second, with probabilities.

But since probabilities are not certainties, we must never impose our own beliefs upon others. The most reasonable attitude between man and man is one of "mutual charity and forbearance." There is no reason why men cannot "maintain peace and common offices of humanity and friendship in the diversity of opinions." Don't fight about your different governments or creeds. Try to reason with your fellows, and then allow them to reason their opinions out for themselves. "We shall do well not to treat others as obstinate and perverse because they will not renounce their own and receive our opinions, [especially] when it is more than probable that we are no less obstinate in not embracing some of theirs." There is no one who, in our state of human fallibility, has a right to set himself up as the sole measure of truth. "For where is the man that has uncontestable evidence of the truth of all that he holds, or of the falsehood of all that he condemns; or can say that he has completely examined [and understood] all his own or other men's opinions?" Our intolerance may be due not so much to the other fellow's as to our own ignorance. At best, it is due to our misunderstanding of one another's words. Therefore, we must learn to express our meaning correctly, to distinguish clearly between opinions and facts, and to practice tolerance toward one another. "There is reason to believe that if men were better instructed themselves, they would be less imposing on others." Live and let live. Be bold to think your own thoughts, but beware of shackling the thoughts of other men.

In short, we must aim at co-operative toleration. It is only through the mutual respect for, and the mutual understanding of, one another's views that we can hope to approximate the truth. Instead of reasoning one against the other, said Locke, let us learn to reason together.

And now, having glanced at the theoretical basis of Locke's philosophy, let us examine its practical application. First we shall consider his discussion of ethics, or the conduct of the individual; and then we shall take up his theory of politics, or the relationship among individuals and among nations.

Ethics: All of us, said Locke, have an instinct for justice —a God-given feeling for one another's rights. This feeling has been implanted in us from birth; it is one of the divine laws of our human existence.

These divine laws are as decisively subject to demonstration as are the principles of mathematics. "The idea of a Supreme Being, infinite in power, goodness and wisdom, whose workmanship we are, and upon whom we depend, and the idea of ourselves as understanding, rational and compassionate creatures . . . would, if duly considered and pursued, establish morality as an exact science . . . wherein, I doubt not, but from self-evident propositions, the measures of right and wrong might be made out."

Among Locke's "self-evident propositions" of right and wrong—to mention but a few—are the following:

All men are born free and equal. Hence no man has a right to look down upon his fellow men.

It is our solemn duty to help rather than to injure one another.

Contracts, verbal as well as written, are sacred; they must never be terminated except by mutual consent.

Parents have a right to control their children, just as they have a duty to educate them—but only until the children have arrived at the age of reason.

The goods of the earth are common to all. They may become the private property of one who has "mixed his labor" with them, *provided* "there is enough and as good left for others."

Here we have a summary of the moral precepts of all the great philosophical and religious systems. But Locke has introduced a new and important note into this universal code. He has translated an ethical ideal into a scientific law—the "intuitive law of divine justice." The individual has a double duty to society: first, to appropriate nothing for which he has not labored; and second, to take only his fair share so that others, too, may enjoy their share.

Good conduct, in other words, is that kind of behavior which leads "toward happiness and fromward pain." But the scientific moral law requires that the conduct of the individual should lead *to the greatest happiness of the greatest number and to the lessening of pain for all.*

Politics. Locke's ideas on politics are a direct outcome of his observations on ethics. Government, he declares, should be a compact of mutual consent to provide the greatest happiness for the greatest number. "Our reason teaches all mankind, who will but consult it, that being all equal and independent, no one ought to harm another in his life, health, liberty, or possessions."

Thus speaks the father of modern democracy. Government is not an imposition of the sovereign upon his subjects, but a trust between man and man. The ultimate power is not vested in the scepter of the king; it remains in the hands of the people.

And therefore the rights of the individual are to be protected rather than restricted by the state. The ruler has neither the divine authority nor the moral justification to set himself up as his brother's keeper. All men are equal in the eyes of God, and must be so regarded under the political laws of the government. It is the height of folly, asserts Locke, for men to rely upon kings (or dictators) in order to protect themselves against one another. It is as if "they protected themselves against polecats and foxes but are content, nay think it safety, to be devoured by lions."

The only safety, then, is for men to unite themselves into governments based upon the consent of the majority. Such governments are to function *for* the people, and their expenses are to be borne *by* the people. But the taxes must be raised only with the consent of the majority.

This sort of government by the majority of the people, declared Locke, should allow freedom of speech, of thought, of election, and of religious worship. And in order that it may be prevented from becoming too arbitrary, this democratic government should be regulated by a system of checks and balances. The government should therefore be divided into three distinct branches: the legislative, the executive, and the judicial. And of these three branches, the legislative should be supreme.

This actually is a blueprint for our present-day government in America and in those other countries which try to follow our system of democracy. A government of this type, said Locke, must never be aggressive; but it must be ever on the alert for its defense.

The political philosophy of John Locke, we must remember, was presented almost three hundred years ago to a world in which democracy was only a dream. It was the seed out of which grew our own Declaration of Independence a hundred years later. It was not Jefferson, but Locke, who first asserted the right of every man to his life, liberty, and pursuit of happiness, and the duty of every man to elect his own government.

But Locke's philosophy went beyond the democratic government of individual states. It outlined the principles of international as well as of national government. The day of real progress, he said, will arise when nations as well as individuals are united in a social contract of *political interdependence*. The trend of human freedom is from national to international democracy—from the cessation of duels among individuals to the abolition of wars among nations.

V

When a king attempts to enforce his autocratic power, declared Locke, the people have not only the right but the duty to resist such usurpation—without bloodshed, if possible. Locke lived to see—indeed, he helped to bring about—such a bloodless revolution. King James II had tried to emulate King Charles I. He had set himself up against the will of the people, and the people decided that the king must go.

Not, however, by violence. At first the king disregarded the people's demand for his abdication. But the people had discovered a new weapon: civil disobedience. This pre-Gandhi method of "peaceful warfare" compelled the king to see the light. His rashness yielded to reason. He gave up his throne (1688) without the firing of a single shot.

The new king, William of Orange, was imported from Holland, the country which had sheltered Locke during his exile. The philosopher was now a free man. The next few years were the most prolific of his entire career. "My life really began at sixty." He sat on the Board of Trade, helped to found the Bank of England, organized the education of the masses, and wrote a number of books and pamphlets defending the rights of labor, the freedom of the press, and the democratic as against the autocratic way of life.

He remained a teacher to the end. He loved to be among "young and eager minds." He preferred the hopefulness of youth to the disillusion of old age. "Two groaning old people make but an uncomfortable concert."

Though he lived to the age of seventy-two, he refused to grow old. "My body—the cottage in which I live—is becoming shaky. The wind is beginning to blow in through the cracks. But the tenant within—my soul—is as young as ever, and eager to move into a new and better home."

PART
5

The "Enlightened" Philosophers

CHAPTER XX

Jean Jacques Rousseau (1712–1778)

ROUSSEAU was a philosopher who tried to abolish philosophy in order to save humanity. "Ever since learned men have appeared," he wrote, "honest men have disappeared." He therefore advocated a return to nature, the life of the "noble savage" as against that of the "depraved civilized man," the superiority of goodness over cleverness, of intuition over instruction, and of the emotions over the mind. Reason, he declared, inclines a man to atheism; but instinct leads him to God.

The philosophy of Rousseau was a mixture of Lao-tse's return to nature, Buddha's compassion for the poor, Isaiah's search for social justice, St. Augustine's progress from licentiousness to love, and Locke's blueprint for a better world. In addition to all these influences, however, Rousseau brought to his work the imagination of a poet and the sympathy of a gentle soul.

II

Rousseau told the story of his life in his *Confessions*—a fascinating texture of fiction and fact. He depicted himself as a scoundrel because he was anxious to shock the public. So let us take his autobiography with a generous pinch of salt.

He was born at Geneva (1712) of poor parents. He lost his mother in his infancy. His father, a fanatical Calvinist, had a twofold career—he was a watchmaker and a dancing master. Apparently he cared very little for his child's education. Jean Jacques left school at twelve, and ran away from home at sixteen. Drifting from town to town in an effort to find himself, he came to a monastery at Turin, where he asked to be converted to Catholicism. It was a physical rather than spiritual hunger, he confessed, that had thrown him into the arms of the Church. "My holy deed was at bottom the act of a bandit."

From Catholicism he turned back to Protestantism; and then he abandoned all organized religion, to live alone "with his conscience and his God."

But for a time his conscience failed to serve him any better than his creed. He got various jobs and stole from his employers, and he fell into dissolute company, male and female.

He worked as the secretary of the French ambassador to Venice, only to be paid in compliments instead of cash. He appealed to the French Government for his wages, and for a long time the authorities paid no heed to him.

This "national disgrace" turned Rousseau against "the organized tyranny of the powerful and the rich." At long last, he said, he had found a definite purpose in life—the overthrow of all government that operated without the consent of the governed.

To show his contempt for the conventions, he settled down (1745) to a life of unwedded domesticity. He entered into a "family relationship" with Thérèse de Vasseur, a servant at his hotel in Paris. He lived with her steadily, though not faithfully, for the rest of his life. He had five children by her, and took them to the foundling hospital right after their birth.

What he discovered in his mistress to attract him, nobody could tell. She was a slattern with an ugly face and an ignorant mind. He taught her to scribble her name; but beyond that, she could neither write nor read. She couldn't even remember the names of the months, or add up her simplest accounts.

And her character was as low as her mentality. She drank, lied, cheated and stole, and ran after the stable boys. "I like them," she said, "because they're my kind." Perhaps Rousseau's attraction toward her was motivated by pity rather than love.

He had a fellow feeling for the distressed and the dispossessed.

At any rate, he put up with his "simple barbarian." After all, she was the ideal of his philosophical dream—the savage who couldn't think evil because she couldn't think at all. Though faithless and dishonest and uncouth, she was an "unspoiled child of Nature" who attended to his needs and provided him with the opportunity to develop his philosophical thought.

III

Rousseau was almost forty when he entered upon his philosophical career. The Academy of Dijon had offered a prize for the best essay on the subject, Have the Arts and Sciences Benefited Mankind? Rousseau took the negative and won the prize. Smarting under a series of insults at the hands of the educated elite, he maintained the thesis that culture is an evil rather than a good. Many of the world's injustices, he wrote, are due to the fact that we have allowed our minds to outstrip our hearts. The wider our knowledge of the world, the greater our thirst to possess it. Hence the ambition of the educated classes leads to the enslavement of the ignorant masses.

The fame he achieved from the publication of this essay had a sobering effect upon him. He withdrew from society, assumed the simple life, and sold his watch. "I shall no longer be a slave to time," he said.

He wrote a second essay—*Discourse on Inequality*—in which he elaborated the ideas of the first. "Man," he said, "is naturally good. It is only his artificial environment that makes him bad." The worst evil of this unnatural environment is the private ownership of property. "The first man who, having enclosed a piece of land, bethought himself of saying 'this is mine,' and found people simple enough to believe him—this man was the founder of all oppressive government."

The only remedy for this "evil," declared Rousseau, is "to

abandon civilization." In their natural state, all men are good. Let a savage have something to eat, and he will be a friend to all his fellow savages. But once he has begun to be educated, he will develop hungers beyond his necessity for food; and he will become envious, aggressive, hateful, spiteful, and eager for a fight. Far better to have a world of peaceful savages, said Rousseau, than a world of civilized warriors.

At bottom, Rousseau was opposed not so much to civilization as to its evil by-products. Like Locke, he was anxious to build a better world for a happier race. He outlined the features of this better world—an exaggerated form of Locke's ideal democracy—in a number of books: a novel, a treatise on education, an essay on religion, and various tracts on history, politics, and ethics.

These books—especially *The New Héloise*, *Emile*, and *The Social Contract*—were destined to serve as a springboard for the French Revolution. They created the fashion for more than two centuries of radical thought.

Briefly summarized, the philosophy of Rousseau may be reduced to two simple themes: the goodness of God, and the equality of man.

God, said Rousseau, is the power for good. "How do I know this? Because I feel it in my heart." The promptings of the heart, declared Rousseau, are clearer than the reasons of the mind. Our emotions of awe and mystery, our sense of compassion for one another, our aspiration toward the beautiful, our instinct for the right, our urge for service, and our joy at the rising and the setting of the sun—all these facts are clear proofs of God's existence and beneficence. "Ah madame," he wrote in one of his letters, "sometimes in the privacy of my study, with my hands pressed tight over my eyes and in the darkness of the night, I think there is no God. But look yonder: the coming of the day, as the sun scatters the mists that cover the earth and reveals the glittering landscape, disperses at the same moment every cloud from my soul. I find my faith again, and my

God, and my belief in His goodness. I admire and adore Him, and I prostrate myself in His presence."

If we listen to God with our heart, we must acknowledge one religion for all, since he speaks to us all in one language—the glory of nature. Heaven is not reserved for the members of any one church—it is the heritage of the entire human race.

So let us follow the guidance of the heart, declared Rousseau, and all men will be united in a single religion. A religion of eternal punishment for none, of ultimate salvation for all. A creed of natural kindliness, universal tolerance, freedom from dogma, and friendly understanding among neighbors and strangers alike.

This "new religion of the heart" exploded like a bombshell among the conservative leaders of France. The rulers of the court as well as the dignitaries of the church assailed him for his idea of an impartial God. For each of them believed that he and his sect alone had found the one true road to salvation. Rousseau had become an object of hatred because of his desire to harmonize the world under a single faith.

But even more explosive than his religious faith was his political creed. The trouble with most governments, said Rousseau, is that they are founded upon a basis of social inequality. The division of society into classes, the unfair distribution of property, the uneven dispensation of justice, the slavish submission to "divine" right and aristocratic privilege—all these evil practices can be abolished if only we realize that "all men are born free." The problem, then, is "to find a form of association which will defend and protect the person and the goods of every associate, and in which every one, while uniting himself with all the others, may still obey himself alone, and remain as free as before." Rousseau calls the agreement for such a combination of free men the "social contract." In this contract, "the rights will be the same for all, and hence no one will have any interest in making his own rights burdensome to others."

Although Rousseau's political theories paved the way for

communist dictatorship, while Locke's showed the way to democratic leadership, both men's theories called for a government based upon the free and friendly collaboration of the entire citizenry. "The government cannot impose upon its citizens any fetters"—or confer upon them any favors—"that are injurious to the community." Such an ideal government will reflect the "general will" of the governed. It will be a corporation into which "every member will be admitted as an indivisible part of the whole." It will have no preferred stock for anybody, but a common stock of equal justice for all.

No preferred stock, and no preferred property. "The state, in relation to its members, is master of all their goods." For the state—that is, the collective will of the people—has the sole right to weave the threads of the individual interests into the pattern of the common good. *Vox populi, vox dei*—the voice of the people is the voice of God.

But, concluded Rousseau on a pessimistic note, a government of political and economic equality such as outlined in the social contract is possible only for a city of angels. "So perfect a government is not for men." In this imperfect world of ours, Rousseau's utopia, like Plato's Republic, is likely to remain a dream for many years to come.

In its own day, *The Social Contract* was met with an avalanche of fury. Rousseau was branded as a scoundrel. The French king ordered his arrest. He escaped to Geneva, where the Democratic Council burned his book and threatened his life. He took refuge in Germany, where an angry mob almost lynched him. He fled to England, and there he found a haven of pity amidst the hurricane of hate.

By this time, Rousseau's suffering had affected his reason. He was tormented by a persecution mania, and he suspected that even the men who had befriended him were trying to put him to death.

Finally his fear of being murdered impelled him to commit suicide. "The minds of men are against me," he said just before he died, "because I teach them to listen to their hearts."

CHAPTER XXI

Voltaire (François Marie Arouet)
(1694–1778)

WHEN ROUSSEAU'S *Discourse on Inequality* was published, he sent a copy of the essay to Voltaire. And Voltaire replied: "I have received your new book against mankind, and I thank you for it. Never was such human cleverness employed to reveal such human stupidity. One longs, after reading your book, to walk on all fours. But as I have lost that habit for more than sixty years, I'm afraid I shall find it impossible to resume it."

This reply hurt Rousseau to the quick. It marked the beginning of a bitter rivalry between the two philosophers. Rousseau accused Voltaire of wasting his talents on his dramas—"the stage is nothing but a school for lechery." And Voltaire ridiculed Rousseau for espousing the cause of the "noble savage who in reality is an ignoble idiot." The two men exchanged a barrage of abusive epithets for a number of years. The "mischievous madman"—Voltaire's name for Rousseau—and the "lofty genius with the lowly soul"—Rousseau's sobriquet for Voltaire—could never see eye to eye. Except for one important thing: they were both consumed with a passion for the underdog. In spite of their differences, the naturalism of Rousseau and the rationalism of Voltaire served as the double mainspring of the French Revolution.

II

His contemporaries called Voltaire "the laughing philosopher." In reply to this, Voltaire said: "I laugh to keep myself from going mad."

And there was much in the world of that period to drive people to madness. The princes oppressed the peasants; the rich trampled over the poor; the workers slaved to create beauty for their masters; and the youngsters were raised merely as fuel for the incessant wars. Diderot, one of the French contemporaries of Voltaire, has given us a vivid picture of the times. Louis XIV is showing off his palace at Versailles to the ghost of his grandfather, Henri IV. The old king looks at the palace and shakes his head:

"You are right, my son. It *is* magnificent. But I should like to show you the hovels of the peasants at Gonesse (the country surrounding Versailles). These peasants sleep on straw; and many of them haven't a roof over their heads or bread in their mouths."

It was Voltaire's genius—and sorrow—to see both sides of the picture. And it was his bitterness that aroused the whirlwind of his laughter. His jests were spiced with the salt of his tears.

His entire life seemed like a sardonic jest. He was so puny at birth that the doctors expected him to die within a few days. Yet he lived to be over eighty. He dedicated his life to the task of ridiculing despotism and superstition out of the world. And he completed with his cynicism the job that Rousseau had begun with his censure. When Louis XVI, just before his execution, looked at the works of Rousseau and Voltaire, he exclaimed: "These are the two men who have destroyed France!" What he meant was that these two men had destroyed the tyranny of France.

And Voltaire, like Rousseau, paid a high price for his devotion to human freedom. He suffered vituperation, exile, imprisonment, the suppression of his books, the loss of his health, and even occasional attacks upon his life. Yet, unlike Rousseau, he retained his sanity and won every battle against him with the weapon of his caustic tongue. As the Danish critic, Georg Brandes, has observed: "Voltaire annihilated with his laughter his own sufferings as well as many of the stupidities of his day."

He was perhaps the homeliest man in Paris, thin as a skeleton, long-nosed, beady-eyed, pock-marked, and forever on the alert for a battle of the tongue. Yet the women idolized him; he had won a reputation for battles of another sort. Though sickly for the greater part of his life, he was a dynamo of energy. Once, at a rehearsal of his play *Mérope* he tried to inspire the leading lady to speedier action. "But," she complained, "to act as you demand, I'd have to have the Devil in me." "Precisely," retorted Voltaire, "you've got to have the Devil in you to succeed in any of the arts."

This was the secret of his success. *"Voltaire avait le diable au corps,"* Sainte Beuve observed. Indeed, he was a combination of the Devil, Diogenes, and Aristophanes, with a generous dash of St. Francis thrown in to soften the spice of his philosophical dish.

In other words, Voltaire was a living paradox. His father, too, was somewhat of a paradox—he belonged to the Jansenists, an unconventional Protestant-Catholic sect to which the conventional Catholics and Protestants were violently opposed. Voltaire thus grew up in an atmosphere of rebellion against the popular religions of the day. Asked, as a boy, what trade he would choose when he grew up, he said: "My trade will be to say what I think."

His insistence upon the free expression of his thought resulted in a prison term at the Bastille when he was still a young man. Here is how it happened:

At the death of Louis XIV (in 1715), the ruling power fell into the hands of a regent. When the regent sold half the horses at the royal stables, Voltaire remarked that it would have been wiser to dismiss half the asses at the royal court. And then he followed this remark with a lampoon against the regent. He was repaid with a lodging in a Bastille cell.

During his stay in prison, he wrote a brilliant epic on the life of Henry of Navarre. Shortly after his release, he attended a dinner party given in his honor at the Duc de Sully's château. He was still shaky on his feet, the result of a recent attack of smallpox. But his tongue was as nimble as ever. At the height of the festivities, one of the favorites at the court, the Chevalier de Rohan, asked in a loud whisper, "Who is this man"—pointing to Voltaire—"who talks so boisterously?" "My lord," replied Voltaire, "he is a man who bears no great name, but who honors the name he has." The Chevalier, offended at the commoner's "arrogance," hired a gang of ruffians to attack him at night. "But," he cautioned them, "be careful not to hit his head. Something good may come out of it yet."

Half-dead and in a towering rage, Voltaire limped his way to the Duc de Sully's château and asked him to report the matter to the police. But the Duc's only reply was laughter. It was a capital joke, he said, to see a poet thrashed by a peer.

As soon as he recovered from the assault, Voltaire challenged Rohan to a duel. But the Chevalier appealed to his cousin, the Minister of Police, to protect him. Once again Voltaire was arrested and sent to the Bastille. Upon his second release, he was ordered into exile in England.

The French nobility witnessed his departure with "outbursts of laughter." And the young philosopher was determined to meet them with their own weapon. "We shall see whose laughter is the loudest and the best."

III

Voltaire was thirty-two when he arrived in England. He found it easy to master the English language, but he retained his French accent and his French clothes. One day he was jeered by a mob for his "outlandish" attire. But he knew how to meet the situation. Mounting a bench, he cried: "My dear friends, please bear with me. Am I not already unlucky enough to have been born a Frenchman instead of an Englishman?" At this sally, the mobsters changed their jeers into cheers.

Voltaire loved England, especially its freedom of speech and its intellectual alertness—this was about forty years after the English Revolution of 1688. "The English," he wrote, "are a civilized nation . . . Not long ago a distinguished group were discussing the question, who was the greatest man—Caesar, Alexander, Tamerlane or Cromwell? Some one answered that it was Isaac Newton. And he was right: for it is to him who masters our minds by the force of truth, and not to those who enslave them by violence, that we owe our devotions."

He stayed in England for three years; and he recorded his impressions of that country in a series of "Philosophical Letters." These letters, contrasting the "independence" of the English as against the "enslavement" of the French, provided one of the initial sparks for the fire of the French Revolution.

Voltaire returned to France after an exile of three years. For a time he remained in hiding. But finally he wrote to the regent, asking leave "to trail his chains in Paris." The leave was granted, on one condition—that the philosopher would hold his tongue. Voltaire made the promise, and forgot it almost as soon as he became a free man again.

IV

It was only two years after his reinstatement in Paris that he got into his next difficulty. An actress whom he had greatly admired, Adrienne Lecouvreur, had just died. The church authorities insisted upon her burial, along with that of other "disreputable people," in unhallowed ground. Voltaire criticized this action in a scathing poem. Threatened once more with arrest, he escaped to a village in Normandy.

But this was not the end of his persecution. His *Philosophical Letters* were published without his consent. The magistrates ordered the book to be burned "in the palace courtyard . . . as being scandalous, contrary to religion, good morals, and the respect due to the ruling powers." Voltaire became once more a hounded man.

This time he accepted an offer from one of his female admirers, the Marquise du Châtelet, to take refuge at her château of Cirey. The castle was situated on the French border close to Lorraine, whither he could escape in the event of pursuit by the gendarmes. Here he lived with his hostess and mistress for fifteen years, the happiest period of his life.

And one of the most scintillating periods in the intellectual history of France. The Marquise was married to a professional soldier who was away with his regiment when Voltaire took possession of his castle and his wife. In those days it was not unusual for a woman to enjoy a husband and two lovers—the husband for her material comfort, the first lover for her physical needs, and the second lover for her mental improvement. This was the sort of *ménage à quatre*—one woman and three men —at Cirey; and it worked without any undue jealousy among the four.

But the two who derived the greatest pleasure out of the arrangement were Voltaire and the Marquise. A student of Latin, a brilliant mathematician and essayist of unusual charm, she spent many an exciting hour conversing and studying with her philosopher.

And now and then engaging in bitter controversy. They were both competing for a prize offered by the Academy of Science for the best essay on the Nature of Fire. And, much to Voltaire's chagrin, the Marquise carried off the prize. He greeted the announcement with an outburst of ridicule that almost put an end to their friendship.

Yet, in spite of their quarrels, they adored each other. The Marquise regarded Voltaire as "the finest ornament of France." And Voltaire esteemed the Marquise as "a great man whose only fault is that she was born a woman."

And thus they insulted and worshiped each other, and worked together in a chemical laboratory which they had built at Cirey, and offered shelter to rebellious souls, and produced private plays to the most brilliant audiences in France, and gave sumptuous dinners spiced with discussions on poetry, science, philosophy, politics, music, and art.

And it was at Cirey that Voltaire began to pour out a veritable cascade of philosophical romances, each of them a jewel of wisdom in a setting of wit. He wrote almost a hundred volumes, and the quality of his output was even more amazing than the quantity.

He worked at a breathless pace, like a man who lived on borrowed time. "We must feed the flame that God has entrusted to us before it dies down." At times his output averaged almost fifteen thousand words a day. And at night he read his manuscripts aloud to his friends.

Let us join one of these readings at Cirey. Note the vivacious little figure of the philosopher, the haggard face, the whimsical upcurve at the corners of the mouth, the nervous hands, the dancing eyes. He acts out every part as he reads. A born mimic, with the cynicism of a devil and the soul of a saint.

He is reading one of his philosophical romances, *L'Ingenu* —*The Child of Nature*—a work not unlike some of Rousseau's books which Voltaire at one time had so flippantly dismissed. *L'Ingenu* is a whimsical satire upon the illogical pretensions of the civilized man as compared with the logical simplicity of the savage. A group of explorers have brought a Huron Indian to Paris; and an abbé tries to convert him to Christianity. He gives him a copy of the Bible, which the Huron reads with the greatest interest. The Indian decides to become a Christian and insists upon circumcision as well as baptism. "For I do not find in your Bible a single man who was not circumcised. It is therefore evident that I must become a good Jew before I can become a good Christian." When this matter is explained to him, though not to his satisfaction, he allows himself to be baptized and asks for the next step. He is told to confess his sins to the abbé. Having done this, he drags his confessor into the penitent's seat. "Now," he declares, "it is your turn to confess to me. For the Bible distinctly commands, 'Confess your sins to one another!'"

After this episode, which only adds to his perplexity over the "antics of civilization," the Huron falls in love with a Frenchwoman. He proposes to her and she accepts. Their friends prepare to get the notaries, priests, and witnesses and to draw up the contracts and the dispensations for the wedding. "Are all these precautions necessary?" asks the Huron.

"Yes, indeed! Marriage must be protected in our civilized society."

"In that case," observes the Huron, "your civilized society must be a mob of scoundrels!"

And so on and on. Voltaire continued to amuse and stimulate his audiences with his satires. His philosophical motto was *rire et faire rire*—to laugh and to make laugh. In another of his stories, *Zadig*, Voltaire concludes that "the human species is a parcel of insects devouring one another on a little atom of clay." In still another of his fantasies, *Micromégas—Littlebig*—he tells about two travelers from other planets who come to visit the Earth. One of these travelers is a 500,000-foot giant from Sirius and the other is a 1000-foot pigmy from Saturn. As they stroll through the Mediterranean, a little puddle that barely wets the Sirian's heels, the two visitors converse with each other.

SIRIAN: How many senses do your people possess?
SATURNIAN: Only seventy-two—hardly enough to give us more than a smattering of knowledge.
SIRIAN: And how long do you live?
SATURNIAN: Just a trifle over fifteen thousand years—a mere point in eternity.

In the course of their stroll, they pick up a ship which the Sirian balances upon his thumbnail. The human passengers appear no bigger than microbes. Bending over them like a cloud, he addresses them: "O intelligent atoms, you must be supremely happy because you are so extremely small. Having hardly any bodies, you must be all soul."

"We enjoy little happiness," replies one of the passengers, "but we do a great deal of mischief . . . At this very moment there are a hundred thousand men, covered with hats, slaying an equal number of their fellow men, who are covered with turbans."

"Scoundrels!" exclaims the Sirian. "I have a good mind to trample the entire nest of such ridiculous assassins under my feet!"

"Don't give yourself the trouble," replies the passenger. "The soldiers are doing this job themselves . . . Yet it is not the soldiers who are to blame but their barbarian rulers who, sitting idly in their palaces, issue orders for the murder of a million men, and then solemnly thank Heaven for their success . . ."

And thus they spent their evenings at Cirey, enjoying the bittersweet laughter of Voltaire, and absorbing the ideas that were to shatter the foundations of the Bourbon throne. The earth, observed Voltaire, is perhaps a lunatic asylum for those who have gone mad on the other planets.

V

Voltaire's happy interlude at Cirey ended with the death of the Marquise. Fortunately for his peace of mind, he received an invitation to come and live at the palace of the Prussian emperor, Frederick the Great.

Frederick, a man of enlightened ideas, found a congenial companion in Voltaire. And Voltaire enjoyed the friendship of the emperor and, it must be confessed, the lavishness of his purse.

For a while they lived in comparative harmony. But Voltaire had enemies at court, men who were jealous of the royal favors he received. The emperor, who regarded himself as

somewhat of a poet, asked Voltaire to correct some of his manuscripts. On one such occasion it was reported to Frederick that
Voltaire had remarked: "Here's some more of the dirty linen
His Majesty wants me to launder." At about the same time,
it was whispered to Voltaire that the emperor had said: "I shall
use him for another year. The way to handle an orange is to
squeeze out the juice and to fling away the rind."

Finally the trouble came to a head. The emperor accused
the philosopher of a shady business deal. And Voltaire replied
in a pamphlet that accused the emperor of disloyalty to his
friends. The pamphlet was burned by the public hangman. Voltaire was sent to jail, and after his release he was ordered to
move on.

He was sixty now—a man without a country. "I find no
more liberty in Germany than in France."

VI

He now took refuge in Geneva. Here he found complete
freedom and produced some of his best work. He signed his
letters "Voltaire the Swiss" and spent much of his money on
building houses for workers. "By selling these houses at cost,
I am ruining myself. But a man could not ruin himself in a more
decent cause." He set up workshops which he managed on a
basis of the highest possible wages and the lowest possible
profit. And he instilled in the workers a sense of dignity and
tolerance toward one another. "In my village," he remarked,
"nobody notices that there are various creeds. They all sub-
scribe to the religion of a friendly human race under one God."

Voltaire himself had developed a hunger for God—the impartial creator and protector of all mankind. He dedicated himself as a priest of this universal faith. He expressed this faith
in a flood of articles and books published under different names.
And the recurring theme song of these publications was,
Ecrasez l'infame! (Crush the infamy!) Destroy the madness of

superstition and sectarianism, and enthrone in their place a religion without ritual or controversy or hate.

And the Bible of this religion—here we find another echo of Rousseau—is to be the Book of Nature. This is the only book that can reveal the majesty of God. "The splendor of creation reveals the Creator . . . Nobody can doubt that a well painted landscape—a mere reproduction of Nature—is the work of a skilled artist. If the copy springs from an intelligent mind, can the original be a matter of chance?"

The only true religion, declares Voltaire, is to worship God by doing our allotted work in this terrestrial paradise—the cosmic garden which it is our business to cultivate in harmony with one another's plans.

And this brings us to the most famous of Voltaire's works, his *Candide*. In this book the philosopher points out that what is wrong with the world is man's inhumanity to man. Then he goes on to explain how we can right this wrong.

This book, like many of Voltaire's other works, is a bitter satire delivered under a jester's mask. Jesters, as Gilbert K. Chesterton reminds us, are often the most serious people in the world. The hero of the book, a rich young nobleman, is a pupil of Pangloss, professor of metaphysicotheologicocosmonigology. "It can be easily demonstrated," declares Pangloss, "that this is the best of all possible worlds"—a parody on the philosophy of Leibniz—"and that there is nothing we could or should do to improve it." For example, continues Pangloss, our legs have been designed to fit into stockings . . . pigs have been made to supply us with pork . . . and fleas have been created to give us the pleasure of scratching. "And therefore," maintains Pangloss, "it is foolish to assert merely that all is well. The truth is, that all is for the best."

While Candide is listening to his professor's lecture, his father's castle is attacked by a Bulgarian army. Candide is captured and drafted into the army.

One day he decides, as a free man in this "best of all possible worlds," to go for a walk outside the camp. He is caught, court-martialed and whipped as he runs the gantlet of the regiment thirty-six times.

After a while he escapes from the army, only to learn that the enemy troops have murdered his parents and destroyed their castle. "But all this was necessary," explains Pangloss. "Out of our private suffering comes the public good."

To avoid further "personal suffering for the general good," Candide escapes to Lisbon. He arrives there just in time to be caught in an earthquake that destroys thirty thousand souls. "How happy the dead must feel that the others have survived!" exclaims Pangloss.

Candide flees from the earthquake into the hands of the Inquisition—"another example of justice in the best of all worlds." And escaping from the flames of the Inquisition, he sails to a Dutch colony where the Negro slaves "enjoy" a bitter life to make sugar for their white masters. One of the slaves, he observes, has lost an arm and a leg. "How," he inquires, "did this happen?" "When we work at the sugar plantation," explains the crippled slave, "they punish us for losing a finger by cutting off an arm. And they punish us for trying to escape by cutting off a leg."

And thus Candide proceeds from misfortune to misfortune, and tries to fit his own and other people's experiences into the picture of "the best of all possible worlds." And the harder he tries the more bewildered he becomes. "Do you believe," he asks a fellow traveler on one of his voyages, "that men have always massacred one another as they do today, that they have always been liars, cheats, traitors, ingrates, brigands, scoundrels, thieves, gluttons, drunkards, misers, murderers, graspers, fanatics and fools?"

"Do you believe," inquires his fellow passenger, "that hawks have always eaten doves?"

"Without a doubt," replies Candide.

"Well, then, if hawks have always retained their nature, why should you imagine that men have changed theirs?"

And thus debating about the characteristics of the human race, they arrive at their destination. Candide settles down as a farmer on a little plot of land. Pangloss is at his side, still trying hard to prove his point to his pupil. "There is a chain of events in this best of all possible worlds," he declares. "For if you had not been kicked out of a castle . . . if you had not escaped from an earthquake . . . if you had not fallen into the hands of the Inquisition . . . and if you had not suffered all the other tribulations . . . you would not now be here eating preserved citrons and pistachio nuts."

"All this may be very well," replies Candide. "But let us cultivate our garden."

This is the crux of Voltaire's philosophy. Cultivate the garden of this world. Don't be satisfied to leave it in the wild state in which you have found it. *Ecrasez l'infame.* Crush out the weeds and the pests that endanger the healthy flowering of the garden. Develop your allotted piece of land and don't cast greedy eyes upon your neighbor's lot. Eat your bread by the sweat of your labor, bend to your plowing, be patient for the harvest, and help build for your fellow workers houses of blessing and chapels of peace.

Just before the end of his life, Voltaire summarized his philosophical creed in a few words: "I die loving my friends, not hating my enemies, detesting superstition and adoring God."

CHAPTER XXII

Immanuel Kant (1724–1804)

HE WAS so precise in his habits that his neighbors looked upon him as their animated timepiece. Every afternoon exactly at three-thirty he left his house for his daily stroll. But one day he failed to appear. "Something very strange must have happened," they thought. Yet this strange interruption to his daily routine was nothing more than a book: Rousseau's *Emile*. For several days Kant interrupted his schedule in order to read and reread this book. He was delighted to find in Rousseau a fellow adventurer out of the darkness of disbelief. They were both aiming to find their way to God—Rousseau through his heart, and Kant through his mind. It was Rousseau that gave the final spur to the philosophy of Immanuel Kant.

II

This philosophy came to flower in a turbulent age—the age of the Seven Years' War, the French Revolution, and the Napoleonic madness. Yet Kant managed to weather the storm. "I am so small and unimportant, the winds pass over me without uprooting me like the higher growths." He was a quaint little fellow, about five feet tall, flat chest, protruding stomach, humped shoulders, head perched to one side, gray hat, gray coat, and gray cane tapping rhythmically toward the avenue of the lindens which the people of Koenigsberg had nicknamed The Philosopher's Walk. Trudging behind him, with an umbrella in hand to shelter his master against a sudden rainstorm, came Lampe, his faithful old servant who needed someone to protect *him* just as he protected Kant. It was for Lampe, as we shall see, that the philosopher was so anxious to create a religion and a God.

III

Kant was born at Koenigsberg, Prussia. Outside of a brief excursion as tutor in a neighboring village, he never left his native city physically, though mentally he ranged over the entire universe. His ancestry was Scotch-German. His father, a maker of leather straps, used them frequently upon his eleven children. "Spare the belt, and spoil the brat." His mother, an overstrict puritan, kept her children entangled in a web of rigorous ritualism. As a reaction against his early training, Kant stayed away from church throughout his adult life. Yet ho always felt a hunger to reach out, in his own unorthodox way, toward the divine.

This hunger led him to the study of the oriental philosophers, who exercised a profound influence upon him. Yet it was not until his reading of Rousseau that he was to find the key to his own speculation. For a number of years he had drifted in a sea of metaphysical doubt. "I have the fortune to be a lover of philosophy; but my mistress has shown me few favors as yet."

And his material progress was as slow as his intellectual development. He began his career in 1755 as private lecturer at the University of Koenigsberg. It took him fourteen years to rise to a professorship in logic and metaphysics. He was a quiet little hunchback with a timid voice that barely carried to the back seats in the classroom. He preferred, he said, to teach the students of medium ability. "The geniuses are in no need of my help, and the dunces are beyond all help." His more successful colleagues on the faculty remarked that he was indeed a mediocre teacher for mediocre minds.

An obscure teacher, two of whose sisters were housemaids;

nothing about the Kants to startle the world. Nobody expected him to create a sensation. He was described as a man who used "sesquipedalian words"—words six feet long—to express unimportant thoughts. One of his students remarked: "He carries us over a sea without shores in a vessel without sails." As a teacher he was beyond the depth of his pupils, and quite beyond their concern.

Or the concern of anybody else.

For nobody knew that there was a volcano of ideas seething within that modest little head. It was not until he had reached fifty-seven that his ideas erupted into the most stupendous philosophical system of modern times.

The work that so astounded the world consisted of three monumental books: *The Critique of Pure Reason, The Critique of Practical Reason,* and *The Critique of Judgment.* These three books may be roughly compared to a three-storied temple—a basement for discarded idols, an auditorium with stained glass windows for the transmission of a mystical light, and a dome which towers into the blue radiance of heaven.

Let us step into this temple.

IV

At first the light is obscure. Kant wrote in a heavy style difficult to understand. The very title of the first book—*The Critique of Pure Reason*—is professorial rather than popular. But we shall try to simplify both the title and the work.

The Critique of Pure Reason means a careful examination of reason in its pure state—that is, when our reason has been liberated from the observations of our senses. Pure reason is the reason of the mind unaided by the experience of the body. Most of our knowledge, maintains Kant, does not come through our senses. "General truths are clear and certain in themselves," regardless of any appearances that our imperfect vision may supply. An idiot observes the same world as a Shakespeare.

But only a Shakespeare can find in the world a pattern of beauty and sense.

The real world, in other words, is beyond our sensory observation. But it is within our intellectual comprehension. We can see the world with our inner eye. We can understand it without the help of our experience. "My question is," writes Kant, "what can we hope to achieve with the intellect when all the material and assistance of experience are taken away?" And he answers the question by asserting that we can hope to employ our intellect—that is, our reason—not merely as a receiver of impressions but as a creator of ideas.

Our reason, therefore, is not a bundle of observations dependent upon our *senses* but a vehicle of independent knowledge revealed through our *sense*. "How far we can advance independently of all experience is shown by the brilliant example of mathematics." No matter what we may see or hear to the contrary, it is absolutely certain that two plus two will always make four.

And so the mind is not a collector, but a director, of thought. It organizes the world, through its knowledge of mathematical and other absolute truths, into an intelligible unit. It enables us to transform chaos into order, random experiences into a patterned unit, individual perceptions into universal wisdom. And to grope from human wisdom to divine light.

Human wisdom, therefore, is *organization*—the ability to use eternal truths for the understanding and the ordering of our temporal affairs. Our wisdom enables us to depend less upon our senses and more upon our sense. Our senses show us a world of appearances, but our sense directs us to the reality behind the appearances—Kant called this reality the *thing-in-itself*. "Kant's greatest contribution to philosophy," declared Schopenhauer, "was his distinction between the *real* world—the thing-in-itself—and the *apparent* world of our senses."

The apparent world is like a jumble of bricks, iron, glass,

wood, and stone scattered over the ground. But the real world is a complete building, constructed out of these materials into a beautiful architectural unit. Our notions about what we observe, our sensory notions about man and nature, success and failure, life and death, these are mere illusions. They have little in common with reality. "It remains completely unknown to us what these may be by themselves and apart from the receptivity of our senses." The same is true of our notions about free will, the soul, and God. We can neither prove nor disprove their existence, owing to the limitations of our senses. We therefore have no right to be positive about any of these things. We shall never understand the exact nature of reality. Even our pure reason, when freed from the senses, can never explain to us the mystery of the world. "It remains completely unknown to us what the world may be by itself . . . We know nothing but our manner of perceiving it." We know merely that the world exists.

How did it come into existence? Has it been created by a supreme artist, and is it guided by a supreme mind? To these questions Kant replies, "There can be no answer dictated by pure reason."

V

But perhaps there is an answer of another kind, dictated by pure emotion? This is the answer Kant takes up in the second book, *The Critique of Practical Reason.* Having failed to find God in his mind, he tries, like Rousseau, to find him in his heart. Is not the existence of God indicated in our feeling for the right? Is there not perhaps an absolute principle of morality just as there is an absolute principle of mathematics? Kant's answer to this question is a hopeful yes. The moral principle, like the mathematical, is inborn. It is prior to, and independent of, our experience as derived from our senses. This moral principle is the basis of our religion, the demand of our conscience, the very center of our existence.

Good conduct is an absolute commandment from within. Mutual kindness is a *must*. We feel—and it is a feeling born with the birth of our body—that we are spiritually bound to one another. We know instinctively that we ought to do our duty. This mutual sense of duty, the feeling that cements the world into a concordant unit, not only guides our minds toward the harmonious procession of the stars, but prompts our hearts toward the proper adjustment of our conduct in all our human relationships.

"The starry heavens above, the moral law within"—these are the two aspects of the selfsame principle that leads our reason and our emotion to a better understanding of the world. The mathematics of the heavenly bodies and the ethics of our earthly existence are the expression of one divine law. The operations of this divine law may be summarized into a single word: God.

And thus, while the mind leads us to question the existence of God, the heart prompts us to declare it. The gentle philosopher, as Heine half-jestingly and half-seriously points out, "created this God of the Heart for the sake of his old servant, Lampe. Hitherto Immanuel Kant had appeared as a grim and inexorable iconoclast. He had stormed heaven, put the whole garrison to the sword, and left the Ruler of the World to swim senseless in his blood . . . And old Lampe stood by with his umbrella under his arm as a sorrowing spectator, and the sweat of anguish ran down his cheeks. Then Immanuel Kant was moved to pity and showed himself not only a great philosopher but a good man. 'Old Lampe,' he observed, 'must have a God, or else the poor man cannot be happy; and people really ought to be happy in this world. Practical common sense *requires* it. Very well, let practical reason guarantee it.'"

As usual, Heine concealed an aspect of the truth behind his comic mask. It *was* the kindness of Immanuel Kant that led him to postulate the existence of God. God *exists* because humanity *needs* Him. In this world of senseless injustice, aggression, and hate, there would be no place for happiness or hope without a Providence that patterned the whole into an ultimate unit of sense. The feeling of the heart is a safer guide than the logic of the head. For the heart, to paraphrase Pascal, has reasons of its own which the head can never understand.

And thus, if we cannot base our belief upon science, we can base it upon morals. Our ethical obligation—Kant calls it "the categorical imperative"—guides our conscience to a definite distinction between right and wrong, a definite divine law for the guidance of our human conduct. This categorical imperative points not only to the existence of God but to the operation of free will. For if we had no free will, we should have no conception of right and wrong, no moral obligation toward one another. And finally, the categorical imperative demonstrates the probability of life after death. For we follow the dictates of our conscience even without the hope of reward in this life. Why? Because we *feel*, and therefore we *know*, that the drama of our present life is but an unfinished act in a larger drama and that the plot, however irrational it may appear in this world, will come to a logical denouement in the next world. Every human life is a complete plot. Every loose thread will be tied up, every frustration will be straightened out, and every intelligent hope will be realized in the end. For this is the verdict of the human heart.

And thus, as we examine the real world of the heart as opposed to the fanciful world of the senses and the mind, we find three important facts emerging out of all our doubts. These three facts are: God, the free will, and the immortal soul.

VI

In this first book, *The Critique of Pure Reason*, Kant doubts God. In his second book, *The Critique of Practical Reason*, he affirms Him. In his third book, *The Critique of Judgment*, he finds Him. And where does he find Him? In the beautiful design of nature, a design based upon the "pattern laid up in the heavens." This is an idea based largely upon Plato and Rousseau. Behind beauty, declares Kant, there is always purpose. The work of art presupposes the artist. When man experiences the beautiful, he feels within himself an infinite power which corresponds to the infinite power outside of himself. Like calls unto like. God has spoken to Man, and Man replies, "I understand." Some men—the humanitarian, the statesman, the painter, the sculptor, the composer, the poet—live always in the presence of this vision. But the layman, too, has his moments of sublime insight. And in such moments he recognizes the presence of God in the two supreme manifestations of His creative power—the mathematical precision of the stars and the moral prescription of the heart.

Morality, like mathematics, prompts us to live in accordance with the harmonious process of life. "Act," observes Kant, "as if the maxim of your own conduct were to become by your will the maxim of all the world's activity." Avoid any action which, if adopted by all other people, would make social life impossible. Are you tempted to break your promise? Your conscience—the commandment of your heart—informs you that a world of broken promises would be like a world of exploded stars. On the same principle, your conscience condemns aggressiveness, cupidity, intolerance, extortion, treachery, malevolence, murder, theft.

Your conscience, in short, prompts you to keep the world organized on the basis of unstinted labor from, and adequate compensation to, every member of society. Let every man be

"an end in himself," instead of an instrument wielded by some-
body else. *Thou shalt not exploit thy neighbor.* "There can be
nothing more dreadful than that the actions of a man should
be subject to the will of another man." This is Kant's declaration
of independence—or rather, interdependence—for the entire
human race.

VII

Kant finished his philosophical trilogy at the age of sixty-
nine. He hoped to settle down to a tranquil old age. But his
hope was not to be realized. His rejection of religion unsup-
ported by reason aroused a storm of abuse. And his insistence upon the duties rather than the dogmas of Christianity
whipped the storm into a hurricane. The Pharisees of the
world called him a dog; and many of them called their dogs
Immanuel Kant. The king of Prussia, Frederick William, demanded that he "cease from undermining the teachings of
Christ." And Kant replied: "Your Majesty, I am merely trying
to *establish* those teachings. Christ sought to bring the Kingdom
of God nearer to earth. But judging by the conduct of most
Christians, He has been grossly misunderstood." And when the
king once more insisted upon his silence, the little philosopher
replied: "Your Majesty, I have had my say."

Yet he did write one more book—*Eternal Peace.* This work,
published when he was seventy-one, was a plea for a world
federation of free states. "Our rulers have no money to spend
on public education"—note the modern ring of the complaint—
"because all their resources are already placed to the account
of the next war." He advocated not only the reduction but the
abolition of all military forces. "Standing armies excite states
to outrival one another in a savage race for victory." The function of government is to advance, not conquest, but co-operation—a sense of respect for every individual in every nation as
an "absolute unit in himself." This means that we must organize

our states on a democratic basis, so that "war cannot be declared except by a vote of all the people." We can hope for universal peace only when monarchs and dictators "who regard themselves as the sole owners of the state are a thing of the past." This, declared Kant, is the goal toward which all humanity is striving. And for this purpose we need the guidance of God. It is the thought of God, the principle of Cosmic Unity, that can bind us into a world federation of understanding friends.

And thus, as one of his biographers has observed, Kant's gentle heart *felt* the divine purpose of life which his brilliant mind was unable to *see*.

CHAPTER XXIII

Arthur Schopenhauer (1788–1860)

SCHOPENHAUER acknowledged three main sources of his inspiration: Kant, Rousseau, and the Upanishads. From Kant he learned that the philosophy of the heart may be more revealing than the philosophy of the mind. From Rousseau he acquired the habit of studying the Book of Nature rather than the books of men. And from the Upanishads he discovered the futility of selfish ambition, since the individual self is but an organic part of the universal self.

Schopenhauer might also have acknowledged his indebtedness to Aristotle, who taught him that every object has a form, or inner urge, that governs its structure and growth. Schopenhauer translated the word "form" into "will." All existence, he said, is the result of a will to live.

Yet there was a difference between Schopenhauer and his teachers. Kant, Rousseau, the writers of the Upanishads, and Aristotle were optimists. But Schopenhauer was a pessimist. The will to live, he declared, is not good but evil. And the best way to abolish this evil is to arrive at the nirvana of nonexistence.

Let us look at this strange man with his interesting, if devastating, philosophy.

II

Arthur Schopenhauer came naturally by his pessimism. He lived in a world of ruins. His age was similar to our own. He published his epic of despair, *The World as Will and Idea*, in

1819. At that period Europe had been turned into a shambles. Frightened human cattle were being driven from one slaughter to another. Humanity seemed to have lost its bearings. The blind leaders of the blind were destroying their followers along with themselves. The will to power, as incarnated first in Robespierre and then in Napoleon, had ended in universal catastrophe. The Holy Alliance of Czar Alexander, which was supposed to establish the brotherhood of man, turned out to be an enslavement of mankind under a dictatorial whip.

Change the names of the leading actors, and you have a similar world drama in our own generation. Substitute Lenin for Robespierre, Hitler for Napoleon, and the communist ideal of Khrushchev for the Holy Alliance of Alexander, and you will understand the cynicism of a Schopenhauer in the nineteenth century just as you can understand the cynicism of a Pasternak in the twentieth.

Schopenhauer's philosophy grew out of the propensity of the aggressors to exert their will over their fellow men. The will to power, he declared, is the greatest evil in the world. For the world, it seemed to him, is governed not by a benevolent God but by a malevolent devil. This devil, or spirit of evil, has imposed upon us a universal plague—an overpowering will to live, and to cheat, rob, and kill others in our effort to advance our own life.

Schopenhauer had personally suffered from aggressive power. He had experienced it not only in the devastation of Europe but in the frustration of his own desires. His father, a successful merchant, had tried to force him into a business career. Schopenhauer detested business. He preferred the quiet of his study to the tumult of the market place.

And even after his father's death—by suicide, it was widely believed—Schopenhauer found no peace. His mother, a brilliant novelist, was insanely jealous of her son's literary ability. "Who ever heard of two geniuses in the same family?" she said. They quarreled and separated and came together again and again, until finally Frau Schopenhauer threw her son down the stairs. (Fortunately there were no broken bones.) The son hurled a bitter insult into her face: "There is only *one* genius in our family. Your ultimate fame will rest not upon your novels but upon my philosophy."

The mother and the son never met again. A hatred of authority and a disdain for women became the basic articles of Schopenhauer's pessimistic creed.

This hatred and this disdain were intensified during his college years. He disliked the dogmatic arrogance of his professors, and they in turn disliked the equally dogmatic impudence of their pupil. He fell in love, only to be rejected as an "unromantic lout." For a time he tried to play host to his neighbors—his father had left him an ample income—but his neighbors accepted his toasts and rejected his thoughts.

And so he withdrew under his own skin, a bitter, suspicious, and cynical porcupine of a man who, to paraphrase his own figure of speech, stayed away from people just far enough to avoid the warmth of their friendship but near enough to sting them with his sarcastic barbs. "A man is your friend only for what he can get out of you. A friend in need is not a friend indeed—he has come merely to borrow your money."

Schopenhauer lived severely alone. He kept his purse and his pipes under lock and key; and he shaved himself because, as he explained, "I wouldn't trust my neck to another man's razor." He never went to sleep without a loaded pistol at his bedside. He ridiculed conversation as "meaningless cackle." He disliked noise of any kind. "The more you can stand noise, the less intelligent you are . . . Noise is a torture to all thinking people."

Yet there was one kind of sound he wanted desperately to hear—applause for his philosophy. And this pleasure was denied him for many years. His books fell like feathers upon a silent sea. The majority of his publications were sold as wastepaper. He was deeply hurt at this neglect, yet he had a ready

answer to account for it. "What can you expect? A book is a
mirror of the reader's as well as of the writer's mind. If an ass
looks in, you can't expect an angel to look out."

For a while he tried to lecture as well as to write. He accepted a teaching post at the Berlin University. But he lectured
to empty seats.

And so he told society to "go hang." He moved into a two-
room apartment at Frankfurt, where he stayed for over thirty
years, deriving great joy out of his revelation of a joyless world.
His only companion was a poodle—"another pessimist like myself." He named the poodle Atma—the Hindu word for World-
Soul. But his townsmen called it Schopenhauer, Junior.

Whenever he was seen walking his dog, people wagged
their heads. "Here come the two philosophers ready to growl
at the world."

In this way Schopenhauer spent the greater part of his life,
examining the world through the blood-tinted spectacles of his
age. And what he found was chicanery, aggression, hopeless-
ness, and pain. "The day of our death," he concluded, "is happier than the day of our birth. But happiest of all is never to
have been born."

III

The greatest misfortune in the world, said Schopenhauer,
is the will to live. It is a blind and useless will. For our human
life—*all life*—is a thing of no value. Man is essentially a creature
endowed with an instinct for suffering. We are the slaves of life.
Driven by our desire to go on living, we are forever impelled
to seek one reprieve after another, and always at one another's
expense.

Our so-called pursuit of happiness is an irrational chase
after phantoms. We never reach the goal of our quest. For the
attainment of every desire is but the transition to another desire. Every success leaves within us a terrible boredom, an

empty void that demands a drive for further success. And thus our existence becomes a pendulum swinging continuously between the suffering of desire and the emptiness of fulfillment. Our hope for happiness is but a dream. We love best the things we haven't got. And after we get them, we learn that they are not what we had hoped for. The goal is still beyond our reach.

In this world of phantom goals, there is only one reality—pain. The Platonic realm of ideas becomes, in the philosophy of Schopenhauer, a realm of one idea—a restless will to persist in a life of frustrated hopes. We can look forward to nothing except a hunger that will never be stilled and a battle that will never end in peace.

Not even in death. For though the individual dies, the race is condemned to live on. Each of us is a part of the cosmic unit of life. The craving for existence is eternal.

And thus the universal will to live—the creation of a malevolent God—plays a perpetual joke upon us. It impels us, before we die, to bring another generation into the evil of life. "The relation of the sexes is the invisible central point in all action and conduct. It is the cause of war and the end of peace." It has been noted that after every great war there is a preponderance of male over female offspring—a ready-made army for the fighting of the next war. "We see the sex urge—the will to life and to strife—sitting upon the throne as the hereditary lord of the world, and laughing at our futile efforts to bind it, or to imprison it, or at least to keep it within reasonable bounds."

It is the reproductive hunger of the species, maintains Schopenhauer, that keeps us continually chained to the wheel of Life. The will to live has deceived us into perpetuating the misery of our race. "Nature has endowed woman with a wealth of charm—for a few years at the expense of the rest of her life—so that during these years of her bloom she may capture the fancy of some man to such a degree that he is carried away into undertaking the honorable care of her . . . Then, just as the female ant, after fecundation, loses her wings . . . just so the woman, after giving birth to a number of children, loses her beauty." The woman and the ant have accomplished their mission.

Hence the individual in love is merely a blind instrument of Nature. And when Nature has served her purpose to bring another group of draftees into the battle of life, she opens the eyes of the lovers. And then comes the bitterness of disillusion. The man is no longer a creative demigod but a clumsy gorilla called "husband"; and the woman has changed from a winged angel into an "undersized, narrow-shouldered, broad-hipped and short-legged creature" called "wife." "Thus the individual discovers, too late, that he has been the dupe of Destiny." His lyric of love has become soured into a growl of disenchantment. "If Petrarch's passion had been gratified, his songs would have been silenced."

There is therefore no free will for the individual. "Everyone believes himself to be perfectly free, even in his individual actions. But this is an illusion . . . Through experience, we find that we are not free, but subjected to necessity; that in spite of all our resolutions and reflections, we do not change our conduct . . . All of us must carry out the very character which we ourselves condemn."

A character in a drama over which we have no control. Its plot is a story of suffering, because pain is its basic theme. The more intelligent a man is, the more pain he experiences; and "the man who is gifted with genius suffers most of all."

Life is evil, because life is strife. Every individual "fights for the matter, space and time of every other individual." This is a universal practice. "The bulldog ant of Australia affords us the most extraordinary illustration of this truth. For if it is cut in two, a battle begins between the head and the tail. The head seizes the tail with its teeth, and the tail defends itself by stinging the head. And this battle lasts until they are both dead or are dragged away by other ants."

We find this passion for mutual murder in every species until we come to the human race. And then the conflict assumes its most diabolical aspect. Humanity has developed almost to perfection the insanity of war as an evidence of our will to live. Head against tail, brother against brother, nation against nation, we are engaged in a perpetual struggle to destroy one another's lives.

War is the ultimate evil of our irrational will to live. For it summarizes all the other evils, all the atrocities, all the sufferings of the world. There can be no inferno after death that can equal the inferno of life. "Where did Dante take the materials of his Hell but from our actual experience here on earth?"

Our life, in short, is a farcical tragedy—a farce if we examine it in part, and a tragedy if we survey it as a whole.

Then what is the remedy? Suicide? No, replies Schopenhauer. "The willful self-destruction of the individual is a vain and foolish act; for the species, the universal will to live, remains unaffected by it, even as the rainbow endures however fast the drops which support it for the moment may chance to fall."

Or is the remedy against the evil of life to be found in race suicide, a sort of nirvana that would absorb the universal will to live into the ultimate peace of death? This would indeed be desirable, observed Schopenhauer, if it were possible. But it isn't. There is no power on earth that can stop all life (Schopenhauer wrote before the day of the nuclear bomb. Were he alive today, he would probably welcome the final conflagration of an atomic war—and after that, the dark).

But, declared Schopenhauer, since individual suicide is impractical and race suicide is impossible, perhaps there is a third way. A wise and calm acceptance of our fate. A philosophical attempt to look upon ourselves objectively. Since life is an unprofitable business, let us stifle our craving for competition and cultivate an instinct for contemplation. "Not struggle but serenity, not wealth but wisdom is the way." Let us concentrate not on what we have, but on what we are. And each of us is, or can become, one of two things—a slave of impetuous will, or a master of tranquil observation. *We can train our intellect to curb our will.* "What the bridle and the bit are to an unmanageable horse, the intellect is to a willful man."

Cultivate your intellect. Not, however, by passive reading but by active thinking. The trouble with many so-called educated people is that they borrow other people's thoughts but have none of their own. "Their education is a sort of vacuum suction." The emptiness of their mind draws into it all kinds of ideas, bad as well as good, that happen to float around. "So it comes about that if anybody spends too much time in [desultory] reading, he gradually loses his capacity for thinking."

Read few books, but let these books be the best. Above all, read the Book of Nature. But use your own experience as your text, and your reading as a commentary.

For, after all, it is your own past that can best serve as the guide to your future. "In the end, every one must stand alone." The only kind of happiness possible in this world of suffering is to find within yourself the strength to endure this suffering.

Stand alone, with philosophy as your staff to support you. Train your intellect to conquer your will. Use your self-control to curb your self-indulgence. "Unselfish Intellect rises like a perfume above the faults and follies of the world of Will." The next best thing to nirvana, or complete departure from the world, is to stand aside and to view the world objectively. Learn to be a spectator, rather than an actor, in the tragedy of life. "The wise man's life is an adventure from [active] suffering to [passive] serenity . . . My gospel is to aim at the peace which is above understanding, the perfect calm of the spirit, the deep rest . . . when the will has vanished and only knowledge remains."

Especially the knowledge of the heart—the understanding of the bond that exists between yourself and the rest of the world. Schopenhauer's gospel is a modern version of the an-

cient Hindu philosophy. "There is no doctrine," declared Schopenhauer, "so beneficial as that of the Upanishads." The doctrine of a calm acceptance of your own suffering and an effort
to mitigate the sufferings of others who are but an extension of
yourself. "Fellow-prisoners in the dungeon of life, let us be kind
to one another."

IV

And thus the pessimism of Schopenhauer ends in a sort of
negative optimism, an intellectual pleasure in making the best
of a bad bargain. It is a philosophy not for children but for mature characters.

Yet Schopenhauer's own character never grew to full ma-
turity. His will to criticize was stronger than his willingness to
contemplate. At times his criticism descended even to physical
violence. One day, in an argument with a servant, he pushed
her out of the room. She fell in the scuffle and broke her arm.
She sued Schopenhauer for damages and won her case. He was
compelled to support her—and cursed her—for the rest of her
life.

He was keenly aware of other people's faults and keenly
insensitive to his own. His chief pleasure was to sit in his study
smoking his pipe, a Turkish contraption that curved almost five
feet from his mouth to the ground, and gazing at the busts of
two congenial spirits, Buddha and Kant. He had the complete
adoration of only one living creature, his poodle Atma. "I feel
most at home," he said, "among demigods and dogs. They alone
are free from the foibles of men."

His cynicism toward the world was really an outcry against
its failure to recognize his genius. It was not until he was quite
old, with his sight and hearing almost gone, his gums toothless,
and his appetite for food and fame no longer keen, that he got
a measure of recognition at last. Applause for a dying man. He
acknowledged it with a wry smile. "After a long life of insig-

nificance and disregard, I am escorted to the grave with trumpets and with drums."

And the rest of the world? Still blowing its trumpets and beating its drums for war, more war. That diabolical will to conquer. 1860. Rumblings in Germany, France, Italy, Austria, the United States. *Homo homini lupus.* Not men but human wolves, ready to spring at one another's throats. The will to be born, the urge to kill, the tempest of life, the peace of death.

Ah, but life, even Schopenhauer's life, *has* been a thrilling adventure! Perhaps the apostle of pessimism was wrong? Perhaps it is better to have loved and lost, lived and died, than never to have loved and lived at all? The laughter of children, the beauty of art, the thrill of devotion, the joy of understanding, the rebirth of spring after winter's death—are not these pleasures worth all the pains of life, and more?

The joy of understanding, the rebirth of spring. What if there is some connection between the two: complete understanding in a new birth? Not nirvana, eternal death, but *vita aeterna*, eternal life. Perhaps Schopenhauer failed to write the final chapter to his philosophy. Our life, he had said, is a farce if we examine it in part, a tragedy if we survey it as a whole. That is, up to the point of death. But what of the final chapter—the possibility of life beyond the grave? With this final chapter— accepted actually by many and provisionally by most of the great philosophers—life is neither a farce nor a tragedy, but an epic.

A glorious epic of promise and hope!

CHAPTER XXIV

Herbert Spencer (1820–1903)

SPENCER'S PHILOSOPHY is a bridge between Schopenhauer's pessimism and Kant's optimism. He begins, like Schopenhauer, with the belief that life is a futile tragedy. But he ends, like Kant, with the declaration that the last word perhaps is not futility but hope. "There is a soul of goodness in evil, and a soul of truth in error." The "Unknown Cause" of the universe is a constructive rather than destructive power. The world undergoes a continual process of evolution and dissolution. But every dissolution is followed by another evolution; every night is an interval between a day and a day; every spring is an awakening from a winter's sleep; every death is a prelude to a resurrection into a new life.

II

This English philosopher of the "recurrent rhythm of existence" came of a line of religious non-conformists and political individualists. The Spencers liked to think for themselves instead of accepting the thoughts of other people. His father, a teacher in a private school, "never took off his hat to anyone"—as Herbert Spencer tells us—"no matter of what rank." He transmitted this characteristic of stubborn independence to his son. Herbert yielded to nobody, not even to his father, who wanted him to acquire an education and to become a teacher. At thirteen he was sent to study under his uncle who also taught at a private school. But Herbert promptly ran away and tramped back from his school at Hinton to his home—a distance

of over a hundred miles—in three days. Throughout this journey, he lived on bread and beer. "Better this fare than a daily
diet of Latin and Greek." Compelled to return to his uncle's
school, he stayed there for three years. This was the sum total
of his systematic instruction until he was thirty. And even then
he picked up his knowledge piecemeal. "The most erudite philosopher of the nineteenth century" was a man without any
regular education.

But his "irregular" education was the result of his amazing
insight. "His curiosity was ever awake; and he was continually
directing the attention of his companions to some notable phe-
nomenon until then observed by his eyes alone."

He was especially interested in the phenomena of biology
—the physical and mental changes that take place in the pageantry of life. It was Herbert Spencer who coined the phrases
"struggle for existence" and "survival of the fittest" in 1852—
seven years before the publication of Darwin's *Origin of
Species*.

His own struggle for existence appeared time and again
to be doomed to failure. The oldest of seven children, he was
the only one who survived his infancy. He grew up sickly and
discouraged about his chances to survive. Compelled to serve
as a mechanic for a living, he suffered a physical breakdown
in his early manhood. He was never himself again. From his
middle age on, he took nightly doses of opium to induce sleep.

Discharged from his job as a mechanical engineer, he decided to try his luck in literature. He went down to London
and got a position on the editorial staff of the *Economist*. While
serving on this staff, he met several members of the London
intelligentsia—including George Henry Lewes, Thomas Hux-
ley, and Marian Evans (known to the literary world as George
Eliot). He took a fancy to Miss Evans, and they kept company
for a time. People waxed romantic about them, expecting an
early engagement. But the only thing that ever came of this
"romance" was the following observation in Spencer's *Autobiog-*

raphy: "Usually heads have, here and there, either flat places or slight hollows; but Miss Evans's head was everywhere convex."

"Spencer is too scientific to be human," observed one of his acquaintances. "The passionless thin lips show a total absence of sensuality, and the light eyes betray a lack of emotional depth." He reduced everything to a physical or chemical or mathematical formula. Once, as a young man, he thought of migrating to New Zealand where he might possibly find "better luck under fairer skies." With scientific precision he jotted down two columns of items—one for and the other against the move—valuing each of the items at a definite figure. The totals came to 110 points for England and 301 for New Zealand. But he decided to remain in England. The dictates of his heart didn't always follow the calculations of his mind.

III

Spencer's scientific coldness was in part a mask to cover his emotional warmth. One day, as he was traveling in a carriage, he sat opposite a laborer who was busy with his lunch. At first the scene aroused in his mind a set of scientific figures—statistics about the wages of labor, the profits of capital, and their impact upon the rest of the world. His next thought was one of repulsion. "The fellow's mode of eating was so brutish as to fill me with disgust—a disgust which verged into anger." But finally Spencer's anger gave way to pity. "I noticed the woebegone expression of his face. Years of suffering were registered on it . . . While I gazed on the sad eyes and the deeply marked lines, I began to realize the life of misery through which he had passed."

This combination of thought and emotion—scientific detachment, disgust at the ugliness of the battle for existence, and pity for the fighters in the battle—lay at the basis of Spencer's "Synthetic Philosophy." It was designed to be a complete philosophy of evolution, dealing with the nature of existence, the principles of biology, psychology, sociology, and ethics, and the fundamental unity in the diverse religious systems of the world.

It was in the midst of physical suffering that Spencer outlined this monumental work. When the outline was finished, his friends got busy securing advance subscriptions. He planned to issue the work in quarterly installments. About five hundred people in Europe and two hundred in America agreed to underwrite the venture. The total amount would produce an income of about $1500 a year—enough to supply Spencer with the necessities of life. As for the luxuries, Spencer had no use for them. "I don't think they're worth the bother."

But even the small amount of $1500 began to melt away after the first book was published. This book attempted to reconcile science and religion—an idea which precipitated a battle among the extremists on both sides. Many of his patrons withdrew their support, and the number of subscribers kept shrinking with every new installment of his work. Spencer was compelled to dig into his own meager savings to pay for the publications. Finally his funds were completely gone. He was ready to quit when he received the following unexpected note from one of his philosophical rivals, John Stuart Mill:

Dear Sir:
On arriving here last week, I found the December *livraison* of your Biology, and I need hardly say how much I regretted the announcement in the paper annexed to it . . . I propose that you should write the next of your treatises, and that I should guarantee the publisher against loss . . . I beg that you will not consider this proposal in the light of a personal favor . . . it is a simple proposal of co-operation for an important public purpose, for which you give your labor and have given your health. I am, Dear Sir,

Very truly yours,

J. S. Mill

Spencer refused the generous offer. He was still determined to give up the work—his body was racked with pain and his mind was distracted with worry. But just then he received encouragement from another source. He learned that his American admirers had bought, in his name, a block of securities of which the dividends were to help defray the expenses of his future publications.

He accepted this offer and for the next forty years he continued to write his "Synthetic Philosophy." In the course of his work, he traveled from boardinghouse to boardinghouse with his manuscripts. At times he was so weak after a siege of illness that he was able to dictate only a few minutes at a time. His physical exercise was restricted to an occasional walk of two or three hundred yards—it was all he was able to do—and a fifteen-minute drive in a carriage with indiarubber tires. And after his days of "too little work and too much suffering," he called his nights good if, with a strong dose of opium, he managed to get three or four hours of broken sleep.

It was under these difficulties that he gradually built up his philosophy of evolution—the development of matter from atom to star, and of life from amoeba to man.

IV

Spencer's philosophy is coldly scientific. It is devoid of emotional or poetical warmth. It is like the reflection of the sunlight upon a polar sea. Yet because of its frigid glow, it sheds a clean light, unencumbered with the mist of metaphysics, upon the riddle of existence.

All existence, believes Spencer, is in a perpetual process of evolution. Sooner or later every operation in the universe (as well as in the human mind) will be explained on mechanical principles. In his early years, Spencer tells us, he was interested in the construction of watches. This interest remained with him throughout his life. He saw the universe revolving on the wheels of a cosmic timepiece. He described this revolution, or rather *evolution*, down to the minutest detail—save for one important item. He failed to explain how the timeclock of the universe got wound up in the first place.

But he offered a logical reason for his failure to explain the origin of the world. "This origin," he said, "is unknowable; and the unknowable is inconceivable." Both the believer and the disbeliever in God are equally unable to substantiate their claim. For if God made the world, who was it that made God? But if nobody made the world, how did it happen to come into existence?

We must therefore accept our mental limitations and refrain from extending our ideas beyond the boundaries of the knowable. We have no right, observes Spencer, to call ourselves either theists or atheists. We are merely agnostics—we don't know. "Ultimate scientific ideas are representations of realities that cannot be comprehended . . . In all directions the scientist's investigations bring him face to face with an insoluble enigma; and he ever more clearly perceives it to be an insoluble enigma. He learns at once the greatness and the littleness of the human intellect—its power in dealing with all that comes within the range of experience, its impotence in dealing with all that transcends experience."

And so Spencer dismissed the transcendental—the mystery beyond our experience—and devoted himself to the actual. He based his philosophy upon the definite evidence of science rather than upon the indefinite suppositions of theology. With regard to these suppositions about the great mystery, the final cause of existence, "the scientist more than any other truly *knows* that he knows nothing."

But within the field of the knowable, the scientist can range at will. And Spencer follows him to the uttermost limits of that field—verifying, classifying, arranging, organizing the entire panorama of human experience into a comprehensive system of philosophy. "Philosophy," to quote Spencer's own definition, "is completely-unified knowledge."

And this unification, declares Spencer, is founded upon a universal principle—the rhythm of motion in a world of matter. All existence is rhythmical. The ebb and the flow of the tides, the succession of the seasons, the birth and the decline of races and men, the vibration of the violin string and the beating of the heart, the circulation of the blood, of the wind, of the planets and the stars—these are but a few examples of the interminable pulse of the universe. And this eternal pulsation measures the recurring phases of existence in accordance with the formula of *evolution* and *dissolution*. "When we examine the entire history of anything," observes Spencer, "we find that it includes its appearance out of the imperceptible and its disappearance into the imperceptible." Out of the nebulae spring masses of flame; they develop into comets and meteors and stars and planets; and then the individual bodies become organized into groups and constellations and galaxies and universes until they merge into a supreme harmony of motion and light. And by the same principle, maintains Spencer, all living creatures arise out of the earth; they develop into fishes and birds and animals and men; the individuals then become assorted into families and clans and classes and states until finally they will harmonize into the co-operative federation of a united world.

So much for the evolution of the rhythmic principle in a material universe. But after the *evolution* comes the *dissolution*. From the individuals to the aggregate, from the aggregate back to the individuals. From death to life, from life to death. Dust thou art, to dust returnest. This is true of man; it is equally true of the world. Every organism will end in disorganization. Every star will be dissolved into ashes. Every man, every nation, every syllable of the recorded achievements of mankind will be blotted out. Every birth is but a summons to the grave.

But—and here comes the hopeful note in Spencer's philosophy—*the rhythmic process goes on forever*. After the completion of one cycle, another cycle begins. The life and death of an individual person or planet or universe is but a single act and not the entire drama of existence. In the rhythmic structure of this drama, the day follows the night just as surely as the night follows the day. Our experience ends at the threshold of the great mystery of dissolution and death. But "there is a reality that lies beyond experience." The world in its essence, Spencer explains in a late edition of his work, "cannot be conceived wholly in scientific terms." Back of it all there must be an inscrutable power—"an Unknown Cause that produces within us a certain faith" not only in the rhythmic recurrence but in the ultimate justification of existence. Every dissolution is a step toward a new evolution, and the final answer to the riddle of the universe is not an eternal death but an eternity of life.

V

Closely allied to the evolution of life in the philosophy of Spencer is the evolution of ethics—the gradual development of an ideal society. In such a society, he declared, there would never be any talk about a mixture of egoism and altruism in the make-up of a man's character. There would be no question as to the relative rights of your pleasure and my happiness. There would be absolute standards of conduct that would apply to all persons, under all conditions, at all times.

And the highest conduct would aim, not at happiness—which is merely an "accompaniment" of life—but at the preservation and the amplification of life itself, in all its "length, breadth, and completeness."

The power which guides us toward this ideal—Spencer would agree with Kant—is an innate moral sense. In its prolonged struggle for existence, the human race has developed certain characteristics—instinctive reactions to its environment that enable it to survive. Such reactions gradually come to be regarded as good behavior. A good act is one that conduces to life; a bad act one that leads to death.

In the earlier period of human history—and unfortunately we have not as yet emerged from that period—men found it expedient to kill in order to live. Cruelty was regarded as courage, vindictiveness as virtue, and warfare as the noblest of human pursuits. But gradually it dawned upon the human mind that it was easier to survive through mutual aid than through individual antagonism. And the idea of justice was born in the world. "The sentiment of justice can grow only as fast as the antagonisms of society decrease, and the co-operations of their members increase." The slogans of war gave way, in a few advanced minds, to the maxims of peace. Slavery was softened into service, obedience into loyalty, licentiousness into license, forwardness into freedom. And the idea of human freedom became molded into a new concept. "Every man is free to do that which he wills, provided he infringes not the equal freedom of any other man."

All men are equally free to exploit the material resources of the earth. From each according to his ability, to each according to his merit. Not, however, to each according to his need, as advocated by the teachers of socialism. Spencer is very emphatic on this point. The socialistic ideal, he maintains, can work only with regard to children, but not with regard to adults. "Within the family group, most must be given where least is deserved, if desert is measured by worth"—that is, by ability to produce. But within the social group of mature people, "benefit must vary directly as worth—worth being measured by fitness (to survive). The ill-fitted must suffer the evils of unfitness, and the well-fitted profit by their fitness." This, Spencer would admit, is an ethic based upon justice rather than mercy. But it is the only ethic possible, he would insist, in a society dependent upon an endless struggle for existence. "If, among the young, benefit were proportioned to efficiency, the species would disappear forthwith; and if, among adults, benefit were proportioned to inefficiency, the species would disappear by decay in a few generations."

And thus Spencer proposes a new code of ethics—mercy toward the young, justice toward the mature. Spencer's ethical code, based upon the Hebraic rather than the Christian ideal, applies not only to the individual group but to the entire family of mankind. In this human family every child has a right to kindly protection and every healthy adult to honest competition. Help the helpless; as for the rest, allow them the freedom to help themselves without encroaching upon the freedom of their fellow men.

The instinct of the human family is for social justice. The sense of duty is an impulse to mutual aid—the formula for the survival of mankind. The evolution of society "will so mold human nature that, eventually, sympathetic pleasures will be spontaneously pursued to the fullest extent advantageous to all." And then there will be one code of ethics, one world federation, and one universal creed based upon the core of identical truth that is to be found in all the great religions of mankind.

VI

After a slow start, Spencer's philosophy of justice through evolution became famous in his own lifetime. His work was translated into most of the European languages. The sale of the various editions made him financially secure. He was showered with invitations to meet distinguished people, but he invariably refused. "No man is equal to his book," he said. "His best thoughts go into his writing. Only his inferior products go into his talk." He associated with only a handful of friends. When strangers insisted on talking to him, he plugged stoppers into his ears and pretended to listen with a silent smile.

But his smile turned a little sour as he grew older. His

popularity declined toward the end of his life. The religious leaders assailed his "irreligious attitude"; the socialists criticized his "capitalistic bias"; and the militarists attacked his stand against war. Slowly his followers deserted him. And he was left late in life, as he had been early in life, pathetically alone.

Yet, just before he died, he asked himself: "Had all my subsequent disappointment and . . . shattered health been known to me when I embarked upon my career, would it have discouraged me from continuing?" And his answer to his own question was a definite and courageous no.

PART

6

Modern European Philosophers

CHAPTER XXV

Friedrich Wilhelm Nietzsche (1844–1900)

LORD BYRON said of Rousseau that he turned insanity into beauty. It may be said of Nietzsche that he turned beauty into insanity. Nietzsche was a mad prophet, the founder of a savage religion without a God. "I am," he exulted, "the most pious of all those who believe not in God." He took the cold philosophy of evolution and set it on fire. The result is a splendor that excites and distresses and blinds, like the sun when you focus your vision too directly upon it. And like the sun, Nietzsche's philosophy taken in too large doses can produce a dangerous sickness. It inflamed too many of his disciples into a fever for war.

Strictly speaking, Nietzsche was not a philosopher but a poet, one of the most imaginative prose poets of the nineteenth century. He advanced no definite doctrine; his thoughts were too paradoxical to be logical. Yet out of the maze of his exaggerations and contradictions there emerges a recipe for poison which, in the hands of his disciples, came near to destroying the human race.

But before we come to the philosophy of Nietzsche, let us take a look at Nietzsche the man.

II

His mad adventure in philosophy was partly the result of a misadventure in love. His oversensitive mind gave way when the woman he wanted to marry rejected him. His feeble body could neither restrain nor satisfy his impetuous will. He was born (1844) in Prussia—a little country which, like himself, was inordinately anxious to become great. He lost his father, a clergyman, at an early age. His mother brought him up on a spiritual diet of fanatical orthodoxy. And he himself remained fanatically orthodox up to the age of nineteen.

And then the pendulum swung to the opposite extreme. Nietzsche turned heterodox, but retained his fanaticism. He became violently antagonistic to Christ, and conceived the irrational idea that he was destined to be Antichrist. He had read Schopenhauer's *World as Will and Idea,* and he had decided that just as John the Baptist was the forerunner of Jesus, Schopenhauer was the forerunner of Nietzsche.

For the philosophy of Schopenhauer, which—as we shall see—he misinterpreted, had thrown him into an ecstasy of self-glorification. "It seemed as if Schopenhauer were addressing me personally . . . In this book I saw my own nature depicted with frightful grandeur." He began to see himself as the founder of a new religion, a religion of hatred as opposed to Christ's religion of love.

At twenty-three he was drafted into the Army. The military life was too strenuous for him, and he was quickly discharged. From that time on, the soldier—the symbol of strength which he himself lacked—became an object of worship to him. "I felt for the first time that the highest Will to Life does not find expression in a miserable struggle for existence, but in a Will to Power, a Will to Overpower, a Will to War."

And thus the young disciple of Schopenhauer began to distort his master's teaching. Schopenhauer had said that our aggressiveness, the will to live, is the greatest misfortune in the world. But Nietzsche declared that this aggressiveness, the will to kill in order to live, is the noblest objective in the world.

The new gospel of Nietzsche—the glory of pushing to the top. But his own hunger for this glory was stifled in a sedentary life. He got a position as professor of ancient Greek literature at the University of Basel. Here he became confirmed in his diabolical philosophy, supported by the Spartan doctrine of military aggressiveness, that the power to destroy is the greatest aim in life.

He was obsessed with the idea of grandeur. Yet in spite of his glowing words about himself, he found no grandeur in his own soul. He began to look around for a hero after whom he might model himself. And at the moment he found this hero in Richard Wagner. In the blatant music of Wagner he saw a spirit akin to his own. The Freudians would probably ascribe this hero-worship to Nietzsche's inferiority complex—his desire to picture himself as a Superman because he had failed to reach the stature of a man.

He became, for a time, a satellite of Wagner. But he left him in anger when Wagner, in his *Parsifal*, "succumbed"—as Nietzsche put it—"to the decadence of Christianity." This sort of "piety and pity" was too much for Nietzsche's anti-Christian soul.

III

And then came his unsuccessful love affair and a breakdown in physical and mental health. He recovered only in part, to become more fanatical than ever before. He traveled to Italy in search of his health, and from Italy to the Alps, and from the Alps to the nebulous fantasies of a world of his own making. He employed, as the mouthpiece for his new philosophy, the ancient Persian prophet, Zarathustra (or Zoroaster).

But here again Nietzsche misinterpreted his teacher. Zarathustra had pictured the world as the scene of a struggle between good and evil. "And the good shall prevail." But Nietzsche saw the world as a madhouse beyond the boundaries of good and evil, a place where the greed of the masters shall prevail over the need of the masses. Zarathustra embraced humanity in his universal love. But Nietzsche engulfed it in his universal hatred.

Nietzsche's book, *Thus Spake Zarathustra,* is one of the most fantastic dreams ever recorded by an insane mind—"a soul," as Nietzsche confessed, "that overflowed all its margins." In his delusions of grandeur, Nietzsche exclaimed: "This work stands alone. Let us not mention other books in the same breath. Nothing like this has ever been produced."

This book is indeed unique. It is supercharged with emotion instead of being filled with thought. And it has swept unstable and dictatorial minds into an orgy of self-aggrandizement at the expense of the world. "Live dangerously!" cries Nietzsche. "Live in a state of war!" He who wants to prevail must break all the old values into pieces. The old gods are dead—they have laughed themselves to death. And there is no new God to take their place. There is only the Superman. "The Superman is a destroyer, not a creator." For him there is only one kind of duty—the determination to be unkind. This is the morality of the *masters* as opposed to the morality of the *slaves.*

Indeed, the slaves must live only to be exploited by the masters. The multitude of men must perish in order that the Superman may survive. To Nietzsche this was perhaps only a poetical hyperbole. But to a madman like Hitler it became a gospel fact. Nietzsche was daydreaming when he saw himself as a savage warrior magnified into superhuman proportions. Hitler transformed this daydream into a nightmare of reality.

For Nietzsche's philosophy is a guidebook for dictators— the monomaniacs who see themselves through a magnifying mirror. They raise themselves upon a pedestal above the rest of the world. They regard themselves as Nietzsche's Supermen —the Blond Beasts who leap over the heights and prey upon the "inferior cattle" in the valleys and on the slopes.

In the effervescence of his imagination, Nietzsche was unaware of the mischief he was doing. He seems to have been more anxious to startle than to teach. Thus, in answer to the idealists who maintained that we have had too much war, he declared that we have had too much peace. "There have not been wars enough to strengthen our souls." A man must be supremely evil, asserted Nietzsche paradoxically, in order to be supremely good. That is, supremely strong in his mastery. "Doth my preaching break all your truths? Let them break! Thus spake Zarathustra."

All history, said Nietzsche, is activated by a will to triumph through ruthless power. "The will saith: 'So did I will it, so shall I will it! *Be not considerate to thy neighbor.*'" Cruelty is the cardinal principle of life. The animal fights to evolve into man; man strives to evolve into Superman. The aim of every creature is to climb upward over the bodies of its fellow creatures. The torture of the many is necessary for the triumph of the few. And this triumph can be attained only through aggressive warfare—the warfare of the superior animal against the common herd; of the superior man, the Superman, against the "bungled and botched" masses of the common people. The noblest occupation in the world is to wage war. "Man shall be trained for war, and woman for the recreation of the warrior. All else is folly." This, contends Nietzsche, is not a criticism of religion. It is not a diatribe against ethics. It is merely a blunt statement of reality—the everlasting struggle for existence, the undying instinct for power. "What is the loftiest soul? *The most selfish soul* . . . They shall rise the highest who can trample upon others the best . . . Thus spake Zarathustra."

These "words of Zarathustra" are repeated, in somewhat different form, throughout the later books of Nietzsche. Unable, because of his supersensitive eyes, to face the daylight, he shut himself up in an attic and drew down the blinds. And in this murky atmosphere he continued to brew the potion of his witches' dream. The entire purpose of this dream was "to destroy the old morality" and "to establish the new immorality." Ambition, ruthlessness, hate—these are the strength of the master class (*die Herren*). Compassion, generosity, love—these are the weakness of the slave class (*die Herden*).

All of Nietzsche's philosophy is dedicated to the proposition that might is the only right. And thus he proposes a "transvaluation of all values." He turns light into darkness and justice into a jest. "Whatever is good for the master is good for the world." The "evil virtue" of the strong, proclaims Nietzsche, must become the acceptable burden of the weak. "All morality must be compelled to bow before the gradations of rank." The ambition of the Superman must become the ethical standard of the world.

And the Superman must steel himself against becoming too soft. He must ever aim to "become better and more evil"—to revert to the "cruelty that constituted the great joy and delight of ancient man." This cruel happiness of the Superman—of Napoleon, for example, an aggressor who was one of Nietzsche's supreme admirations—"is the greatest blessing that can come to the worthless herd of mankind."

For "not mankind but Superman is the goal." The world, as Nietzsche beheld it through his sickly eyes, is a huge laboratory in which tons of rubbish must be wasted to produce an ounce of gold. Don't protect the average, or help the mediocre, or pity the underdog. They are the expendables in Nature's experiment for the best. They are the muck that must fertilize the soil in order that "the seed of man may grow into the flower of Superman."

Away, then, with the "softness" of Christianity—the "enervating" doctrine that all men have equal rights. The masses of men have only an equal duty—to refrain from rebellion against their masters and to leave them "free, in their wild-beast innocence, from every social restraint."

This aristocratic, "wild-beast innocence" of the Superman, as Nietzsche apprehensively confessed, is endangered by the spread of democracy. He called it the "Judaeo-Christian mania" for treating all men alike. "We must destroy this Christian democratic notion before it is too late."

And the pity of it is that the dictators who followed Nietzsche took him at his word. Those distorted little paranoiacs, mistaking themselves for Nietzsche's Supermen, attempted to turn all human values upside down. Note Nietzsche's words about the "Ideal" Ruling State—a perfect picture of nazism, fascism, or communism: "a State of blond beasts of prey, a race of [would-be] conquerors and masters, with military organization . . . unscrupulously placing their fearful paws upon the people of the world . . ." The "Superman-ruler" of such a state has no need of the consent of the public, no contractual understanding between his people and himself. "What has he to do with contracts who is master by nature, who is able to command with violence in attitude and action?"

This "Blond Beast," this Superman-ruler—what a far cry from Plato's Philosopher-king!—must try to "rescue" the world from the "democrats, the Christians and the cows" otherwise known as *die Herden*, the Herd.

And the purpose of all this is "to overthrow the old society and to build the new." This new society, said Nietzsche, "must be constructed like a pyramid. It must stand upon a solid foundation of willing mediocrity at the bottom, with a commanding apex at the top." And the commander at the top must be the "Ego whole and holy—selfishness supremely blessed."

In this philosophy of supreme selfishness, based upon the "ruthless laws of evolution," Nietzsche forgot one important thing. The survival of the fittest depends not upon mutual destruction, but upon mutual service. The evolution of man is not a struggle for existence, it is an organization for coexistence. Darwin himself has defined this urge for co-operative organization as the "permanent instinct" of humanity. Interdependence is the predominant factor in nature—in the motions of the stars and in the morals of men. The world is not merely a battlefield in which the weak are exterminated by the strong, the sluggish by the swift, the simple by the cunning, and the timid by the bold. It is also a school for progress, a classroom for socialization, a platform for inculcating the lessons of longevity, intelligence, companionship, beneficence, sympathy, and love. The process of evolution teaches us not only how to live, but how to live together. Nature is by no means an illustration of the triumph of physical force. It is rather a demonstration of the ascendancy of spiritual endowment. The struggle for survival is not between man and man, but between societies of man on the one hand and the destructive powers of nature or of ill-willed individuals on the other. And in this struggle it is not the predatory but the peaceful peoples that survive. For peace leads to union, and union to strength. This mutual-aid instinct is always at work in man. "It is," as Darwin has observed, "the origin and the basis of our human conscience."

Nietzsche's Superman, on the other hand, is an inhuman creature without a conscience. The aim of man is to develop not the conquering individual self but the co-operating social self. This, as Nietzsche failed to realize, is the ethical factor that underlies all religion and all philosophy. It is the cement that binds the human race into a unit of mutual compassion. It enables us, slowly but surely, to understand not only the identical direction of all human aims, but the essential identity of all human life.

IV

For all his brilliance, it is a sickening experience to read Nietzsche today. His worship of the Blond Beast is a religion for madmen like Nietzsche himself. The older he grew, the more unbalanced he became. He looked upon himself as greater than Wagner, greater than Napoleon, greater than Christ. He regarded his books as the "supreme literary achievement of all time."

His self-glorification was equaled only by his self-mortification. As time went on, he became more and more derisive about humanity, more and more bitter about himself. Indeed, his laughter was but the outcome of his bitterness. "Perhaps

I know best why man is the only animal that laughs," he wrote
in one of his lucid intervals. "Man alone suffers so excruciatingly
that he has been compelled to invent laughter."

And so Nietzsche went on laughing and railing and rhap-
sodizing as his body was racked with pain. His sight grew gradually worse until at last he was almost blind. And in his hal-
lucinations he began to cry out that he was a pagan god nailed
to the cross of human stupidity.

One day, in the winter of 1889, his madness became unmanageable. They took him to an asylum—"the right man," as
the German critic, Max Nordau, remarked—"in the right place."

After a while they released him in the custody of his
mother. But he was a complete wreck now. He was no longer
able to write, or even to think. He merely babbled incoherent
phrases. Now and then a brief quotation from his own work
would come stumbling across his clouded mind. "Say thy word,"
he whispered on one of these occasions, "and break in pieces."

And at last, in 1900, death gathered up the broken pieces
and swept them out of the world.

But the evil had been done. The mischief-makers of the
world had found an eloquent advocate. And mankind is still
suffering from the chain reaction of his destructive thoughts.
It was Nietzsche's philosophy that inspired Hitler's aggressiveness. From the madman with the pen it was but a short step
to the madman with the gun.

CHAPTER XXVI

Henri Bergson (1859–1941)

BERGSON, like Nietzsche, based his philosophy upon the Darwinian theory of evolution. But unlike Nietzsche, he saw in evolution a positive force for good rather than a negative force for evil.

In the philosophy of Bergson, evolution is not a mechanical process; it is a creative impulse, a subconscious growth toward the divine. Man blunders as long as he strives; but through all his blundering he possesses the instinct of the one true way.

This instinctive turning toward the light, just as a plant turns toward the sun, is brought home to us through the intuition of the philosopher, the devotion of the martyr, the inspiration of the poet, the hope and the faith and the charity of the common man. The human spirit, maintains Bergson, is forever on the upward march.

This Jewish-French philosopher brought a guiding light to a perplexed world. He wrote at a time when men's minds had become lost in the labyrinth of materialism. Life seemed nothing more than a machine set in motion by no hand and moving toward no goal. But Bergson tried to show the way out of this labyrinth. Taking up the thread from the old oriental philosophers, he traced it all the way through Plato and Aristotle, St. Augustine and Spinoza, Rousseau and Kant and Schopenhauer, up to his own day and declared that the three entities—matter and mind and spirit—are really one. He demonstrated the essential unity in the diverse systems of philosophy and discovered—or, rather, rediscovered—that nearly all superior thought

points in one direction: from energy to the atom, from the atom
to man, from man to God.

II

Born in Paris, Bergson started as a mathematician and
ended as a philosopher. He was a brilliant student and won
practically every prize at the schools he attended. He entered
the École Normale Supérieure at seventeen, and continued to
amaze his teachers with his mental versatility. He was equally
at home in ancient literature and in modern science. And he
brought to all his studies the glowing imagination and the sty-
listic perfection of a poet.

At first he was an agnostic poet like Lucretius, the Roman
disciple of Epicurus. Bergson's inclinations at college were
"ruthlessly materialistic." There is no spiritual purpose in life,
he maintained, and no basis for hope. "A single glance into the
microscope will dispel forever the vanity of the most ardent
believer in human salvation." Once, when he served as librarian
for his class, his teacher upbraided him for the untidiness of
his bookshelves. "How can your librarian's soul endure such
disorder?" asked the teacher. Whereupon his classmates cried
out in chorus: "Bergson has no soul!"

Upon his graduation from college, however, he began to
doubt his own doubts. He had accepted a position as teacher
of philosophy at the Lycée of Clermont-Ferrand, in the picturesque province of Auvergne. Here he took long walks over
the countryside, and gradually dropped the attitude of his scientific skepticism. At heart, he concluded, he was not a lifeless
measuring rod but a living thinker. He began to distrust the
test tubes of the laboratory, the formulas of the physicists, and
the precise definitions of the pundits. How could they ever explain the one essential thing that defied explanation—the meaning of existence? How did life begin? How could the philosophy
of materialism solve the mystery of consciousness? How could

the majesty of the hills on the horizon—and his own appreciation of their beauty—be ascribed to a fortuitous whirlpool of atoms? What mechanical power made him catch his breath when he saw the sun rising over the treetops?

Bergson's transformation from a materialist to an idealist was not the matter of a moment. At first he couldn't explain, even to himself, just where his thoughts were leading him. But little by little he began to feel that a sort of instinctive "poetical realization" had taken hold of him and was striking out "through every fiber of his body and every cell of his mind." He became more and more convinced that the human mind is not a machine. Could a mechanical combination of natural forces produce the dramas of Shakespeare? Could a mathematical arrangement of the letters of the alphabet create the Sermon on the Mount? Could the chemical and physical formula called Henri Bergson explain the eloquence of his lectures and the responsiveness of his audiences? And what scientific process could account for the transformation of Bergson from a cold materialist to an ardent idealist?

III

He tried to convey to his students something about the transformation within himself. In one of his lectures dealing with scientific research, he said: "You have all handled a microscope and may have noticed in its box those little slips of glass each of which encloses some anatomical preparation. Take one of these preparations, put it under the lens and look. You will see a tube divided into compartments. Slip the glass along and observe how one cell succeeds another cell, each clearly distinguishable. But what is the object, and what have you seen? If you want to get the answer to this question, you will be obliged to abandon the microscope and to consider, as a whole, with your naked eye, that ugly spider's foot which you have been examining in part." Life is more than what meets the eye, even under the analysis of a microscope.

The trouble with scientific analysis in the past, declared Bergson, is that it told only a part—and a very small part—of the story. The tendency of the scientific mind was to look upon the world as an object in space rather than as a motion in energy. Indeed, the modern development of scientific thought seems to have corroborated Bergson's idea. Matter is beginning to appear more and more like energy. The atom is melting into the electron, and the electron is dissolving into a non-material force of life—Bergson called it *l'élan vital*. Yet many of us even today, he said, fail to realize that the world not only exists in space but also moves in time. It has temporal duration as well as physical extension. "Duration," he explained, "is the continuous progress of the past which gnaws into the future and which swells as it advances." No moment of time is ever lost. "The past in its entirety is prolonged into the present and abides there actual and acting." All history is our common heritage and our individual stimulus. Our conscious memory may recall only a few incidents of the past; but our subconscious instinct enables us to use all the accumulated experience of mankind in the solution of our current problems. And thus each of us is not merely a wheel in a mechanical process; he is rather a focus of creative evolution gathering all the rays of the past to spread a new light upon the future.

Our memory, however inadequate, performs a useful function in the service of our instinct. "The primary purpose of memory is to evoke all those past perceptions which are analogous to the present perception, to recall to us what preceded and what followed them, and so to suggest to us that decision which is most useful.

"But this is not all. By allowing us to grasp in a single intuition multiple moments of [the creative impulse of] time, it frees us from the movement of the flow of things, that is to say, from the rhythm of necessity. The greater the number of these free moments our memory can recall, the firmer is the hold which it gives us on matter." A man's memory, in other words, measures his power for creative action.

And our memory, or consciousness of the past, is not necessarily connected with our body. During our lifetime, to be sure, our minds depend upon our brains. But this is true only in the sense that a coat depends—or hangs upon—a nail. The coat does not exist *because* of the hanger. Remove the nail, and the coat goes on existing as a coat. "It is not necessary to have a brain in order to remember, just as it is not necessary to have a stomach in order to digest." An amoeba, for example, can digest its food without a stomach. A man's brain, like his stomach, is merely a temporary device but not an indispensable organ for eternity.

Why, then, are we accustomed to regard our thoughts as the product of our brains? Because, declared Bergson, the "intellectual" aspect of our thinking has developed into an instrument for understanding the world as a material object in space. "Our intellect, in the narrow sense of the word, is intended to secure the perfect fitting of our body to its environment, to represent the relations of external things among themselves—in short, to think matter," to measure and analyze physical objects, to see the body but not the spirit of life. Our intellect fails to understand the correlated essence of the world, the growth of time as well as the extension of space in the eternal unity of existence.

Hence our so-called exact sciences are merely approximate guesses. They can explain matter but not energy, the brain but not the mind, the object conceived by the thinker but not the essence of his thought. Our intellect, in short, is geared to a mechanical, materialistic world. We laboriously build machines to carry our bodies a thousand or a million miles into space. But our minds, unhampered by any mechanical carriers, can circumnavigate the entire universe—covering innumerable billions of miles—within a single moment.

Our ideas, in other words, are not material objects traveling in the world of space. They are non-material entities of *persistent creation*—or, as Bergson puts it, *progressive duration* —in the realm of time.

This world of ideas—here Bergson comes close to Plato— is the world we see, not with our intellect but with our intuition. ("Intuition" comes from the Latin word *intueri*, "to see steadily.") Intellectual observation gives us only a part of the truth; but intuitive reflection gives us the whole truth. It enables us "to sound the depths of life, and to feel the harmonious pulse of its spirit." It shows us that our thought is not a molecular motion of the brain, but an eternal stirring of the spirit of life.

Yet the intellect, according to Bergson, is not to be taken too lightly. It, too, has its necessary function. It helps us to understand the world of matter and space, while the intuition enables us to grasp the inner meaning of life. The horizons of the mind are far wider than those of the intellect. "To explore the most sacred depths of the mind, to labor in the sub-soil of consciousness—this will be the principal task of philosophy in the centuries to come."

IV

Bergson's philosophy deals with the evolution of human thought. His concept of evolution is something altogether different from Darwin's idea about the survival of the fittest in the struggle for existence. Evolution is not a blind process of destruction, but rather an intentional power of creation. It is "the continual elaboration of the absolutely new." The progress of life, from the lowest to the highest forms, is more than the movement of a machine constructed out of hit-or-miss material. It is an impetus for growth; every seed has "an instinct within it that reaches and towers, and comes to a soul in grass and flowers." There is a design in everything. It is, as Aristotle had observed, an *inner* design, an instinctive collaboration of the parts to produce a more harmonious whole.

Life is "always and always a productive and reproductive urge" to something better than before. In the process of evolution there is no such thing as accident. Every living creature is patterned—to a great extent, self-patterned—for progress. The purpose of life is not security but adventure. "In the evolution of life, just as in the evolution of human societies and of individual destinies, the greatest successes have been for those who have accepted the heaviest risks."

One of the greatest risks of life is the freedom of human thought—the effort to bring man ever closer and closer to the image of God. But this greatest of risks can produce the greatest of rewards. This is the true meaning of the struggle for existence—the creativeness of life struggling against the inertia of matter. "Creation, so conceived, is not a mystery; we experience it within ourselves when we act freely." When we thus try to improve ourselves—that is, to make us more acceptable to our better selves—we follow the urge of the *élan vital* within us. We yield to the power of creative evolution as against the forces of obstructive dissolution.

And let us not forget that thus far we are still in the kindergarten of our school in creative evolution. Our human existence on earth has covered but a pinpoint of time in the eternal duration of our progressive growth. The theater for our future achievement is infinite in scope. And the drama in which we play a part is beyond the power of words at the present stage of our development. In one of his most eloquent passages, Bergson describes the spectacle of creative evolution as he sees it: "The animal takes its stand on the plant, man bestrides the animal, and the whole of humanity, in space and time, is one immense army galloping beside and before and behind each of us in an overwhelming charge able to beat down every resistance and clear the most formidable obstacles, perhaps even death."

V

When Bergson lectured to his classes—he was now teaching at the Collège de France—he frequently looked up from his notes and remarked to his students: "Try to understand part of this with the mind and to divine the rest—with the heart."

It was with his mind and his heart that the Jewish philosopher of eighty-one reacted to Hitler's fight against the creative forces of history. The Nazi-inspired French Government of 1940 had ordered the resignation of all Jewish professors in the state universities. Bergson was offered an exemption from this order. He refused to accept the favor. "I am ready to suffer along with the rest," he said. "But in spite of our sufferings and your triumphs, the creative march of evolution will go on."

CHAPTER XXVII

Benedetto Croce (1866–1952)

FROM BERGSON, the mystic, we now come to Croce, the skeptic. Yet these two philosophers, though they travel over different roads, arrive at the selfsame truth—that through our intuition we can find a beautiful pattern in the universe and in human history. Following the idea of John Keats, both Bergson and Croce maintain that "beauty is truth, truth beauty," and that this is all we know or need to know.

Croce was a more universal philosopher than Bergson. Like Plato and Aristotle and Francis Bacon, he undertook a complete survey of human thought, aspiration, and hope. But this survey, Croce believed, could best be made by a philosopher who stepped out of the professorial ivory tower and into the stirring turmoil of life.

And so Croce plunged into the center of life's hurricane in order to find the secret of its motion. He played an active part against the upheavals of fascism, nazism, and communism. He showed that violence among individuals, classes and nations is against reason, and that the happiness of mankind consists in a wise reconciliation or "harmonization"—the old Platonic doctrine—between materialism and idealism, infidelity and faith, the stability of tradition and the mobility of transition. In other words, Croce advocated a wise acceptance of what was good in the past and an active readiness to work toward something better in the future. All this, however, must be done in an atmosphere of peace and not of war, in a meeting of constructive minds rather than in a race for destructive arms.

II

Croce's philosophy was born in a cataclysm. In 1883 his father, a wealthy Neapolitan landowner, was spending his vacation with his family on the island of Ischia. They were caught in an earthquake which killed the Signore and his wife and their only daughter. His two sons, however, were rescued after they had remained buried in the debris for several hours.

The older of the two sons, Benedetto, was seventeen at the time. "The catastrophe," he wrote, "broke my bones and left my health shattered for many years. But it sharpened my mind." His long convalescence gave him time to think about the physical and the spiritual earthquakes that so dramatically interrupted the ordinary business of life.

Benedetto's own life was destined to be filled with spiritual earthquakes and political storms. He was born (1866) in the midst of a revolution. It was the turbulent age of Mazzini, Garibaldi, and Cavour. Naples had overthrown the monarchy, Italy had torn itself away from the grip of Austria, the state had cast off the excessive power of the Church, and thoughtful people everywhere looked forward to a united Italy, a united world. The Croces were not immediately involved in the upheaval; but their cousins, the Spaventas, were up to the hilt in the fight. And it was at the house of one of the Spaventas that Benedetto came to live when his parents were killed in the earthquake.

He was a "studious and pugnacious" lad, more keen, however, for a mental duel than a physical brawl. As a result of the tragic death of his parents and his sister, he had abandoned his belief in God; and his eagerness to assert his disbelief kept him out of tune with the world. "Those were the saddest and darkest years," he wrote. "Often, as I laid my head on the pillow, I keenly desired never to wake again."

He was suffering, at that period, from a mental conflict

now recognized as *ambivalence*. His mind was torn between piety and atheism. He had been brought up as a devout Catholic, and in his heart he felt the need of a guiding hand even in the hours of his disbelief. Having lost his earthly father, he longed for a revival of his faith in a Heavenly Father. He was desperately in search of the God whose existence he denied.

He entered the University of Rome, where he failed to find the proper food for his soul. He left the university (in 1886) without a degree. For a time he withdrew from the world —studying, brooding, waiting for something to turn up.

And something did turn up: a visit to the Spaventas from Professor Labriola, a member of the faculty at the University of Rome. Labriola told his hosts about a book he was preparing on Karl Marx. "I asked the professor for the manuscript," writes Croce, "and I read it . . . My mind was fired . . . I came to believe that the march of history has the right to crush individual men . . . in the service of mankind . . ."

But he soon lost this political enthusiasm for an abstract humanity as against concrete individuals. He became revolted at the idea of "killing a man in order to set him free." Violent revolution was too much like an earthquake. It might temporarily readjust the surface of the earth, but at the cost of too much suffering. The philosophy of Karl Marx was based upon the theory of destruction. What Croce wanted was a system that would promise to save, instead of threatening to destroy, human lives.

He therefore decided to elaborate a philosophy of his own. It was toward the turn of the century—the proper time, he thought, for a complete survey of human history, aspiration, faith, and hope.

First of all, he re-examined the past in the light of the present. In the course of his reading he had become interested in the theory of an earlier compatriot, Giovanni Vico, that all history is a spiral of progress. Humanity, Vico had declared, advances not in a straight line but in an upward march—a spiral, so to speak—around a mountain. In this spiral cycle of development, there is never any turning back toward the starting point, but every step and every turn is higher than the one before. Thus history never repeats itself; what seems to us a repetition is merely a re-view of an old landscape from a loftier position that enables us to look into wider horizons. As we keep going higher and higher in our cyclical climb, our outlook will become broader, our sympathies more inclusive, our hearts more friendly, and our contacts more free.

With this spiral-ascension view of history—an idea closely allied to the Bergsonian picture of the mounting cavalcade of creative evolution—Croce formulated his philosophy of enlightenment. "Learn to see better as you rise in the scale of progress." He started with the publication of a magazine, *La Critica,* in which he tried to depict the world from a superior point of view. From the very outset, he made his magazine the arsenal for a battle of ideas against the warriors of the world. "We intend to fight for a definite order of life," he wrote in the first issue, "a general reawakening of the philosophic spirit . . . unhappily interrupted after the Italian Revolution of 1860."

His associate in this "venture toward sanity in an insane world" was another young philosopher, Giovanni Gentile, an intellectual firebrand who, as Croce was to learn later on, was endowed with more heat than light.

For the present, however, Croce and Gentile lashed out against the aggressions and oppressions of the "misleaders" of the world. Croce selected as his principal target the arrogant militancy of such writers as Gabriele D'Annunzio and other superpatriots who were trying to incite their countrymen to new and destructive wars.

Then came the tragedy of World War I, when Italy, along with many other countries, was plunged into a whirlpool of blood. But after the war, there was an interval of sober reflection. A man of peace, the sedate and moderate Giolitti, was

called to the helm of the Italian government. He selected
Croce (in 1920) as his Minister of Education.

This was the sort of career Croce had always dreamed
about—the pursuit of philosophy from the center of practical
life. At last, he hoped, he would be able to bring about a vital
regeneration in human thought.

But his hope was short-lived. It was only two years later
that Mussolini seized the government. And the man whom the
dictator named as the new Minister of Education was none
other than Croce's former coeditor, Giovanni Gentile.

Croce had parted company with Gentile even before the
war of 1914. When he saw the approaching crisis and the danger of Italy's involvement in the conflict, he had raised his voice
in a passionate plea for peace. But Gentile had joined the military party; he had become infected with the insanity against
which he had fought in his earlier days. He regarded the war
as a holy crusade. And later on, when the dictatorship of Mussolini stifled the voice of freedom, Gentile allied himself with the
fascists as the "founders of a new military order." Croce drifted
farther and farther away from the man who had once served
as his fellow crusader for peace.

The final breach came when Gentile supplanted him as
Minister of Education under the terrorism of Mussolini. Croce's
bitterness against Gentile was motivated not by his personal
ambition but by his devotion to the public interest. "It is sad
enough," he wrote, "to misgovern the old without the added
evil of misguiding the young."

Croce's courageous stand against fascism aroused not only
the anger of Gentile but the enmity of Mussolini. Yet the dictator refrained from arresting him. The public wouldn't tolerate
the imprisonment of their favorite teacher. As a lame excuse for
his failure to "liquidate" the philosopher, Mussolini pretended
that he knew nothing about Croce's ideas. "I have never read
a page of any of his works," he declared. Whereupon Croce
retorted that the dictator had often quoted him. "But, of course,

Mussolini may be telling the truth in this case. He does not quote me personally. He merely reads the speeches which are written for him by others."

Even though Mussolini left the philosopher alone, some of the other fascist leaders delighted in tormenting Croce. They broke into his home and destroyed his books and manuscripts. They hinted that if he went outdoors, he would be attacked by "unnamed patriots who resent his subversive ideas." And anybody who dared to visit him was branded as "an enemy of the State."

III

But Croce, regardless of his personal safety, continued with his program for restoring the sanity of a world gone mad. Quietly, fearlessly, persistently, "the sole master of himself" kept pouring out book after book on history, literature, philosophy, science, and art. Blueprints for the rebuilding of society after an earthquake. He who had been buried alive under the ruins of Ischia had nothing to fear from the catastrophes of nature or the cruelties of men. When he walked through the streets of Naples, people whispered to one another—they dared not say it aloud—"There goes the hero who defies the Duce."

It was the defiance of a man who, in the midst of ugliness and evil, saw beauty and goodness at the heart of things. And he developed this fundamental idea—which he had inherited from the greatest ancient and modern philosophers—in a series of more than fifty books. The beauty of goodness, the goodness of beauty, and the harmony that weaves all the different threads of the universe into the tapestry of truth. And the substance of this truth is easy to grasp: The world is one, all life is one, and all men are members of the single body of mankind.

Yet Croce's philosophy, he modestly observed, was not meant to offer a system of organized thought. It was rather a loose collection of random observations.

In one of his first books—*The Materialism of Karl Marx*—
he pointed out that the Marxist theory of economics is neither
good philosophy nor good science. The field of economics is
not, as Marx would have us believe, a battleground between
classes and masses, capital and labor, the seller and the buyer,
the rich and the poor. It is much more important than that.
Economics is a theory of human values, a view of history in
terms of supply and demand—in short, an aspect of philosophy
in motion.

Indeed, all history, whether economic or social or spiritual
or political, is philosophy in motion. It is a pageant of human
values, ideas, and deeds. The true philosopher, the true historian, must note every possible phase of the pageant, the bad
as well as the good, in order that he may instruct his own generation how to improve its part in the pageant for the better
instruction of the coming generations. For history is a re-vision
of the past for the enlightenment of the future. The reason we
so consistently repeat our past stupidities and errors is that our
historians have improperly observed them and inadequately
interpreted them. The historians give too little time to their
task, and the world produces too few historians. For to write
the history even of a single period (like the nineteenth century), or of a single phase of the human pageant (like economics), requires lifetime study by several observers who must
examine the different aspects of that period or phase from their
different points of view.

But to return to the economics of Karl Marx in the nineteenth century: this apostle of the proletariat, declared Croce,
failed to realize his limitations. He tried to speak for all people at
all times. From his own point of view, Marx saw economics as
a *rivalry*. But from a wider point of view, we can learn to see
it as a *collaboration*. Every transaction between a buyer and a
seller should be an exchange of goods and good will. Each
transaction involves the universal choice between egoism and
altruism, dishonesty and honesty, suspicion and trust. The sci-

entific principle of economics, therefore, is coextensive with the philosophical problem of the good, the beautiful, the true. The economic adjustment of society will come about not through a violent conflict between class and class, but through a trustful understanding between man and man.

And thus Croce subordinated the material to the spiritual values of life. He made utility the servant of beauty. He translated the Platonic idea of justice into a modern concept of economic and social harmony.

IV

In Croce's philosophy—the composite view of history through different eyes at different times—economics is to be regarded as a branch of esthetics, the science of art, and of ethics, the study of morals.

Among one of Croce's most important works is his book entitled *Esthetic*. Art, he explains in this book, is the science of sciences. Some of the other sciences—like mathematics, for example—take us away from individual facts to universal abstractions. But art brings us back from universal abstractions to concrete persons, definite objects, individual facts.

The creation and the appreciation of art writes Croce, in common with Bergson—belongs not to the intellectual but to the intuitive part of our mind. "Art is the product of the imagination (or intuition) surveying the world. It does not qualify objects, it does not define them; it feels and presents them— nothing more." This idea, Croce might have added, applies not only to art but to religion as well. Our intuition does not define nor measure God; it merely feels his beauty, his goodness and his truth.

Intuition, continues Croce, is prior and superior to knowledge. We imagine before we reason; hence we are artists before we are scientists. *Before*, and *after*. Art precedes, follows, and finally embraces science. The great artists, said Croce, understood this fact. "One paints not with the hands," observed Michelangelo, "but with the heart." The creation of a masterpiece is a matter of intuition; its production into a painting or a statue or a poem or a song is merely a process of mechanical technique or manual skill. "When we have mastered the internal word," said Croce, "when we have vividly and clearly conceived a figure or a statue, when we have found a musical theme, expression is born and is complete, nothing more is needed. If we open our mouth, and speak or sing . . . if our hands strike the keyboard of the pianoforte . . . if we take up pencil or chisel or brush . . . what we are doing then is to execute laboriously and outwardly what we have already executed briefly and rapidly within."

As for those of us who have no talent for creation, we can cultivate our ability for understanding—"for bringing ourselves into harmony with the music of the world." Every one of us, if he wills it, can qualify himself for the degree of A.B.—Appreciator of Beauty—in the University of Life. In our financial transactions (the field of economics), as well as in our intuitive perceptions (the realm of art), we can learn to form the correct images of our individual relationships to the world. Economic justice and esthetic beauty are the result not only of the scientist's or the artist's genius, but of the layman's ability to conceive and to apply the true images of a consistent world.

A world consistent—from the Latin *consistere*, "to stand together"—with economic justice, esthetic beauty, and an ethical spirit of free play.

V

And this brings us to Croce's ethics. The important thing in life, he maintains, is not only to conceive the right image, but to perform the right act. "It is only the spiritual act that can be regarded as beautiful, logical, useful and good." Though he frequently criticized the established religions of the day, Croce was at heart a man of the deepest religious faith.

He expressed this faith most clearly in his essay, "Why We Cannot Help Calling Ourselves Christians." "Christianity," he observed, "has been the greatest revolution in history." For it has inspired mankind to a new way of life—from justice to mercy, from mercy to love. Christianity represents the spiritual aspect of democracy, for it emphasizes the equal dignity of all men.

What is true of Christianity, observes Croce, is equally true of all the other great religions of the world. To be sure, the advance of Christianity, like that of any other great religion, has become cluttered up with "mummeries and myths." Yet in spite of these superfluities, it has retained its original ethical truth. We must appreciate it for the purity it has preserved instead of blaming it for the infections to which it has succumbed. "We read Homer," Croce reminds us, "not for his errors but for his truths."

And the true value of Christianity, of any great religion, is that it preserves a center of stability in the whirlpool of our human passions. Let us not criticize it for its rituals, but let us rather honor it for its righteousness. Even science and philosophy are not free of error. And are the religious rituals altogether erroneous? Have not the services and the sacraments of the various Christian denominations helped to educate barbarians and to emphasize the superiority of moral principles to material expediency?

Christianity, like Judaism, Buddhism, and Mohammedanism, "lives on in spite of its defects because it has a vital function and satisfies a universal need."

And thus the churchmen sustain the order of the past, while the philosophers and the scientists are trying to devise a better order for the future. Don't destroy the old house before you have finished the new. "None can say whether another revelation or religion, of equal or higher rank, will light upon humanity in a future of which we now discern no glimmer." But unless and until such a revelation arrives, "let us live within the limits of our present faith."

So let there be an understanding instead of a clash between the guardians of tradition and the champions of transition. Let them support one another toward an orderly progress in the upward march of life.

This harmony between order and progress, religion and philosophy, the zest for the old and the quest for the new, is but a part of the universal harmony that Croce hoped to see established in the ethical relationship between man and man. Croce wrote a series of essays dealing with the adjustment of the individual to the religious and the philosophical demands of civilization. Both religion and philosophy speak the same ethical language: "Adapt yourself to the logical world of reality, and don't live in an illogical world of fitful dreams." Are you frustrated, ill-treated, ill-employed? Don't jump from the frying pan of temporary evil into the fire of permanent hate. Do you think it would make you happy to see the death of the enemy you fear? If so, you have not escaped from your enemy. You have not even escaped from your own fears. You have merely lost your chance to face the enemy courageously and, if possible, to convert him into a friend.

Take another example of practical ethics. Everyone you love is destined to die. Should you steel yourself against the loss of your beloved by limiting your love? No, declares Croce. On the contrary, true love in this realistic world of ours will accept the pain as well as the joy. Indeed, the one is but the contrast to the other, as the night is to the day and the winter to the spring. Our sufferings are but the hurdles that exercise our souls. "True happiness is to be won by learning to love with such elevation of spirit as to attain the power to stand up to grief"—the ability to "surpass the old love with an even greater new love."

The purpose of love, of devotion, of all ethics, is to fortify the individual against his own weakness and to fit him as a well-adjusted character into a rational pattern of life.

VI

Croce was opposed to every sort of outbreak—nazism, fascism, communism—that threatened to destroy this fundamental pattern. To the end of his days he hated explosions and earthquakes. During the turmoil of the fascist explosion he tried to shape the minds of men toward a new government of reason. When Mussolini fell and Victor Emmanuel came back to the throne, Croce refused to truckle to him. The brutality of despotism was as distasteful to him as the barbarity of fascism. He was foremost among those who insisted upon the dethronement of the obstinate king.

But throughout these political upheavals, Croce was intent upon a peaceful return to stability. When the anti-fascists assassinated Gentile, Croce expressed his horror at the violent death of his enemy. "I had hoped . . . to insure his personal safety, and to guide him back to the studies which he had deserted."

Here we have Croce's philosophy in a nutshell. Protect your enemies, and by so doing try to turn them into friends. In the battle between good and evil, teaching is a far more potent weapon than killing. Upon the abdication of King Emmanuel, Croce was urged to return to the political fight. The people wanted him to become President of the new Italian Republic. But he refused the honor. His own days as a statesman-philosopher were over. From now on, he wanted to remain a teacher.

And his vigor as a teacher remained undiminished to the end. At the age of eighty (in 1946) he began a series of lectures for postgraduate students—to repay him, as he said, for his enforced departure from his teaching during the fascist regime. At eighty-four he was on the point of death from a cerebral hemorrhage. But he recovered for another two years of lecturing and writing and pointing the way to a life of greater utility and beauty and faith. And when he died, one of his disciples described his beloved Don Benedetto as a man "with the rugged face of a fighter and the sensitive eyes of a saint."

PART
7

Modern American Philosophers

CHAPTER XXVIII

Ralph Waldo Emerson (1803–1882)

EMERSON was the leading American disciple of the old Hindu idea of "the Highest Law—the oneness of mankind." He may be regarded as the American architect of the United Nations, the teacher of universal tolerance toward individual liberty, of mutual collaboration as against mutual distrust among all the members of the human family. On July 15, 1838, he delivered an address before the senior class of the Harvard Divinity School. In this address he pointed out the great American weakness—national preoccupation with the manufacture of better trinkets instead of better teachers. But he also pointed out the great American potential strength. For America, he declared, can become the scene of the world's noblest experiment —"the patron of every new thought, every unproven opinion, every untried project" which may lead the human race in a united march toward friendly coexistence and peace.

In short, he placed the ethical code of humanity upon a practical American basis—*to live, let live, and help live.* And thus he translated the ancient Eastern—and much of the modern Western—philosophy into the Yankee dialect.

II

Emerson lost his father when he was still a child. His mother opened a boardinghouse in order to support her five little sons. From the very beginning, therefore, Ralph learned to know and to like people. And he also acquired an optimistic outlook on life, a knack for being cheerful in the midst of poverty. In the winter he and one of his brothers had but a single overcoat between them, and they were obliged to wear it on alternate days. Ralph made the best use of his indoor confinement by listening to the conversation of the grown-ups and reading the books in his mother's library. Before he had reached his teens, he was familiar with Plato, Pascal, and the philosophy of the Upanishads.

But his physical nourishment was at times unequal to his spiritual fare. His mother found it difficult to make ends meet. She could have lived more cheaply in the country; but she insisted on staying in Boston, because, as she said, her children were "born to be educated" and "to enter the pulpit like their father." She put Ralph into the Boston Latin School, the oldest public school in the country, and then she "scrimped and scrubbed" to put him through Harvard. He was only eighteen when he graduated, tall and thin as a lamppost and with a lamplike glow in his eyes. It was the fire of genius that burned in those eyes, and the flame of disease. He had fallen a prey to the Emerson plague—consumption—which had killed his father and was soon to destroy two of his brothers. For twelve years he lived "in the House of Pain," fought desperately against death and strove to find a financial as well as a physical foothold on life. He tried teaching among the hills of Roxbury, a suburb of Boston, "where men in the bush with God may meet." He wrote poetry that sounded like prose, and prose that sang like poetry, and failed to sell enough of either to make a living. He was invited to preach at various churches where he enchanted the members of the congregations with his voice—a soft and golden instrument that melted away the frost of New England fundamentalism like an April sun. "Oh Sally!" wrote a Northampton lady to her sister, "we thought to entertain a pious indigent; but lo, an angel unawares!"

Yet this Yankee angel was too much of a non-conformist to please the "pillars of the church." He was too much of a Christian to be a theologian. The religious observance of the people, he declared, had too much form and too little soul. The sexton at one of the churches complained that Emerson couldn't make "the proper impression at a funeral."

No, Emerson was not the man to preach lugubriously about death. He was the poet of life. So he resigned from the pulpit and went out to search for the meaning of life. He took long walks in the country. He tried to attune his ear and his heart to the music of Nature. And before long he made a strange discovery. He learned that the heart of Nature was beating in unison with his own heart. He was, as the old oriental philosophers had hinted, *an intimate part of a living world.* His mind was an important cell in the World-Mind—or, as he preferred to term it, the World-Soul or Over-Soul. And this abstract rediscovery of an old truth led him to a practical philosophy. He noticed, when he thought about the intimate relationship between himself and the rest of the world, that his whole being was electrified with a surge of power, an overmastering confidence in himself and in his fellow men. This power seemed infinite. He felt himself at one with the world. All history was an everlasting Now, and every man was an eternal image of God.

This power which he sensed in his communion with Nature was always at his beck and call. He could draw upon it at will. *And he could teach others to draw upon the same power within themselves.* Each of us, he concluded, possesses the spiritual capital for developing an enormous business—the business of acquiring and exchanging beauty and joyousness and hope and friendship and peace. "The trouble with most men," he said, "is that they are like children unaware of the heritage which is theirs." Assert your heritage. It is there for the asking!

It was a philosophy admirably suited to the pioneer spirit of America. We are forever, he said, "on the verge of all that is great." Trust in yourself. Claim your share of the greatness of life. Recognize your relationship to the divine. Surrender yourself to the power within you. Dare to become the master of your own fate.

Emerson had found his business in life. He was to become a traveling salesman of hope—"a Professor," to use his own expression, "of the Science of Joy."

III

Emerson's own life was not a life of unmixed joy. He fell in love and married and lost his wife, all within eighteen months. For two years after her death, he paid a daily visit to her grave. He expected that he himself would follow her shortly—his painful cough was "like a sexton singing a funeral dirge in his chest."

But Emerson's philosophy was a call to life instead of death. He took a trip to Europe, in order to learn more about life from the masters of the Old World. And then he returned to America to become the teacher of the New.

He found a new kind of schoolroom, the village lyceum. Here, unbound by the shackles of conventional creeds, he expressed his ideas about everything under and over the sun. It was not an easy road he had chosen to travel. The Brahmans of Boston and Cambridge were determined to stop his "subversive" teaching. Once they shouted him off the platform when he attempted to lecture at Harvard. But the simple folk understood the sincerity of his voice even when they failed to understand the meaning of his words. They had the feeling, when they listened to him, that here was a man whose soul was attuned to their own.

His lectures brought him about eight hundred dollars a year, enough to satisfy his modest needs. Indeed, he felt himself quite rich. He bought a small house—he called it a "mansion" —in Concord, Massachusetts, married a second time, and settled down to bring wisdom within the reach of the average man.

The little town of Concord was, in Emerson's day, one of the spiritual garden spots in the history of the world. For some strange and inexplicable reason, the gods occasionally select a little spot on earth and people it with the citizens of heaven. This happened in Athens during the fifth century B.C., the age of Aeschylus and Euripides and Phidias and Socrates and Plato; in London during the reign of Elizabeth, the period of Beaumont and Jonson and Fletcher and Bacon and Shakespeare; in Germany during the early years of the nineteenth century, the era of Goethe and Schiller and Mozart and Beethoven and Brahms; in Russia during the latter part of the nineteenth century, the generation of Turgenev and Dostoyevsky and Chekhov and Tchaikovsky and Tolstoy. In a somewhat lesser sense, perhaps, we see a similar flowering of the human spirit in Concord at the time of Emerson. Among the intimates of Emerson were Nathaniel Hawthorne, "the conscience of America"; Margaret Fuller, a female Merlin who played with ideas as a juggler plays with colored balls; Bronson Alcott, the peddler-prophet who "combined the wisdom of Plato with the warmth of Saint Francis"; Henry Thoreau, the devout vagabond whose income was about twenty-five dollars a year but whose capital was an infinity of love; and "Aunt Mary" Emerson, a living flame of four-feet-three who, dressed in a white shroud and a scarlet shawl, galloped on her horse over the fields of Concord, "a mental adventuress" whose wit could tear into shreds the pomposity of the learned pundits at Harvard.

With his congenial neighbors and friends in Concord, Emerson exchanged ideas about mice and men and the meaning of the world. And then he went into his study and minted these ideas into the golden coin of his lectures and his essays. And he displayed his thoughts under a mystic light which, like the sun, had risen in the East. A light which illumined and warmed and gladdened the heart. "Rejoice and rejoice, for your destiny is greater than you think!" The Blessed Immortals, declared

Emerson, echoing Zoroaster, are swift to meet those who believe in themselves.

Emerson spread the sunlight of his philosophy over New England, in the South, and across the continent into California. He talked to all sorts of people, teachers and tradesmen and laborers and poets and pioneers, and to many of his listeners he brought a message of personal hope. He inspired them with a serenity founded upon his own supreme faith. Faith in the justice of American freedom and in the heroism of the average American man.

IV

Emerson's philosophy, like his character, was informal. He proposed no erudite plan for the regeneration of mankind. He took men as he found them, with all their faults, and aroused within them the divine spark which, as he assured them, every one of them possessed. He scattered his ideas throughout his essays, making no effort to correlate them. "Let them fall like seeds out of the hand and into the wind. Wherever they reach a fertile spot, they will bear flowers and fruits."

And the flowers and fruits of his philosophy formed a landscape with a definite pattern. This pattern may be briefly summarized as follows:

America must throw overboard the old beliefs of a dying world. "We live in a new land, new men, new thoughts." We need a new kind of virtue—virtue "with guts in it." Pride in our work, and justice for our workers. For the workers are the channels through which the aspiration of the few flows into creation for the many. This is to be a country of great ideas and great deeds. Free, dynamic, daring deeds not only of independence but of interdependence. Let us all work fearlessly together for the common good. "The heart in thee is the heart for all."

Are you afraid, in pursuing your new course, that you will be misunderstood? "It is a fool's word. Is it so bad then to be misunderstood? Pythagoras was misunderstood, and Socrates, and Jesus, and Luther, and Copernicus, and Galileo, and Newton, and every pure and wise spirit that ever took flesh. To be great is to be misunderstood."

Let us "bow and apologize never more" as we go ahead with our great American experiment. Our country is to be dominated by the strong, stern will of our pioneers and guided by the wise and gentle counsel of our philosophers. And the goal of our experiment? Complete democracy, social, political and economic. A future hope, founded upon past mistakes. Use your past not as a platform to stand upon, but as a springboard from which to advance. Accept America as a land of groping and stumbling, yet forward-looking and self-reliant souls. Keep on trying and blundering and failing, but do not despair. In spite of your failure, in spite of your sufferings, in spite of your discouragements, keep "antagonizing on." The race is not to the swift, but to the resolute. Have you been pushed aside? Have you stumbled? Never mind the ridicule, never mind the defeat; up again, old heart! "Be of good cheer . . . Patience and patience, we shall win at last."

This world, declared Emerson, belongs to the energetic. To the daring. Dare to assert yourself as an accredited citizen in the great Republic of Mankind. Your birth into this world has been no mistake. You are an invited guest to the banquet of life. And he who has sent you the invitation is no niggardly host. Divine generosity is hidden somewhere behind the mystery of creation. "There is intelligence and good will at the heart of things."

And how can you best adjust yourself to the intelligent goodness that lies at the heart of things? In other words, how can you best help yourself at this banquet of the gods? By helping others, Emerson maintains. And this, to Emerson, is no mere Sunday School maxim. It is the very essence of his philosophy. We are all, he believes, parts of one body. And all humanity has but a single soul. To be self-reliant is to fit yourself harmoniously into the united body and soul of mankind—to enable others, or rather *other parts of yourself*, to enjoy the good things of the world. *Life is a mutual interrelationship.* He is most true to himself who is most true to others. There is one universal lesson that all of us must learn—and that is the art of being friendly.

Friendship, to Emerson, is the most sublime thing in the world. And, he declares, it is a gift within the reach of us all. "My friends have come to me unsought. The great God gave them to me."

The essence of friendship, writes Emerson, is "entireness" —the fusion of different personalities into one essence. This fusion enables us to rejoice in one another's triumphs. "I feel pride in my friend's accomplishments as if they were mine." The soul seeks for friends in order that, through them, it may become better acquainted with itself.

"Happy is the house that shelters a friend!" for it is on the way to becoming a complete unit. A unit of love. In the presence of friendship, therefore, "let us be silent—that we may hear the whisper of the gods." And it is in the music of that whisper that we can feel "the flowing of two souls into one."

But let us not put a false interpretation upon friendship. Let us not confuse it with a selfish alliance for some sort of personal profit. "I hate the prostitution of the name of friendship to signify modish and worldly alliances." True friendship is far above these hollow formalities of social intercourse. It is a substance of such reality and duration that compared to it "the Alps and the Andes come and go as rainbows."

Cultivate the art of friendship and you come close to the heart of reality. True friendship brings you in touch with the divine meaning of life. Is the object of your friendly overtures unable to receive or to reciprocate them? "It never troubles the sun that some of his rays fall wide and rain into ungrateful space, and only a small part on the reflecting planet. Let your greatness educate the crude and cold companion." Even if he is unworthy, "you are enlarged by your own shining . . . and you soar and burn with the gods."

And thus, when you give yourself as a friend, you stop looking at the shadows and begin to see the true source of light. "If man could be inspired with a tender kindness to the souls of men, and should come to feel that every man was another self . . . this feeling would cause the most striking changes of external things; the tents would be struck; the men-of-war would rot ashore; the arms would rust; the cannon would become street posts; the pikes, a fisher's harpoon; and the marching regiment would be a caravan of peaceful pioneers."

Peaceful pioneers. This was the dream of Emerson—a world of brave, interdependent, joyous, loving and adventuring friends.

V

It has been erroneously asserted that Emerson has nothing to teach to our present generation. If Emerson has nothing to say to us, then Isaiah has nothing to say. Or Buddha, or Plato, or Spinoza, or Jesus, or St. Paul. Indeed, as Father Taylor, "the Workingman's Apostle," reminds us, "Emerson was more like Jesus than any other man in American history."

CHAPTER XXIX

William James (1842–1910)

WILLIAM JAMES continued in the mainstream of philosophy that flowed from the East to the West. The world, he agreed, is one body and one soul. But like Emerson, he expressed this thought with an American accent. In our effort to arrive at the truth, he said, let us apply our philosophical ideas to the practical problems of life.

In 1898, he was engaged in a series of lectures at the University of California. One morning he saw a coyote that had just been shot dead. He wrote about the incident in a letter to his children.

This letter is a summary of his philosophy as an intrepid adventure against the afflictions of life. "The heroic little animal," wrote James, "lay on the ground [near the hotel], with his big furry ears, and his clean white teeth, and his jolly cheerful little body, but his brave little life was gone. It made me think how brave all these living things are. Here little coyote was, without any clothes or house or books or anything, with nothing but his own naked self to pay his way with, and risking his life so cheerfully—and losing it—just to see if he could pick up a meal near the hotel. He was doing his coyote-business like a hero, and you must do your boy-business, and I my man-business bravely too, or else we won't be worth as much as that little coyote."

"You must do your boy-business, and I my man-business, bravely." In writing his philosophy William James courageously performed his duties in spite of physical suffering. He was an invalid for the greater part of his life. For several years he thought of committing suicide. A man, he observed, is not psychologically complete unless he has at one time or another contemplated self-destruction. The complete man is he who has stood "on the perilous edge," and who has dared to turn back and *face* the universe.

William James is a practical philosopher who teaches us how to "hold ourselves erect and keep our hearts unshaken" in the hazardous game of living.

II

Born in New York, James grew up in a big-city atmosphere —with its rough-and-tumble education for survival in the midst of crowds. No rooted flower but a restless creature on the wing, he went inquisitively from place to place and got much of his experience through an exchange of blows. As a child, he was full of mischief and rough games. To Henry, his younger brother, who was rather on the quiet side, William said: "Me, I like to play with boys who cuss and fight."

He picked up his formal schooling piecemeal in various countries of Europe. His father, Henry James, Sr., was a mystic who loved to travel physically as well as spiritually over the world. London, Paris, Bordeaux, Geneva, Bonn —a kaleidoscope of people, languages, experiences, customs, and ideas. William James acquired a linguistic facility and a cosmopolitan outlook on life.

He was especially interested in the art galleries of Europe. For a time he thought of becoming a painter. He studied under the artist William Morris Hunt, who was friendly enough to advise him that this was not his field.

So he laid down his brush and began to prepare himself for a scientific career. He entered the Lawrence Scientific School of Harvard—an eager and sociable but sickly young fellow of nineteen who looked forward to only a few years of activity in a world of pain. "One year study in chemistry," he wrote, "then one term at home . . . then a medical education, then five or six years with Agassiz [the great Harvard naturalist], then probably death . . ."

His college course, like his earlier education, was full of interruptions. He was in the Harvard Medical School when the Civil War broke out. Enlistment in the Army was out of the question for a man of his precarious health. But he joined Agassiz in a scientific expedition to Brazil, and almost died in Rio de Janeiro. When he returned to the United States, he suffered another breakdown and went to Europe in search of health. Added to his physical illness—a weak heart—was a mental depression which (as we have noted) drove him almost to the verge of suicide. Unable to recover his health in Europe, he returned to Cambridge where he managed through sheer grit to complete his medical course in 1869.

But he never practiced medicine. He had neither the inclination nor the strength to undertake the rugged career of a doctor. He just settled down to the "declining years of an invalid's life." He spent only a few hours a day in reading; his physicians forbade any excessive strain to his failing eyesight. And he was allowed to make only a few social calls, a terrible hardship to a man of his friendly disposition.

This was the unhappiest period of his life. He wrote a vivid account of his mental depression at the time: "I went one evening into a dressing room in the twilight . . . when suddenly there fell upon me . . . a horrible fear of my own existence . . . There arose in my mind the image of an epileptic patient whom I had seen in the asylum, a black-haired youth with greenish skin, entirely idiotic, who used to sit all day on one of the benches . . . against the wall, with his knees drawn up against his chin, and the coarse gray undershirt, which was his only garment, drawn over them and inclosing his entire figure . . . This image and my fear entered into a species of combination with each other. *That shape am I*, I felt, *potentially* . . .

"I became a mass of quivering fear . . . For months I was unable to go out into the dark alone . . . The fear was so invasive and powerful that if I had not clung to scripture-texts like 'The eternal God is my refuge,' etc., 'Come unto me, all ye that labor and are heavy laden,' etc., I think I should have grown really insane."

The thing that finally saved him was his reading of Charles Renouvier's essay on free will. The exercise of free will, Renouvier had declared, is "the [act of] sustaining a thought *because I choose to* when I might have other free thoughts." James found his reason for further living in this exercise of his free will—his *willing choice to believe* that his salvation lay within himself. "My life shall be [built upon] doing and suffering and creating"—in spite of suffering.

James had stopped drifting and was ready to swim, to do his man-business, bravely, Active daring, and not passive moping; courageous fighting, and not cowardly defeat. And so, in spite of his physical illness, James threw himself fearlessly into the current of life.

III

He married and began to teach physiology at Harvard. From physiology he moved on to psychology, and from psychology to philosophy. From the moment of his own salvation, he remained an active worker for the salvation of mankind.

Philosophy, as he pointed out to his students again and again, is not a final answer to the one great problem of the universe—the ultimate meaning of our existence. It is rather a practical guide to the solution of the many problems that arise in our daily activities.

He was not interested in founding a school or in winning disciples. He wanted everybody to be his own master. His favorite quotation was from the prophet Ezekiel: "Son of man, stand upon thy feet, and I will speak unto thee."

And he spoke to the world in a colloquial style that everybody could understand. It was said of the two James brothers that Henry wrote novels like a philosopher and William wrote philosophy like a novelist. There was little of the professor about William James. Slender, animated, and short, he looked like "a little boy with a beard." There was something puckish about his personality that endeared him to his students. They followed him like the Pied Piper of Hamelin from the lecture hall, across Harvard Square, to his home, pelting him with questions and chuckling at his wise and witty answers. He always subordinated his scholastic dignity to his sense of humor. He enjoyed telling about an incident that illustrated this point. At one of his lectures he was emphasizing a philosophical idea with a homely metaphor when a student interrupted him: "But Professor, to be serious for a moment!"

He rarely stood still as he lectured. He paced over the platform, drew diagrams on the blackboard, and gesticulated with his hands when he wanted to bring a point home. One day he had only a small portable blackboard with him. At first he held it with one hand and wrote with the other. Finding this procedure rather cumbersome, he knelt on the floor as he wrote. But even this was not enough; and so he finally stretched out on his stomach and kept writing and lecturing to his students who listened with the utmost absorption and never even cracked a smile.

His students idolized him because he spoke to them as man to man. They called him "a genuine guy" who taught them "genuine stuff." He took philosophy out of the classroom and turned it into an adventure in living. Every one of us, he maintained, is a philosopher. Whether we know it or not, we are always called upon to make decisions about the things that concern us. And this necessity to make our own decisions, to stand on our own feet, is what makes philosophers of us all.

In view of this universal fact, James developed a philosophy that would be helpful in the solution of our everyday perplexities. He called this philosophy *Pragmatism*—a name which is derived from the Greek word *pragma*, an "act," and which means a philosophy based upon practical action. It is the philosophy of business—not in the narrow sense of exchanging goods in the market place, but in the far wider sense of honest understanding and fair dealing in all our human transactions.

The idea of Pragmatism is very simple. It submits our entire conduct to a single, concrete test: *Does it pay?* What is the "cash value" of anything we may desire to do?

"But don't misunderstand this idea," declared James. "By cash value I do not mean the return in dollars and cents. I mean rather the payment in terms of a healthier body, a stronger mind, a more courageous soul."

It was out of his own need that James devised his practical philosophy. In the days of his depression, he had referred to himself as "a suffering vegetable, if there be such a thing." His philosophy of action was a means of self-defense, a challenge to his own soul to pull him out of his "vegetative" state.

Act! Experiment! Grow! Exercise your free will! Choose to be strong! This is but a paraphrase of Emerson's injunction to rely upon yourself. Yet at first, James approached this philosophy with a cautious mind. Practical American that he was, he wanted to prove its validity before he accepted it himself.

Hence he applied himself wholeheartedly to the various activities of his life, *and found that the idea worked.* His philosophy gave him a stronger incentive for living, a wiser tolerance toward others, a clearer outlook upon the universe, wider horizons, deeper satisfactions, greater peace. He was then ready to teach his philosophy to the world. "Since it has been helpful to me, the chances are it will be helpful to you, too."

IV

Suppose, then, we test this philosophy in the light of our own experience. How can Pragmatism help us in our work, our attitude toward our family, our belief (or disbelief) in God? Finally, what answer can this philosophy give us to the most vital of all questions: Is life worth living?

First, let us consider Pragmatism in relation to our work. James cautions all of us not to overemphasize the importance of "that bitch goddess, success." Don't aim at success, he warns us, to the exclusion of everything else. Whether you are a worker or an employer, the thing that pays best is friendly cooperation rather than aggressive competition. "The bigger we grow, the hollower, the more brutal we become . . . So I am against all big successes and big results, and in favor of underdogs always."

Don't hunger after too much money for yourself at the expense of your neighbors. It doesn't pay. "Of what good is profit to me if it means loss to my fellow men?" Whatever your occupation, you are laboring not only for yourself but for society. And you will find your greatest happiness in a society of mutual helpfulness and honesty and trust. In such a society—which it is your business to help create—your activity will receive the highest wages in the world. The currency of a mind at peace.

The Pragmatism of the office and the shop is closely allied to the Pragmatism of the home. "My philosophy," said James, "has taught me to be quieter with my own lot." He was a sociable soul, but he found his deepest contentment in the family circle. There is "cash value" in a harmonious family—the accumulated capital of unstinted love. "The road of ascent," writes Dean Inge, echoing the philosophy of William James, "is by personal affection."

We have little to fear, declares James, so long as we sustain our affections, so long as we have a home to play *in*, and a family to play *with*. This is the meaning of Pragmatism—the philosophy of the practical life—as applied to our family relationships. The family satisfies our universal hunger for "the dear togetherness." In mutual service, every member of the ideal family arrives at its fullest spiritual growth. He finds that *it pays* to make our home cheerful with the brightness of love.

In the development of his pragmatic idea about family relationships, James widened the boundaries of the home to those of the world—here again we have the philosophy of a united mankind. The world, he observed, is our common home, and all its inhabitants are the members of our single family. The most profitable business of life, therefore, is the friendly exchange of affection and good will among all men.

And this brings us to the idea of Pragmatism as applied to religion. The perfect religion would be that which could unite the entire human race into a family worship of one God.

At present, said James, we belong to different religions because we have different conceptions of God. No man, in the present state of our imperfect knowledge, can have a monopoly of *the* truth. Each of us is a spectator looking upon the universe from a different point of view. And no one has the right to assume that *his* is the only point of view which is infallible. "Neither the whole of truth nor the whole of goodness is revealed to any single observer, though each observer gains a partial superiority of insight from the peculiar position in which he stands."

Therefore, instead of fighting about our different points of view, let us, through the partnership of man under the guidance of God, combine them into a comprehensive vision. But in our everyday life, every man's faith, every man's church, every man's conception of God is for him true if it enables him to cope honestly with his daily problems.

Just what is the whole truth about God, we shall perhaps never know. Our idea about the nature of God, said James, is like the idea of an animal about the nature of man. But let us not be dismayed on that account. In a letter to his daughter about a dog who was his household pet he wrote: "He doesn't understand who or what I am. But he feels I am his friend. His tail keeps wagging all the time, and he makes on me the impression of an angel hid in a cloud. He longs to do good."

You and I, too, are like angels hid in a cloud. We are the house pets of God. However obscure the mists that surround you, you can be confident of one thing: If you believe in God, this belief in itself will make God a reality in your life. The pragmatic value of your religion, therefore, is the spiritual cash value of your reliance upon a friendly moral power greater than your own.

It is a "good investment" to believe in God. It pays you the dividends of a tranquil soul. It puts a definite purpose into your life. For it provides you with a powerful guide toward your nobler aspirations.

But if you expect God to be on your side, it is up to you to be on God's side. And here we come to one of the most important aspects of James's pragmatic philosophy:

Is life worth living? "It depends upon the *liver*," writes James with one of his habitual flashes of humor.

But then, reverting to his more serious mood, he provides us with an inspiring answer to this question. Our life is decidedly worth while, he maintains, if we plan to live *with God's help and as God's helpers*. James is neither a pessimist nor an optimist. He is a "meliorist"—a philosopher who doesn't blink his eyes at the evils of the world but who believes that we can, if we will, ameliorate these evils and make the world better. Following the ancient philosophy of the East, especially of Zoroaster, James declares that our life's purpose is to serve as cobuilders with God in the construction of a perfect world.

For the world we live in is not yet finished. There is much important work to be done before it is complete. And God is relying upon us to be his faithful employees in this work, just as we are depending upon him to be our friendly employer.

Do a good job, therefore, as a collaborator with God. Help to eliminate the imperfections in the unfinished house that has been rented to you for a lifetime, and try to turn it into a more secure, more beautiful, and more livable home.

Your life, then, is an adventure in sweeping away the old and building the new. "It is a real adventure, with real danger . . . Yet we may win through if each several agent does his own level best." And then James proceeds with a personal challenge to every one of us: "Will you join the procession? Will you trust yourself and trust other agents enough to face the risk?"

The philosophy of Pragmatism, in short, is a call to your individual effort in the progressive construction of a superior world. This is the meaning of your life—the cash value of your labor in the currency of joy. In trying to make the world better, you can make your own life happier.

This, observes James, is not an absolute promise; but it is a definite possibility. The important thing, after all, is not the glory of the conqueror but the courage of the fighter. Especially when the fight is against odds. And there is always the chance of victory.

So, in spite of every obstacle, turn your life into a spiritual as well as a physical adventure, and keep adventuring on!

V

James kept "adventuring on" throughout his life. In 1906, he was serving as an exchange professor at Stanford University. On the morning of April 18, the day of the San Francisco earthquake, he took a train to the devastated city—a man of sixty-four with a sick heart—"to do his mite" for the victims of the catastrophe. For twelve hours he struggled amidst the roaring flames and the crashing walls, bringing aid to the stricken and gathering material for his philosophy as a call to perseverance in the depths of distress.

This activity during the disaster at San Francisco was characteristic of his entire career. James was a philosopher of deeds as well as of ideas. He threw himself into many movements to improve the political, social, and economic conditions of the world. He worked not only for abstract causes but for individual men. His own courage against ill health was a spark that fired others into an equal courage. All of us, he declared, have a reserve energy which many of us never use. Take advantage of this reserve power within you, and you will be amazed to discover your capability for solving your most difficult problems. *Stand upon your own feet.* And face whatever dangers may confront you. "Take life strivingly." Fight against your own afflictions and the abominations of the world.

True to this philosophy, James fought against the bigotry of anti-Semitism, the injustice of the sweatshop, the scramble for material success, the aggressiveness of imperialism, and the insanity of war.

He hated war. Yet he realized that our human instinct for fighting is perhaps ineradicable. He therefore advocated the channeling of this instinct into a "battle against nature." Let every young man, said James, enlist for two years in a fighting army—not for destroying but for building. Let us clear the forests, drain the marshes, irrigate the wastelands, span the rivers, conquer the floods, grow food for the hungry, and provide shelter for the homeless. Let us devote our energies and our funds, so tragically wasted in killing, to the more humane adventure of healing. Let us march together toward a friendlier, happier, and healthier life.

His own health, always precarious, finally gave out. In 1907 he resigned from his professorship at Harvard. A final trip to Europe, and he came back just in time to die.

But his mind was still eager for the business of showing others how to live. He left the notes for a book which he was no longer able to write. The tentative title of this book was *The Futility of Jingoism.*

To the very end, a crusader in the war against war!

CHAPTER XXX

George Santayana (1863–1952)

THE PHILOSOPHY of Santayana, one of the greatest American thinkers, was universal instead of national. He was interested in eternal ideas rather than in temporary problems. "The longer we think about the world," he said, "the more surely we return to Plato and his oriental teachers. We need no new philosophy; we need only the courage to live up to the oldest and the best."

The old philosophy of harmony, justice, mercy, love. Brought up as a Catholic, he built his philosophy upon the foundation of a world-embracing intellectual trinity—the True, the Beautiful, the Good. To be a philosopher, he observed, is to *recognize* the True, to *desire* the Beautiful, to *establish* the Good. "This is wisdom; all else is folly."

Santayana's life, like his philosophy, was an echo of the past—the reverberation of a bell down the corridors of time. Though born in Spain and educated in the United States, he was more than merely a Spaniard or an American. He was mentally, as well as temperamentally, a citizen of the world of united thought. His ideas were a summation of the substantial agreement that lies at the heart of all the different systems of philosophy and faith.

II

Before Santayana's birth (in Madrid), his father had served as a Spanish official in the Philippines. He had sailed several times around the world, and he had stocked his mind with many a story of exotic places, persons, and ideas. He told these stories to George, whose eager mind absorbed them like a sponge. The boy grew up in an atmosphere of wonder at all the different peoples in the world, and he imagined in his childish way that all of them were his "cousins"—members of one vast human family. He never outgrew this feeling of relationship toward all mankind.

When George was nine years old, his mother separated from her husband—it was her second marriage—and migrated with her four children to America.

George was educated at the Boston Latin School and at Harvard. He took no active part in the sports of the other boys, but he enjoyed watching them from the side lines. He was especially interested in football. A game on the gridiron was like a living poem to him. "Here upon the broad-backed earth," he wrote, "away from the town, nothing but sky and distant hills about you, where the wind always blows, the struggle has an added beauty . . . Here the heroic virtues shine in miniature and the simple joy of the ancient world returns as in a dream."

This is how Santayana watched not only the football contests of his fellow students but the competitive struggles of his fellow men. The world in which he lived appeared to him as the memory of an ancient dream. *Plus ça change, plus c'est la même chose.* Different characters, different lines, but the same old plot—in ancient Persia, India, and Greece, in modern Spain, Germany, and the United States, in all places and at all times —an endless struggle to reach the goal, but with orders for a strict adherence to the rules of the game.

Unlike James, who was an active participant in the contest, Santayana preferred to remain a passive spectator. Yet the two were essentially alike in their fundamental belief. It is good, they said, to flex the muscles of your body for a healthy but honest fight, and to clean the windows of your soul for a clear and comprehensive view of life's struggle throughout the ages.

And the purpose of this struggle? James saw it as a quest for justice; and Santayana regarded it as a search for beauty. For James looked upon the world as a pragmatist, and Santayana as a poet.

A poet who tried very hard, but unsuccessfully, to be prosaic in his outlook. An idealist who professed that he was a materialist but who confessed that perhaps matter is identical with energy, and energy is identical with life.

Santayana was thus a modern disciple of the ancient hylozoists—the philosophers who believed that the material universe is alive.

III

Santayana wanted to spend his life in "quiet conversation with the great philosophical spirits of the past." But he was compelled, by a trick of destiny, to become a teacher and to spend his time talking to college undergraduates. "I always hated to be a professor," he wrote in his later years. Yet no one would have suspected it from the serenity of his lectures. It was the privilege of the author of the present book to study under Santayana at Harvard. The experience was unforgettable. The scientist-poet-philosopher sat on the platform at Emerson Hall, pale hands folded on his desk under a pale face, black pointed beard giving his features an ethereal El Greco unreality, a spirit from afar flashing out of two fiery Spanish eyes, and a voice filled with a cadenced wisdom that descended upon his students like a benediction. He spoke fluently but in a patient, unhurried tempo, as if he had all eternity for the delivery of his message. And every word fitted into the context of his message like a flawless jewel in a perfect setting.

At times he criticized others for what he looked upon as their wrong ideas. But his criticism never descended to the level of vituperation. He was amused rather than angered at the follies of mankind.

He cared little for the diversions of society. He never married and spent most of his spare time in the company of his books. His closest friends were the immortal spirits of the ages, whom he joined in their never-ending quest for truth.

Yet he retained his one concession to the "mummeries of contemporary life." He was still interested in college athletics. One of his students, familiar only with Santayana's classroom aloofness, was astonished when he saw him, "in his foreign cape and with his foreign cane," walking into the stadium to watch the football game on a Saturday afternoon. "Imagine Zoroaster or Plato," exclaimed the student, "giving a regular cheer for Harvard!"

But aside from his occasional excursions into the contemporary world of action, he lived mostly in the eternal world of thought. He distilled the wisdom of the past into a helpful guide for the future. His books, such as *The Sense of Beauty, The Life of Reason, Skepticism and Animal Faith, Interpretations of Religion,* and *The Realms of Being,* are masterpieces of philosophical prose that scan like rhythmic poetry. Indeed, he began his writing career as a poet. But all his writing, whether poetical or philosophical, reveals a strange admixture of Platonism, atheism, and Catholicism. And, interestingly enough, he weaves these three apparently irreconcilable threads of his thought into a consistent pattern of wisdom.

Let us glance at this pattern, in which we see evidence of the magic that enabled Santayana to transform the perplexed disharmony of his mind into the serene harmony of his soul.

IV

First of all, he looked upon existence as a coherent unit—an upward march of creation toward the sublime. "Perhaps," he said, "matter is not material." Most likely, "it is an electric charge"—an all-pervading surge of vitality that produces "the endless order of the universe."

And this substantial order, he maintained along with Plato, is based upon a harmony of ideas—as in a great painting or symphony, for example. The idea is the important thing; the object that reveals the idea to our senses is but its imperfect image or copy. (Thus, Beethoven's *Ninth Symphony* gives us only a blurred picture of the idea in the composer's mind that produced it.)

Santayana had a new name for Plato's ideas. He called them "essences." The essences of Santayana, like the ideas of Plato, are the original forms, or eternal blueprints, of all the things that exist. And every one of us, said Santayana, can learn to perceive the ideas that form the basis of things—the secret of growth in the unfolding of a flower, the summons to life in the rising of the sun, the stimulus to faith in the laughter of a child, the call to the divine in the performance of a beautiful deed. In these flashes of our clearer perceptions, we experience an *ecstasy*, a "standing away from ourselves." As we struggle over the narrow road of our existence from life to death, blinded as we are by our ignorance, our spirits can and sometimes do lift us above ourselves, so that in a revealing moment we behold eternity. At such moments of self-forgetfulness we see "the Essences laugh from their Platonic heaven at this inconstant world into which they peep for a moment."

Yet this heaven with its "laughing Essences" seems, to Santayana, to be a beautiful estate without a supervisor. Like the astronomer Leland, he "examined the universe with a telescope and failed to discover God." But this is like saying that the scientist examines the brain with a microscope and fails to discover the mind. Actually, the mind is the *Essence* of the brain; and—as Santayana hinted on several occasions—God is the *Essence* of the universe. "Our reason," he said, "is our imitation of divinity." What sort of divinity? Not an anthropomorphic God—a divine being in human form—but an all-inclusive, all-pervasive, all-creative spirit that fashions the universe into a pattern of beauty.

This conception of God as developed in the philosophy of Santayana is not atheistic but rather pantheistic. Santayana is not only a Platonist; he is also a Spinozist. He regards Spinoza as the greatest of the modern philosophers. God is everything, Spinoza had declared, and everything is God. And Santayana echoes this thought when he says that matter and spirit and God are one.

The world, to be sure, is a machine, but it is a *thinking* machine. All creation, believes Santayana, begins to look more and more like a sublime thought. Every atom is imbued with a vital purpose—an urge to combine with other atoms into the continuous pattern of life.

And thus this believing unbeliever sums up his philosophical faith. He disagrees with the scientists who reject religion but who fail to explain the human hunger for religion. The instinct of hunger, observes Santayana, presupposes the existence of food. "The universal *quest* for the divine is a good proof of the *existence* of the divine." The recognition of this fact brings every atheist—including Santayana himself—face to face with the reality of God. Indeed, the human mind feels itself "akin to God."

Hence Santayana admitted, though reluctantly, that his poetical reason prompted him to abandon his scientific skepticism. "Religion is so profoundly moving because it is so profoundly just."

He found this profound justice in his own religion which he had abandoned as a young man. The beauty of his Catholic faith—of all faith—had sunk deeply into his soul. As one of his critics wittily observed: "Santayana believes that there is no God, and that Mary is His mother." He had discarded the material ritualism of religion, but he retained his love for its spiritual beauty. And following Plato again, he felt that the beautiful is synonymous with the true.

Hence, he said, religion is more than a myth, and the world is more than a machine. Existence is an entity not of construction but of growth. No machine as yet has grown like a flower out of a seed.

V

Such is the inconsistent consistency of Santayana's philosophical system. The material world of our experience, he declares, is but an image, a mere hint, of the essential world of our spirit. We glimpse this essential, real world in our moments of ecstasy. At such moments we realize that the world is a coherent unit of life, moving in harmony toward the divine. The fragmentary discords that we experience from time to time —such as frustration, sickness, death—are but the clashes of the individual notes that are being composed in the over-all symphony of the world. And this over-all symphony is true, beautiful, good.

As for the question of our personal immortality, Santayana suspends his final judgment. But he consoles us with the thought that what we do know about this question is in itself true, beautiful and good. Our capacity for love, he observes, makes us immortal. The stream of our existence flows on to our children. They are the newer and fairer copies of the blotted and discarded manuscript of our lives.

And it is the bond of love between ourselves and our children, between all the members of the human family, that reveals to us the meaning of life. Our material body is but an image of our essential soul. And "the soul is akin to the eternal and ideal." It is akin not necessarily to a personal God but to an eternal harmony, a universal spirit of love.

This mystery of our divine relationship is best revealed to us in the ecstasy of religion. And thus, even though some of us may reject the *rites* of religion, all of us can accept its *rightness*. Our belief in religion is so universal because religion is such a universal need.

VI

It was with this "detached though friendly attitude toward man and God" that Santayana lived his entire life. He was the head of no family, the patriot of no country and—after 1912, when he resigned from Harvard—the professor of no school. Shortly before the First World War he left America and went to live in Europe. This was not only a withdrawal to another hemisphere but a retirement to another world—the ancient world to which he believed that he had always belonged. He settled down in Rome, because there he felt "closer to the past than anywhere else." He adopted a quiet routine, walking in the "ignoble present" like the "spirit of a nobler day." He rented a modest suite in a hotel. When someone suggested that he buy himself a home, he replied that "a man is enslaved by his possessions." His habits were simple. "I am the child of my father," he said. "I once asked him why he always traveled third class, and he replied, 'because there is no fourth class.'"

Santayana was a simple aristocrat and a devout skeptic. He had almost completely divorced himself from his Church. "Sitting in a pew," he remarked, "made me tired in the small of my back." But he frequently went to the ruins of the Pantheon to see the statues of the ancient gods, and to San Pietro, to enjoy Michelangelo's Moses, "the supreme achievement of modern religious sculpture."

His favorite haunt was a bench near the ruins of the temple of Aesculapius, the ancient god of healing. Here he sat for hours and dreamed himself back to the springtime of the world from which he had been "so sadly exiled" by the vicissitudes of fate.

Yet there was always a touch of humor in his sadness. He contemplated his own frustrations, like the frustrations of other people, with an impersonal chuckle. Speaking of the poor sale of his books—prior to the publication of his only novel, *The Last Puritan*—he laughingly remarked: "*The Sense of Beauty* is my first book and still my best seller . . . about a hundred copies a year."

And so he gazed with a sad but amused and philosophical calm upon that "mysterious spectacle" called life. Whatever misfortune may befall us, he said, let us remember that it is fugitive. "This, too, shall pass." The important thing is to retain our serenity in the midst of the storm.

Yet this advocate of serenity had one strong aversion—he hated our human propensity for war. "It is war," he declared, "that wastes a nation's wealth, kills its flower, narrows its sympathies, condemns it to be governed by adventurers and leaves the puny, deformed and unmanly to breed the next generation . . . [Therefore], instead of being descended from heroes, modern nations are descended from slaves."

In one of his sonnets he wrote: "Heaven it is to be at peace with things."

To attain this preview of heaven in peace, he ultimately returned to his first love—the Church. During the Second World War he went to live at the Convent of the Little Company of Mary in Rome. Here he found the essential answer to his philosophical quest: "In the final analysis, nothing is real but the harmonious beauty of the world."

PART

8

The Completed Circle

CHAPTER XXXI

Mohandas K. Gandhi (1869–1948)

GANDHI, like Santayana, declared: "I have nothing new to teach to the world." His philosophy re-echoed the wisdom of the ages. Most of the great thinkers had subscribed to it. "Truth and non-violence," wrote Gandhi, "are as old as the hills."

Yet in Gandhi this old philosophy found a new voice. He not only *taught* the truth, he *lived* it. As a young man he set out in search of God; and he found him in his brother's face. "I know that God reveals Himself more often in the lowliest of His creatures than in the high and mighty. Hence my passion for the service of the suppressed classes . . . I am no master, no prophet, no sage; I am but a struggling, erring, humble servant of humanity."

The story of Gandhi's service, both in word and in deed, is the epic of a philosopher's pilgrimage to the City of God.

II

His pilgrimage took Gandhi physically from India to England, to South Africa, and back again to India; and spiritually from the Upanishads to Buddha, to Jesus, to Spinoza, to Tolstoy, and back again to the Upanishads.

He was descended from a race of "fighters and forgivers." His father, head minister to the rajah of the Hindu province of Porbandar, was a man of fearless independence. He once went to prison for his daring to speak the truth. His mother, though less independent, was more gentle than her husband. She believed ardently in the religious principle of "Ahimsa"—non-injury to all living things. Gandhi, the youngest of the children, inherited his father's independence and his mother's gentleness.

When he was seven years old, his parents moved to the province of Rajkot. Here he entered school and learned the alphabet by tracing the letters with his fingers in the dust. The authorities couldn't afford to supply the pupils with writing materials.

At thirteen, he was married "in accordance with the Hindu custom." It was a triple wedding, arranged for Mohandas, his brother, and a boy who was related to them. Their parents had decided to have "the last best time of their lives" in this "sacred ceremony of the clan."

Mohandas and his child wife—her name was Kasturbai—remained "sacredly and devotedly wedded" for the rest of their long life. At the outset, however, Mohandas found it difficult to be a good husband, a dutiful son, and a dedicated scholar. He was eager for an education, but for a time it looked as if his family burdens would compel him to leave school. Fortunately, however, his older brother helped to support him so that Mohandas was able to go on with his education.

As a young student, he "sowed his wild oats," as he confessed. These "wild oats" were, from our Western point of view, tame enough. He ate meat, he swore, and he smoked—three things that were taboo among the pious Hindus.

But he soon gave up his "evil ways." At one time he had yielded to a "goat-eating banquet," together with a school chum, in a lonely spot by the river. During the following night he felt, as he wrote afterwards, "that the goat was bleating inside of me." He confessed his "crime" to his mother and to his wife, who "shamed" him into returning to the vegetarian diet of the Hindus.

These two women, especially his wife, succeeded also in curing him of his other bad habits. "When I tried to bend Kasturbai to my will, she turned the tables on me with her resistance to my will on the one hand, and with her quiet submission to the suffering I caused her with my stupidity on the other hand. It was this determination to convert others through her own suffering that taught me the most important lesson of my life—the value of non-violence"—the power of rebellion through the peaceful practice of religion.

And thus he continued his education in the home as well as in the school until his nineteenth year. In 1888, thanks to the financial assistance of his brother, he sailed for England to study law at the University of London.

III

In London, Gandhi decided to act like an Englishman. Free from his home surroundings, he "dressed like a dude in silk hat and plus fours," learned to dance, and tried to gain a foothold in British society. But he couldn't free himself from his color or his race. The British rejected him as a "foreign and inferior person." His experience in England taught him something more than the Western code of jurisprudence. It inspired him to seek for a universal code of justice.

He returned to India determined to devote his life to this universal quest. Shortly after his arrival in Bombay, he read a stirring article about a fellow Hindu, Vivekananda. This disciple of the ancient Hindu philosophers had gone to America to attend a Parliament of Religions at the Chicago World's Fair. When he arrived at the railroad station in Chicago, he didn't have the price of a hotel room. He spent the night in a dry-goods box at the train shed.

At daybreak Vivekananda started out to look for the Parliament of Religions. Several times he lost his way. But he arrived just in time for the opening of the first session.

He went to the platform and turned to address the audience. He had no notes, and had not even prepared any speech. He began in a low, hesitant voice:

"My sisters and brothers of America . . ."

Encouraged by the outburst of applause that greeted his friendly salutation, he went on: "I profess a philosophy, and I belong to a faith, whose sacred language, the Sanskrit, has no word for *exclusion*. The divinities we worship are all human beings, all living things throughout the world."

Vivekananda's speech, as Gandhi noted in the article about him, had electrified the American audience. They had never heard anything like it. Yet to Gandhi, as to Vivekananda, the thought was familiar. It was but a modern translation of the Upanishads, the wisdom of the ancient Hindus. "There is no word for *exclusion* in the fellowship of all living things." What if he, Gandhi, were to take up the work where Vivekananda had left off? What if he were to teach this simple lesson anew to the people of his own generation?

IV

Before long he got an opportunity to start his teaching. He had taken a trip to Pretoria, South Africa, to represent a client in an important trial. At that period there were about 150,000 Hindus in South Africa. They were subjected to all sorts of indignities at the hands of their "civilized" white governors. Gandhi himself was treated like "the scum of the earth." He was thrown out of the first-class carriage in a train. When he took a stagecoach, he was compelled to sit with the driver. And when he tried to register at the Grand National Hotel in Johannesburg, he was told to "move on."

He took these personal insults in stride. But when the government decided to pass an act that would disfranchise all the Hindus in South Africa, he rebelled.

And his rebellion assumed a strange form. Abandoning his legal practice that netted him about $25,000 a year, he organized a non-violent strike against violence—the opposition of soul-force against brute-force. He became the leader of a new type of army—peaceful soldiers who refused to kill but who were not afraid to die. And he equipped his army with a new kind of weapon—the spiritual weapon of non-violent non-co-operation. "This is how the early Christians won their victory against the Romans, and this is how we shall win our victory against the South Africans."

A new kind of weapon, and a new kind of war. Relying upon the effectiveness of philosophy against force, Gandhi went far beyond the idea of mere passive resistance. He not only *forgave* his enemy, but *helped* him when he was in distress. He acted upon the principle that the best way to win a war is not to kill your enemy, but to kill his enmity. In the midst of the Hindu rebellion against the government in South Africa, a plague broke out in Johannesburg. Gandhi immediately suspended hostilities and organized his followers into a hospital corps to give aid and comfort to the foe.

At first neither the Hindus nor the whites could understand this new kind of warfare. Gandhi was attacked by the fanatics on both sides. He was beaten, imprisoned, and at one time almost stoned to death. Yet Gandhi and his followers never raised their hands to strike back. They repaid injustice with mercy, violence with pity, and hatred with love.

But they refused to obey unjust laws. And the idea worked. Gandhi and his army of non-violent non-co-operators shamed the enemy into defeat. At first General Smuts, the leader of the forces against Gandhi, had looked with contempt upon his unarmed adversary. But before long the general began to realize "the power of Gandhi's weapon that heals as against our own powerless weapons that kill." Finally Gandhi triumphed in his bloodless revolution. "I do not like your people," declared General Smuts, "and do not care to assist them at all. But what am I to do? You help us in our day of need. How can we lay hands upon you? I often wish you took to violence, and then we would know at once how to dispose of you. But you will not injure even the enemy. You desire victory by self-suffering alone, and never transgress your self-imposed limits of courtesy and chivalry. And that is what has reduced us to sheer helplessness."

In 1914 the Hindus in South Africa became a free race. Gandhi had gained a complete victory against violence. And he had accomplished this feat, not by resisting the evil but by cultivating the good in his adversaries' souls.

V

When he returned to India, Gandhi organized his non-violent warfare upon a much larger scale. The Hindus were smarting under the oppression of their British rulers. Again and again they had attempted to rebel, but with no success. Their resorting to force had resulted in their defeat by a stronger force. Gandhi told them to try his new method. "My authority for this method," he said, "is the voice of religion—of all the great religions in the world . . . Many people have acquired enough religion to *hate* one another, but not enough to *love* one another. It is my purpose to apply the formula of love to our daily problems."

He was fond of quoting the words of a Hindu poet, Shamlal Bhatt:

> The truly noble know all men as one,
> And gladly pay with good for evil done.

If people only understood and practiced these words, declared Gandhi, a new era would dawn upon the human race.

And so he set out to convert his nation, by his own example, to the practice of the universal Golden Rule. "I have tried to teach my countrymen a new kind of revolt. A hatred not against our rulers, but against our rulers' hatred. I will minister to them as my brothers, but I will not submit to them as my overlords."

True to this philosophy, he began his "war" against England with a campaign of "friendly enmity." In 1914 he organized an Indian ambulance corps as a help in England's war against Germany. And England, in return, promised India her independence after the war.

But when peace was declared, the British imperialists went back on their promise. Some of them were motivated by a spirit of selfish greed. India was too rich a prize for the aggressive exploiters to give up. Others, however, were sincerely convinced that India was not ready for independence. To set her adrift at that time, they felt, would only invite civil war. At any rate, the disillusion of the Hindus was terrible. The flames of rebellion blazed up in many parts of the country. Gandhi's non-violent methods, insisted his Hindu opponents, had failed.

Gandhi, however, had learned the patience of the East. "Wars," he declared, "are not won in a day." He continued with his plan of peaceful non-co-operation. He enjoined upon his followers—they numbered only a handful at the time—a solemn oath of Satyagraha, or Soul-force, as their only weapon against brute-force. And he began to train them in the principle of ahimsa, the return of love for hatred. He built a camp at Ahmedabad for his "soldiers" and their families. Here he taught them to make shoes and clothes for a living; and he opened a school of non-violence for the children of the camp as well as for their parents. To this camp and school he admitted not only the higher classes, or castes, but the so-called untouchables, or outcasts.

Gandhi's acceptance of the outcasts into his camp aroused a storm of fury even among his closest friends. Some of his associates, refusing to be "polluted by the dregs of society," abandoned his camp. The wealthy merchants of Ahmedabad who had supported the colony withdrew their funds. And even his wife Kasturbai insisted upon the expulsion of the untouchables from their settlement.

But Gandhi stuck to his principles. He threatened to leave his family and to move into the "untouchable" slums of Ahmedabad. Finally his wife yielded to his "better judgment"; an anonymous friend sent him enough money to meet the expenses of the camp; and Gandhi was able to go on with his peaceful war against injustice and hate.

VI

On April 15, 1919, there was a national holiday in India. Gandhi had declared a *hartal*—a public cessation of work—throughout the land. In the city of Amritsar a throng of people—men, women, and children—gathered in a peaceful demonstration on a public thoroughfare. The commander of the British forces in that city, General Dyer, ordered an attack upon the unarmed Hindus. His soldiers fired upon them with machine guns and strafed them with bombs from airplanes. About five hundred people were killed in the massacre.

This tragedy put Gandhi's doctrine to the severest test. "Of what avail," cried many of his countrymen, "is your faith now against the force of the enemy's bullets and bombs?"

But Gandhi persisted in his plan. "It was no white road along which I promised to lead you to victory . . . This is war . . . The soldiers in *every* war are ready to be killed . . . Indeed, all of us ultimately lose our lives in the universal battle of existence. *Our* battle, however, will be won not by the number of enemies we can kill, but by the number of enemies in whom we can kill the *desire* to kill."

And thus he continued his strange war against war. "The foreigners are welcome here as guests; but they are not wanted here as usurpers." He returned a gold medal he had received from the British for his humanitarian work in their behalf during World War I. The British Government took back his medal and presented him with another gift—a prison term. He was arrested together with 25,000 other Hindus. They sang as they were marched off to jail.

At his trial, Gandhi pleaded guilty. "Having rebelled

against your government," he said to Judge Broomfield, "I have deliberately broken the law . . . I do not ask for mercy . . . The only course open to you, sir, is to inflict upon me the severest penalty to which I am liable for what in law is a deliberate crime but for what appears to me to be the highest duty of a citizen."

Judge Broomfield replied with equal chivalry. "It would be impossible," he said, "to ignore the fact that in the eyes of millions of your countrymen you are a great patriot and a great leader. Even those who differ from you in politics look upon you as a man of high ideals and of noble life."

And then, having praised Gandhi for the justice of his cause, the judge sentenced him to prison for the illegality of his conduct. The battle lines in the case had been strictly drawn—the violence of the temporary law of the land against the non-violence of the eternal law of humanity.

And in adherence to this eternal law, the philosopher-warrior pursued his peaceful fight against oppression. Again and again he was jailed; but every time he was released he plunged right back into the battle. Gandhi had now added an additional weapon to his arsenal—fasting. "By my suffering I shall soften the hearts of my enemies."

On several occasions, in his painful march over the highway to peace, he became dangerously ill. These spells of sickness, aggravated by his protracted periods of fasting, brought him frequently to the point of death. On one occasion, when he expected to die within a few hours, he said: "My last message to India is that she will find her salvation through non-violence; and through non-violence alone India will teach the way of salvation to the rest of the world."

VII

Gandhi was a philosopher upon whom destiny had imposed the burden of politics. His concern with the destiny of his country was but a part of his greater concern with the destiny of mankind. His chief objective was to serve as the apostle of world peace. "I am wedded to India," he wrote, "because I believe that she has a mission for the world . . . My quest for peace, justice, truth . . . has no geographical limits. I have a living faith in it which transcends even my love for India herself."

Gandhi's philosophy, stemming from his faith, was based upon the principle that not only all men but all living creatures are members of a single family. One of his strictest injunctions was to cultivate a reverence for life. "Thou shalt not destroy life in any form . . . Since we have no power to create, we have no right to kill."

Following the earlier Hindu—and many of the later Western—philosophers, Gandhi believed that "all life is one." Every living thing was to Gandhi "a poem of pity," and he understood with equal tenderness the language of human distress and the inarticulate cry of the beast.

Gandhi's sympathy for all living things was also based upon his belief in reincarnation. Every individual soul, he said, is embarked upon a pilgrimage of many successive lives—at times in the form of a man and at other times in the form of an animal. Every deed in every incarnation determines the form of the next incarnation. If a man honors justice and loves mercy, he will be reborn a nobler and happier man. But if he embraces evil, he will be degraded into "a weasel or a rat." Heaven and Hell, therefore, are not beyond us but within us. And reward and punishment for every deed are not merely ethical abstractions but practical facts. A single human life, like a single chapter in a book, is fragmentary and confused. But the complete succession of a man's lives is like a completed book, with a logical plot that is woven out of every thread in every chapter. If a man is treated unjustly in his present life, it is because he has acted unjustly in a former life. This is the law of karma—the dispensation of due reward for every virtue and due punishment for every vice.

And the consummation of a man's life is to complete all the chapters in his book, to cleanse his soul of its selfish hungers, and to blend his separate self into the Universal Ocean of Existence—that is, the Soul of God. This will mark the end of his successive rebirths into his individual lives.

In the long run, declared Gandhi, all men have an equal destiny. "All are born in order that they may study how to serve God's plan." Every one of our lives is a special task assigned for our education in co-operative living. And our greatest duty is to teach and to befriend our less fortunate brothers. Especially the "outcasts" of society. "I do not wish to be reborn," he wrote, "but if I have to be reborn, I should want to be one of the outcasts so that I may share their sorrows . . . and that I may endeavor to free them from their miserable condition."

The purpose of a man's life, in short, is to lighten the sufferings of his fellow men.

VIII

It was in this supreme service that Gandhi lived and died. His non-violent war against the British was merely a practical application of his philosophy. And this philosophy stemmed from the universal truth inherent in all the great religions. "The only effective weapon against hatred is love." With this weapon he had won independence for his fellow Hindus in South Africa in 1914. And finally, in 1947, he secured the independence of his entire Hindu nation with the selfsame weapon of non-violent resistance. On August 15 of that year, the British formally recognized India as a free and independent country.

His people hailed him as their savior. "Not since Buddha has any man in India been so universally revered." Yet Gandhi took his personal triumph, as he had taken his personal suffering, with quiet humility. "I am called *Mahatma* (Great Soul)," he modestly observed, "but I am an ordinary man. I have blundered and committed mistakes." Yet he had demonstrated what he regarded as a profound truth. "The world's salvation will come not through *body-force* but through *soul-force.*"

His victory in India had come about through the utmost discipline of his soul. "Wherein is supreme courage required," he had written in his *Sermon on the Sea*, "in blowing others to pieces from behind a cannon, or with a smiling face to approach a cannon and to be blown to pieces?"

It was only five months after his victory that Gandhi met the supreme test of his courage. His people had become restive as a result of their independence. The Moslems and the Hindus of his country had begun to fight against one another to settle their political and religious disputes. Gandhi tried his best to stop the quarrel between these two factions. One morning, while visiting a friend in New Delhi, he made his way through the garden to hold a prayer meeting dedicated to the establishment of national co-operation and peace. A Hindu fanatic, who hated the Moslems and resented Gandhi's friendship toward them, rushed up to the Mahatma and fired three bullets into his body. The philosopher-prophet of a hateless world died within thirty minutes after the attack.

"But my idea," Gandhi had declared, "will live on. For the sword of passive resistance is twice blessed. It blesses him who uses it, and him against whom it is used."

And in the long run "this weapon of non-violent warfare, without shedding a drop of blood, will bring nothing less than victory to the world."

CHAPTER XXXII

Conclusion—Help from the Philosophers

AND NOW we have completed the circle. We have started our survey of the world's great philosophers with an important question: Do the various systems of philosophy, in spite of their many contradictions, provide a common pattern of wisdom that may serve as a guide to the perplexed?

In other words, is there a general basis of agreement in the different philosophies of the world, just as there is a general basis of agreement in the different religions of the world? The answer to this question is an emphatic yes. And the agreement comes precisely at the point where philosophy meets religion. Wisdom, like faith, is a united stream that flows down to us across the centuries. The different philosophers are like observers stationed at different points of the stream. And so they see the truth from various angles. But the truth, from whatever angle we may examine it, remains essentially the same.

We shall realize this common philosophical truth as we briefly review the various ideas of the great philosophers. These ideas may be summarized under three general heads: Metaphysics, or the Riddle of Existence; Ethics, or the Meaning of Morality; and Theology, or the Mystery of God.

Let us look at this threefold quest of the philosophers.

THE RIDDLE OF EXISTENCE

From the earliest dawn of philosophical speculation down to the present day we find an instinctive belief that the entire universe is alive. "Heaven lies about us in our infancy"—the infancy not only of the individual man but of all mankind. The early Egyptians, Persians, Hindus, Chinese, Hebrews—all of them came by different roads to the same conviction: There is a universal life-force that is all-inclusive, all-pervasive, divine. This life-force is a single ocean divided into many waves, a single rhythm composed of many beats, a single soul diffused into many bodies, a single existence observed through many minds.

This universal stream of life receives various interpretations in the various schools of the early philosophers. Stationed as they are at different points, they may quarrel about one another's angle of vision. But they do not quarrel about the central fact. Thus, the Egyptian view of the stars as conscious bodies with flaming souls, the Persian description of the forces of Nature as the living collaborators with God in the progressive building of the universe, the Hindu doctrine of the identity between the individual soul and the World-Soul, the Chinese conception of the ceaseless current of living energy from the whole to the part and from the part to the whole, and the Hebrew picture of one God as the Creator of life and light out of chaos and darkness—all these conceptions add up to one basic idea: *Everything is alive, and life moves progressively on.*

Along with this basic idea, we find two supplementary theories in the work of the early philosophers:

1. Life keeps on developing like a plant. It grows—or evolves—from lower to higher forms. The spirit of man, like a flame, leaps forever upward. Whether in the form of transmigration or of evolution, the process of life as envisioned by the philosophers is constantly on the move to break away from the petty selves of the many and to join the sublime Self of the One.

2. We are able to grasp this sublime and universal sense of existence, as the early philosophers tell us, by means of a sixth sense—our sense of introspection. We can see the truth not with the outward eye of the body but with the inward eye of

the mind. The philosopher, the prophet, the artist, the poet, the seer, and almost everybody else in his rare moments of insight, has experienced this ecstatic oneness of the individual with the universal, of man with God. Philosophy thus tries to establish by reason what religion accepts on faith.

And thus we find an internal agreement in all the external disagreements of most of the early philosophers. Examining the world from their diverse points of view, they converge upon a single focus of progressive energy in a living world—or of life moving eternally onward to a supreme goal.

When we advance from the earlier philosophers to Plato and Aristotle, we find the focus substantially unchanged. The world of Plato is a world of living ideas—an ordered design of goodness and justice and beauty which we instinctively try to incorporate into our daily lives. Existence, in other words, is the pursuit of an ideal—an upward movement of the soul toward the sublime. The world of Aristotle, in spite of his apparent departure from Plato, is the same Platonic world under a different name. Plato referred to the essence of life as an idea conceived by a divine plan; Aristotle regarded it as a form perceived by the human mind. And thus, in spite of their apparent discrepancy, the two philosophers agree on the central point; and on this point they are at one with nearly all the other ancient philosophers: Life is a sublime down-flowing from heaven to earth, and an eternal up-reaching from earth to heaven. There is a living, driving purpose—or pattern—that shapes and guides our destiny.

After Plato and Aristotle we come to the Skeptics and the Cynics. Strictly speaking, these men were not serious philosophers but disinterested observers of the cosmic scene. The Skeptics dismissed the riddle of existence as beyond their understanding, and the Cynics merely laughed at what they couldn't understand.

The next important Greek thinker, Epicurus, was the father of materialism as opposed to the idealism of some of the earlier philosophers. Yet the materialistic substance in the Epicurean philosophy has an idealistic design. The world, said Epicurus, is built out of atoms. But these atoms are not lifeless bits of mechanism. On the contrary, they are imbued with a living purpose, a free will to move in a direction of their own choosing, and to combine with one another into a pageant of progressive evolution.

As we move on from the materialism of Epicurus to the Stoicism of Aurelius, we come again to the central thought of a living world. This world, declared Marcus Aurelius, has not only a physical body but a spiritual soul. And the function of the world-soul is to unite all men into the fellowship of mankind and all mankind into fellowship with God.

The next great philosophical system, Christianity, is a supreme revelation of the selfsame truth. This philosophy is adequately expressed in the Epistles of St. Paul—the student of the East and the teacher of the West. The spirit of man, according to St. Paul, is deathless. For the soul of man is embarked upon a pilgrimage to the Soul Divine from which it came. God is forever creating the world out of his eternal love; and all created things are forever prompted, through love for one another, to become as godlike as possible.

With the dawn of the scientific age, we find our philosophical vision extended through the telescope, the microscope, and the test tube. Yet the center of the truth, as observed through these new instruments, remains the same. The philosophers of the Renaissance saw the world as a universal living substance that moves under the guidance of a universal mind. The individual life is a thread endowed with a will to weave itself into the divine pattern of the whole—the creative plan of God.

This divine pattern continues to be the rallying point in practically all the philosophical systems that come after the Renaissance. Francis Bacon, Descartes, Spinoza, and Locke—each looking at the world from the observation tower of his own individual mind—came to a unanimous conclusion. This conclusion, though described by the different philosophers in different terms, may be summarized as follows: At first glance the world appears as a trinity of matter and spirit and God; but in the final analysis the trinity becomes a living unity— matter and spirit and God are one.

This nearly universal verdict of the philosophers receives further corroboration in the systems of the so-called enlightened thinkers of the eighteenth and the nineteenth centuries. The idea of a universal will to live is the common verdict of Rousseau's naturalism, Voltaire's rationalism, Kant's intellectualism, Schopenhauer's pessimism, Spencer's determinism, and Nietzsche's realism. Whatever definitions the dictionary may give to the various words by which the ideas of these philosophers have been labeled, the essential meaning of their philosophy is the same: In all the illusions of our existence we find a basis of reality—universal life. Our journey through the world is but a fleeting scene in a vast drama. And the theme of the drama has been well expressed by the philosophical poet, Tennyson, who assures us:

> That nothing walks with aimless feet;
> That not one life shall be destroyed,
> Or cast as rubbish to the void,
> When God hath made the pile complete.

This idea lies also at the core of the more modern systems of philosophy, from Bergson to Gandhi. These latest philosophers end exactly where the earliest philosophers began. From first to last, every one of the philosophers has examined the world from a different observation tower. Our own view today, therefore, is a composite picture of their various viewpoints. And this, as we now see it, is the philosophers' answer to the Riddle of Existence:

The world is a unit of matter, energy, and spirit—mass, motion, and life. These are not separate entities but one essence under different forms. The more we study about matter, the more clearly we see it as a form of energy; and the more we learn about energy, the more distinctly we recognize it as a form of life. Bergson, the standard-bearer of the religious idea in modern philosophy, defines the three-in-one essence of the world as the *élan vital*—a living impulse, creative evolution, divine growth. And even Santayana, the protagonist of the scientific fact, admits that "perhaps matter is not material." Most likely "it is an electric charge," an all-pervading flow of energy, "the endless order and vitality of the world in which I live."

And thus the verdict of the philosophers is that matter, energy, spirit, mass, motion, and life are but different terms that define the selfsame reality. This reality, examined under one of its aspects, appears as a cloud, a rock, a forest, a meteor, a planet, a star. Examined under another aspect, it appears as a poem of Shakespeare, a symphony of Beethoven, a formula of Einstein, a parable of Jesus, an aspiration of the human for the divine. And when examined in its entirety, it becomes revealed as an eternal life-stream flowing from, and returning to, God.

THE MEANING OF MORALITY

Morality is the philosophy of righteousness in human conduct. The word "morality" has a religious rather than a legal meaning. The distinction between what is legally permissible and what is morally right is well illustrated in the following little story: One day a Harvard professor of law explained to his students a court decision about a questionable act performed by a public official. "This decision, sir," observed one of the students, "seems legal all right. But is it just?"

"Young man," said the professor, "this is the Law School. If you want justice, go across the street to the Divinity School."

In their quest for justice, the philosophers have sided with the religious teachers rather than with the professional lawyers. And at the core of all the ethical teaching of the philosophers we find a single aim—to establish an honest formula for justice. In other words, the philosophers ask a question that concerns every one of us: "Is there a definite law that determines the difference between right and wrong?"

At first blush it would seem that even a child knows the answer to this question. Yet Bernard Shaw, in his *Major Barbara*, points out that no human mind has yet discovered the secret. Two characters in the play, Undershaft and Stephen, are talking about the idea of morality:

> *Undershaft:* Is there anything you know or care for?
> *Stephen:* Yes, I know the difference between right and wrong.
> *Undershaft:* You don't say so! What, no capacity for business, no knowledge of law, no sympathy with art, no pretension to philosophy; only a simple knowledge of the secret that has puzzled all the philosophers, baffled all the lawyers, muddled all the men of business, and ruined most of the artists: the secret of right and wrong. Why, man, you're a genius, a master of masters, a god!

What seems right to one man may seem wrong to another. What appears good in one age or locality may appear bad in another locality or age. In the Orient it is a mark of respect to cover the head; in the Occident, to uncover it. In Melanesia it was considered ethical to kill the sick and the old in order to relieve the "burden" of the healthy and the young. In China it was dutiful to present an ailing relative with a coffin. In the Solomon Islands it was no sin to fatten young women, like young turkeys, for the slaughter. And even in Europe and in America the standards of morality keep shifting from time to time. For example, the vices of peace, such as cheating, robbing, and killing, become the virtues of war. The question of right and wrong, therefore, is largely a matter of time, place, circumstance, and individual point of view.

Largely, concede the philosophers, but not wholly. For in all the changing scenery of our moral concepts there are certain fixed principles—signposts that point the way out of the jungle of human passion toward the light of human reason. These principles may be grouped under six subjects: duty, reciprocity, friendliness, justice, mercy, and love. And all these subjects may be further reduced to a single precept: Kindness is the light that leads the march of mankind.

This is but another way of stating the Golden Rule—treat others as you want others to treat you. From first to last, all the great philosophers have advanced this idea as the basis of human conduct. "Live in the house of kindliness," wrote the Egyptian Ptah-hotep. "More precious than riches in your storehouse is sympathy in your heart."

The Persian philosopher Zoroaster, who lived about one thousand years before Christ, expressed the same idea in words very similar to those of the Golden Rule. "That man alone is good," he declared, "who will not do unto others whatever is not good unto himself." For all men belong to a single family.

In the philosophy of the Hindus we find a parable that illustrates the close relationship between man and man. A hunter, we are told, was once overtaken by a heavy fog. Suddenly he beheld in the haze the indistinct outline of an unfamiliar beast. The frightful monster was advancing rapidly upon him. In his panic, the hunter raised his javelin and hurled it at the animal. The javelin struck home and the animal fell dead.

And then, as the hunter approached his victim, the fog lifted. And to his horror he saw that the "unfamiliar and frightful beast" was his own brother who was coming to visit him from a neighboring town.

This parable about the fog of misunderstanding can be applied to the Chinese as well as to the Hindu system of ethics.

The philosopher Mo-ti summarizes the idea as follows: "The mutual attacks of state on state, the mutual usurpations of family on family, the mutual robberies of men on men, the want of tenderness between father and son and between brother and brother—these are the things that destroy the happiness of the world." Lao-tse defined this idea as the search for the Way of Righteousness, and Confucius refined it into another version of the Golden Rule. "What you would not have done unto yourself, do not unto others." He called this interchange of good will "the great harmony of mutual understanding."

The Hebrew philosophers translated this idea into the Ten Commandments. And they based the Commandments upon a central foundation—one universal law of reciprocal rights.

The Greek philosophers, from Plato to Epicurus, emphasized this ethical principle in their picture of the ideal man. To Plato, the ideal man is a man of justice—a person whose inward thoughts and feelings are in harmony with one another, and whose outward interests are in harmony with the interests of the world. To Aristotle, the man of justice becomes a man of equanimity—a person of even temper who is able to control his excessive ambitions and passions. Aristotle's gentleman is a gentle man. And to Epicurus, the ideal man is a man of affection—a person whose genius for friendship cements the world into a community of good neighbors.

The early Christians developed this idea into history's supreme example of the perfect life. The Christian communists —so different from the communists of the present day—tried to live in accordance with the Golden Rule. Translated into everyday language, this rule may be epitomized in the words spoken by Jesus at the Last Supper: "A new commandment I give unto you, that ye love one another." The early Christians literally enjoyed the common ownership of goods in a united community of good will.

The next important interpreter of kindness as the badge of mankind was Spinoza. This Jewish philosopher has been called "the greatest Christian after Christ." His ethical system is based upon what is now defined as "enlightened selfishness." "A man's happiness," said Spinoza, "consists in this, that his power is increased through love of self"—not, however, the exclusive self of the individual, but the inclusive self of the human race. Together with St. Paul and the Hebrew prophets, and in keeping with the other great philosophers of the East and the West, Spinoza believed that we are parts of one another, and that when any man injures another man he injures himself. Therefore, "under the guidance of reason a man will desire nothing for himself which he will not also desire for the rest of mankind."

This universal code of ethics prompted Locke to his philosophical Declaration of Independence. All men, he said, are born into a world community of free and equal brothers. Every individual, therefore, has a double duty to society: first, to appropriate nothing for which he has not labored; and second, to take only his just share of the world's goods so that others may also enjoy their just share. In other words, the moral law as interpreted by Locke requires the greatest happiness of the greatest number and the lessening of pain for all.

This idea of the greatest happiness for the greatest number became the categorical imperative of Kant. Our sense of duty, according to Kant, is an inner voice which tells us that a life of mutual kindness is a must. The only true happiness consists in making others happy. In a society built upon this principle, observes the German philosopher, the individual will be regarded not as a means toward another individual's greed, but as "an end in himself"—a master in his own right who performs his honest labor and receives his honest reward. The ethics of Kant may be summarized in one supreme commandment: *Thou shalt not exploit thy neighbor.* "There can be nothing more dreadful than that the actions of one man should be enforced by the will of another man."

In the ethics of Spencer we find the same idea re-enforced

by the science of evolution. In the earlier periods of history, Spencer points out, it was often necessary to kill in order to live. But as we advance toward civilization we begin to realize that we can best survive through mutual aid rather than through mutual antagonism. Peace, and not war, is the foundation of human progress. When we become fully civilized, maintains Spencer, we shall bend all our efforts toward the building of a world at peace. And this ideal condition will be based upon a simple formula: Every man will be free to exercise his will but not to interfere with the freedom of his fellow men. In other words, we shall advance together but we shall not step upon one another's toes.

As we come to the twentieth century, we see a definite shift from individual toward social ethics. And this is but a modern restatement of the old moral principle; individual salvation depends upon mutual help. Bergson, Croce, James, and Santayana are equally insistent upon extending the Ten Commandments from the singular "thou" to the plural "you." Our instruments of rapid communication and transportation have contracted the world into a single neighborhood. The remotest islanders in the Pacific are within a day's journey of our own back yard. And their hopes are included within the family circle of our own hopes. Their hunger is our hunger; their welfare, our welfare; their pain, our pain. In the words of William James, "There can be no difference *anywhere* that doesn't make a difference *everywhere*."

In other words, the highest morality today prescribes not only a man's personal duty but also his social responsibility. He must obey the good laws and try to change the bad laws. As for what is good and what is bad, the unfailing criterion is not the joy of the individual but the happiness of society as a whole.

And this carries us forward to the last and back to the first of the oriental philosophers. Vivekananda and Gandhi, like Buddha and Zoroaster and Confucius, see humanity as one

body and one soul. "I profess a philosophy," declared Vivekananda, "whose language has no word for exclusion." And Gandhi
echoed the same idea in his principle of a new kind of resistance to evil—the resistance of non-violence. "Don't kill your
adversary with the sword, but kill his hatred with love. In this
way you will have destroyed an enemy and gained a friend."

This is the moral principle, just as it is the metaphysical
law, of creation. Our daily human activity, like the eternal
movement of the stars, is a process of evolution from discord to
concord. When every man has learned this truth, agree the philosophers, Heaven will have become established on earth.

THE MYSTERY OF RELIGION

The early philosophers, like the early religious leaders, believed in one God. The many gods of the so-called pagans were
but representations of the manifold powers of the one central
Ruler of the universe.

This monotheistic idea arose in Egypt about fifteen hundred years before the birth of Jesus. "In reality," said the Egyptian philosopher, Ikhnaton, "there is but one Lord of the
universe, one God, one Father to all mankind."

The Persian philosophers continued this monotheistic idea
in their representation of Ahura Mazda as the supreme Lord
of Light. This Lord is "the Creator of the universe who determines the paths of the stars, sustains the earth and the heavens,
binds the waters in their courses, and directs the minds of men
toward divine wisdom." The God of the Persians, in other words,
is the sum total of the forces that perpetuate the beauty and
the glory of the world.

The Hindus subscribed to the selfsame picture of God as
the Creator of all things and as identical with His creation. All
forms of life are one; they seem different only because of our
imperfect perception. To illustrate this point, the Hindu philosophers told the story of six blind men who laid their hands

upon six different parts of an elephant. To the one who touched the ear, the elephant was a winnowing fan; to the one who touched the leg, he was a round pillar; and so on, each describing the animal as something different yet none comprehending it as a unit composed of separate parts.

The Chinese also pictured God as a unit—Shang-ti—the supreme creative and ruling power of the universe. Heaven, they said, is not a place separate from the earth, but the beneficent will of God. And he who directs his life in accordance with this divine will does not bring himself to heaven, but brings heaven to himself.

The Hebrews are generally credited as the founders of the idea of one God. But, as we have seen, they merely rediscovered—or, rather, continued to point out—an old truth recognized by the philosophers throughout the world. The earlier prophets feared God as a stern king; Amos and Hillel regarded Him as a gentle Father; and Isaiah revered Him as the Prince of Peace. But all of them agreed that God is the Creator of one world and the guiding spirit of one universal nation—mankind. "And it shall come to pass"—when the human race understands this truth—"that all nations shall flow into the Lord's house, and He will teach us His ways . . . And they shall beat their swords into plowshares, and their spears into pruning hooks. Nation shall not lift up sword against nation, neither shall they learn war any more."

The age-old philosophical quest for concord. The Greek philosophers, like their oriental predecessors, recognized this universal principle of concord as the creative plan of God. It is interesting to note that while the Greek public believed in polytheism, the Greek philosophers adhered to the idea of monotheism. Socrates, for example, uses the singular word *theos*—God—when he refers to the "divine voice" that speaks within his soul.

From the founding of Christianity to the present day, the monotheistic idea has become established as the foundation of philosophy as well as the basis of religion. Most of us recognize one divine center, though many of us may quarrel about the various roads that lead to it. Religion, speaking with the tongue of faith, assures us of God's personal care in all our tribulations. "Comfort ye, comfort ye, my people; for I am always with you." And philosophy, urging with the voice of reason, reassures us of His divine care. "God's presence is manifest in all that liberates and lifts, in all that humbles, sweetens and consoles."

This idea is admirably expressed in the words of the religious and philosophic poet, Elizabeth Barrett Browning:

> Earth's crammed with Heaven,
> And every common bush afire with God.

But, insists Mrs. Browning, it takes vision and thought to realize this universal truth:

> . . . only he who sees takes off his shoes—
> The rest sit round and pluck blackberries.

For a time the so-called realists were more concerned with the picking of the blackberries than they were with the flaming of the bush. They were too busy with the material aspects of life to recognize its spiritual truths. Voltaire, Marx, and Nietzsche tried to establish a philosophy of reason without faith. Yet the more modern thinkers have rejected this "realistic philosophy." They have returned to the idea of the Upanishads and St. Paul. The modern verdict of philosophy as a confirmation of religion has been summarized in the teaching of Santayana. This Catholic-atheist spent his life searching for the God whose existence he denied. And toward the end of his life he had this to say of his quest: "I disagree with the enlightenment common to young wits and worm-eaten old satirists, who plume themselves on detecting the scientific ineptitude of religion . . . but leave unexplored the habits of thought

from which those tenets [of religion] sprang." Santayana felt
that the universal instinct for the divine is a good proof of the
actual existence of the divine. What really matters, he said, is
the fact that "all thinking people are hungry to discover a reason and a plan for our earthly life"—in other words, they have
a passion to find God.

And thus there is an intimate relationship between philosophy and faith. As our concept of the universe expands, so
too does our belief in a universal guide. Together with the ma-
turing of our reason comes a mature attitude toward religion.
One religion for all—the revelation of a cosmic design in harmony with beauty, the promise of a personal destiny in conso-
nance with hope.

True philosophy, therefore, is religious; and true religion
is philosophical. The philosophical as well as the religious life
is a life of active devotion among all the members in the congregation of the world. The spirit of man seeks a continual out-
let in noble activity. And it is the verdict of the world's great
thinkers that this spirit must never be stifled under the brush-
wood of selfish interests, stagnated dogmas, or antiquated
creeds. Our instinctive human desire for friendly communion,
the philosophers tell us, must be given free play in all our
public and personal contacts.

For life is a procedure toward "infinite companionship."
We have everything to gain from the wisdom of mercy, everything to lose from the stupidity of malice. It is not only immoral
but impractical, as William James reminds us, to outwit or hate
or kill our fellow men. History has yet to show a single persecution or murder or war that has paid off in the end.

And thus we find, both in philosophy and in religion, the
selfsame injunctions: "Let there be light!" We need a more
enlightened outlook upon the true relationship between the individual and society. This idea is well expounded in the words
of the French philosopher, Auguste Sabatier: "The society

which, to maintain itself, oppresses individual souls and sacrifices their rights and their culture to its own tranquillity is like a mother who would devour her children. The individual who, by his own selfishness, exploits or destroys the social bond is the perverse or heedless child who, to warm himself, sets fire to the house of his fathers."

What, then, is the function of the individual? Good will. And the function of society? Co-operative good will. And the design of the universe? Infinite good will. And the practical purpose of philosophy? To will and to live the good life—the life of friendly, sympathetic, social usefulness. In other words —to *live, let live, and help live.* For you are a part of a divine pattern. So is your neighbor, whether on this or on the other side of the national boundary. Whatever his language or his creed, the color of his skin or the shape of his nose, both of you belong to the same universal body, the same universal soul. Ask yourself what have been the red-letter days of your existence. The days on which you have pushed yourself? or crushed a competitor? or vented your hatred or intolerance or contempt? Certainly not! Our royal days are those on which we give freely of our good will. The days on which we open ourselves to the ecstasy of comradeship. For then we touch heaven with our fingertips. It is then that we experience our reason and our religion at their best.

And thus we have come to the end of our philosophical survey. And as we have seen, the great philosophers who have lived at different times and in different places have been able to arrive at the same conclusion. They have reached this unanimity in spite of the fact that many of them could not possibly have read, or heard of, one another's works. Yet their general consensus is no accident. For all of them studied the same universal textbook—Creation—written in syllables of flaming stars and aspiring souls.

And this is the identical solution the philosophers have

found to the mystery of the Cosmic Drama: one God, one living world, one human brotherhood, and one supreme law. Confucius and Plato and Santayana called it harmony. Buddha and St. Paul and Gandhi called it love.

Index